Intimacies

Intimacies

LOVE AND SEX ACROSS CULTURES

Edited by William R. Jankowiak

COLUMBIA

UNIVERSITY

PRESS

NEW YORK

Columbia University Press
Publishers Since 1893
New York   Chichester, West Sussex

Library of Congress Cataloging-in-Publication Data
Intimacies : love and sex across cultures / edited by William R. Jankowiak.
        p. cm.
    Includes bibliographical references and index.
    ISBN 978-0-231-13436-1 (cloth : alk. paper) — ISBN 978-0-231-13437-8 (pbk. : alk.
paper) — ISBN 978-0-231-50876-6 (ebook)
    1. Sex—Cross-cultural studies.   2. Intimacy (Psychology)—Cross-cultural studies.
3. Love—Cross-cultural studies.   4. Interpersonal relations—Cross-cultural studies.
I. Jankowiak, William R.   II. Title.
  GN484.3I68 2008
  306.7—dc22

                                            2007037939

CONTENTS

ACKNOWLEDGMENTS

*T*his book represents the second part of a planned trilogy on the topic of love and sex. The first book, *Romantic Passion: A Universal Experience?* (Columbia University Press, 1995), focused on exploring the expression and manifestations of passionate love in a variety of ethnographic contexts. This book seeks to examine the interplay between sex, comfort, and passionate love in a number of different societies around the world. The final book planned is tentatively titled *A Case for Emotional Monogamy,* in which Thomas Paladino and I will argue that humans as a species are less sexually monogamous than they are emotionally monogamous.

I owe thanks to a number of people who have read all or portions of the manuscript or who otherwise provided assistance, advice, or inspiration. They include Jim Bell, Dan Benychek, Paul Bohannan, Robert Boyd, Donald Brown, Robert Carson, Victor De Munck, Shanshan Du, Carol Ember, Ted Fischer, Helen Fisher, Vanessa Fong, Stacy Garretson, Helen Gerth, Patrick Gray, Peter Gray, Thomas Gregor, Elaine Hatfield, Terry Hays, Barry Hewlett, Bonnie Hewlett, Libby Hinson, Sadie Hinson, Charles Lindholm, David Lipset, Robert Moore, Steve Myers, Alan Redd, Alice Schlegel, Daniel Smith, Martin Spencer, Pam Stern, David Suggs, Donald Symons, Jennifer Thompson, Geeta Tiwari, and Holly Wardlow.

I would like to extend special thanks to the able leadership of Anne Routon, editor at Columbia University Press, who shepherded the manuscript through its paces in a timely matter. In addition, special thanks go to our fierce and relentless copy editor, Polly Kummel, whose dedication to accuracy made all our chapters that much better. A special thanks also to Steve Myers, who read and extensively commented on the introductory and U.S. spouse exchange chapters. His keen analytical eye helped to push the analysis and thus produce a stronger point of view.

So while Emerson sat writing in his study,
Thoreau paddled up the dark river . . .
And at the mid-stream of voyage—
The remembered bed in a hellish limbo—
Bogs down,
    location drifts into a composite landing.

—Thomas Paladino

Intimacies

1. Desiring Sex, Longing for Love
A Tripartite Conundrum

William Jankowiak and Thomas Paladino

"Marriage ought to be based primarily on affection—love if you like—and only if this is present does marriage offer something that is . . . sacred."

"That's exactly what I'm talking about, the preference for one man or for one woman above all others, but what I'm asking is: a preference for how long?"
—Leo Tolstoy, *The Kreutzer Sonata*

CULTURE'S DILEMMA

No culture is ever completely successful, or satisfied, with its synthesis or reconciliation of passionate companion (or comfort) love and sexual desire. Whether in the technological metropolis or in a simple farming community, a tension exists between sexual mores and proscriptions governing the proper context for love. Western societies are not unique in their ambivalence. At various times sexual passion has been preferred to romance as well as companionship. No ethnographic study has reported that all passions and affections have been regarded as equally valuable. The official ideal, and thus the preferred idiom of conversation, is the sexual, the romantic, or the companionship image. No culture gives equal weight to the use of sexual, romantic, and companionate metaphors. One passion is always regarded as a subset of the other. No matter how socially humane, politically

enlightened, spiritually attuned, or technologically adapted, failure to integrate sex and love is the name of the game. The paramount passion is easily
recognizable from examining conversational idioms. Conflicts about issues of propriety, etiquette, and social standing inevitably arise whenever a
break occurs in the cultural understanding and consensus regarding things
sexual and romantic. To some degree dissatisfaction is everywhere: its dis-
sonance sounds in all spheres of culture.

Whatever the posture of a culture (i.e., its patterns of human activity
and the symbolic structures that give such activity significance) toward sex
and the many facets of love, ambiguities, conflicting emphases, perplexities,
unclear strictures, and downright quandaries litter the cultural landscape.
The diversity of ambivalence, tension, and contradiction around the globe
is infinite and (when viewed collectively) bewildering in its range of differences. But what human communities have in common is a universal
compulsion to make a working peace with the three-way conflict of ro-
mantic/passionate love, comfort/attachment love, and physical sex. Every
culture must decide whether to synthesize, separate, blend, discount, stress,
or ignore one or the other. For example, some ethnic groups in Papua New
Guinea believe that sexual intercourse is an intensely unhealthy and deeply
polluting experience that should be avoided. However, sex remains, in the
words of one man, "something that feels so good but is so bad for you"
(Terry Hays, personal communication, 1991). In a different Papua New
Guinean culture, men often run to the river to slice their penis with a
bamboo knife to let the contaminated blood flow from their body after a
sexual experience (David Boyd, personal communication, 1984). Contradictory or seemingly conflicted attitudes are evident among the Huli of
Papua New Guinea, where men abide by traditional taboos in their marriage while seeking out "modern" erotic experiences in their extramarital
life (see chapter 8; Wardlow 2006). Such conflicts can also be found in Igbo
men's need to develop an intimate comfort or attachment love with their
spouse while also seeking sexual pleasure through sexual variety with several partners (see chapter 9).

Because of the two distinct types of love—companionship (sometimes
call comfort love or attachment love) and passionate love or romantic love
(Hatfield and Rapson 1993) have their own logic and endocrinology—
many social tensions, conflicts, and individual moral ambivalences arise
from the efforts of each person or community to balance the twin forces.
By comfort love I mean a deep affection felt toward "those with whom our

lives are deeply intertwined. It involves feelings of friendship, understanding, and concern for the welfare of another" (Hatfield 1988:193–94; see also
Hatfield and Rapson 1996; Harvey and Wenzel 2001). In contrast, passionate love involves idealization of another, within an erotic setting, with the
presumption that the feeling will last for some time into the future. This
does not mean companionate love is without its passions. Percy Bysshe
Shelley, the nineteenth-century poet, thought passion was an integral aspect of both loves; albeit romantic love tended to be more physical, companionate love was more spiritual. Although both forms of love are present
in every culture, they are often not equally valued, celebrated, or honored.
This results in a tension that extends beyond the simple contrasting of two
desires and is, rather, a tripartite conflict of the sexual imperative, the romantic, and the companionate.

The cauldron of ambivalence is immediately apparent in the contradictions that flourish where passionate love is proclaimed as the authentic ground for relationships and marriage. In some societies the connection of love to sexual desire is only silently acknowledged (e.g., Mormon
Fundamental polygamous communities, Lahu, Tamil Nadu), whereas it is
doubted in others (e.g., Marri Baluch, Inuit Eskimo), and openly avowed
in still others (e.g., the United States, urban China). The tension between
passionate love and sex is echoed in Birgitt Röttger-Rössler's account in
chapter 6 of the Makassarese society of South Sulawesi, Indonesia, and its
struggle to reconcile societal duties with individual desire. Makassarese associate falling passionately in love with an illness, and treatment is considered essential. Contradictions are evident in high Himalayan polyandrous
societies where men and women are often caught in the grip of passionate
or excited love and forsake dyadic exclusivity so that the wife can manage
her relationships with all her husbands. Although some women can live, if
not thrive, in a plural marriage, every woman interviewed mentioned how
her life "is emotionally challenging . . . [which is why] many women prefer
monogamy" (Geeta Tiwari, personal communication, 2006). Unstated is
the presumption that the emotional quality of the husband-wife relationship is enhanced in a dyadic, as opposed to a plural, arrangement. Conflict
abounds among the Aka foragers, a society in which men and women are
engaged in competing reproductive strategies: Aka men, many of whom
feel a deep comfort love for their spouse, are still engaged in a "walkabout"
to find a second wife with whom to have more children, whereas wives often resort to physical violence to prevent their husband from leaving. The

Aka understand the wives' anguish while also respecting men's right to seek another wife (see chapter 2).

The discrepancy between the pull of romance and the tug of sexual passion is nicely delineated in Blanche DuBois' admonishment of her sister, Stella, in Tennessee Williams's play *A Streetcar Named Desire*. Blanche expresses her horror at Stanley Kowalski's obvious sexual appetite, saying: "A man like that is someone to go out with—once—twice—three times—when the devil is in you. But live with? Have a child by?" In this case the issues are erotic adventure and excitement versus the stability of domesticity and family. The irony in Williams's vision is that while Blanche argues for the latter as the ideal, much of her life has been consumed by the former. Blanche's problem is not uniquely American: Chinese literature is full of stories concerned with the difficulty of separating or blending the two emotions. In Li Yu's *Be Careful about Love*, written before European contact, a Qing dynasty emperor is attracted to the beauty of one woman while yearning for emotional intimacy with another. The emperor insists that "sexual love [is] a product of admiration of the other's good looks and talent [while] true love [is] the unalterable state that arises from that love" (Hannan 1988:144). The comments of both Blanche and the Qing emperor are representative of the conflict that lies at the heart of the push-pull tension between erotic attraction and a yearning for deeper emotional attachment.

Throughout history there have been various responses to the tripartite tension. For example, contemporary American swingers have institutionalized a set of ritual practices designed to uphold the primacy of the pair bond or comfort love, prevent the formation of a passionate love entanglement, and remain open to experiencing sexual pleasure with strangers. For swingers this is the ideal solution to the competing demands of the tripartite passions (see chapter 10). Another contemporary response is found in the development of sex tourism throughout the Caribbean, Southeast Asia, and other parts of the world. The construction of what Denise Brennan calls sexscape zones (see chapter 7; Brennan 2004) enables people, mostly men, to pursue a variety of sexual encounters rather inexpensively. In the case of mature European and American women, these zones enable some the opportunity to construct an imagined romance, however momentary, with someone who is unsuitable for a long-term comfort love relationship.

These societies, like societies everywhere, have constructed an often uneasy arrangement between the forces of passionate love, comfort love, and sexual desire. This arrangement requires continuous adjustment at the individual and societal level. In the domains of love and sex, society is never stable. The emotional tug between the competing and often contradictory desires ensures that every generation will revisit, renegotiate, and modify its "traditions" that account for the relationship between love and sex. Less known, and even less recognized, are the social constraints placed on the expression of different types of love and sex. Because the demands of passionate love and comfort love often differ from the push of sexual desire, their interrelationship or separation presents different structural problems, psychological dilemmas, and ethical issues for the individual and his or her community. This, then, is this book's central focus: To examine the opportunities, constraints, competing rationales, and social negotiations, voiced and unvoiced, about the appropriate relationship between the expression of passionate (and comfort) love and sex as they are manifested in a variety of ethnographic settings: as deeply felt authentic, albeit often antagonistic, realities.

LOVE: A CONTESTED DOMAIN

Throughout the twentieth century a war of ideas raged about the significance of love. The battle raged not just in regard to the origins and value of romantic passion but about whether attachment love was also real. Most academics did not consider love vital to psychological integration, personal contentment, and well-being. Although some scholars considered love an important value, they regarded it more as an artifact of personal philosophy than a biological imperative. Unless a culture taught otherwise, humans could do just fine without being loved. This was the predominant position, Deborah Blum points out, of mainstream psychology, which regarded affectionate mothering as irrelevant to a child's emotional well-being (2002:57). As a result psychologists advised parents not to develop too close an attachment with their children, lest the parents undermine the socialization process. B. F. Skinner (1974), influenced by the early work of John B. Watson (Buckley 1989), built upon this position to develop his theory of conditioned behavior. For Skinner, and his numerous disciples, Freud's insistence on the existence of an inner consciousness at odds with social circumstances was not only wrong but morally incorrect. Until the late 1970s Skinner's operate conditioning theory was the predominant psychological model taught in most U.S. university psychology departments.

Alternative theoretical frameworks, such as John Bowlby's attachment theory, challenged the Skinnerian paradigm. Bowlby believed that human infants have a biological need to form close loving bonds with a primary caretaker. He thought this behavior had its origins in human evolution. It evolved out of the parent-infant relationship, whereby an infant who was attached to specific individual(s) was more likely to survive (Bowlby 1982). Attachment theory, however, was received with deep skepticism and was severely criticized for advancing a theoretical model that lacked data.

Harry Harlow and R. R. Zimmerman's 1959 research on mother-infant attachment among different monkey species (e.g., rhesus, spider, Cebus, etc.) would change all that. It provided the data (as did other studies that focused on children raised in orphanages) necessary to support Bowlby's insights into the nature and importance of the attachment process. Until Bowlby the conventional wisdom held that "a baby's relationship with its mother was based entirely on being fed by her" (Blum 2002:57). Harlow and Zimmerman's research demonstrated that love matters and thus that the attachment process is essential to human well-being (Blum 2002:58). The development of evolutionary psychology, with its emphasis on discovery of human universals, provided further support for Bowlby's theoretical model (1982). We now know, as Bonnie Hewlett and Barry Hewlett point out in chapter 2, that "the attachment process and the ability to empathize and feel compassion for others influenced" the way humans bond with one another. Today the consensus among mainstream psychologists and anthropologists is that Bowlby and Harlow and Zimmerman got it right: the need for attachment is a human universal.[1]

The attachment theory has moved away from the study of the infant-parent bonding process to focus on how early childhood history shapes an individual's outlook and behavior in adulthood. James Chisholm (1999) has argued that a child's early home environment (e.g., families' access to material, natural, and emotional resources) can predict when a child will become sexually active as well as the child's ability to sustain lasting pair-bond relationships. In materially rich and stable home environments, Bonnie Hewlett and Barry Hewlett point out in chapter 2, children tend to develop a reproductive strategy that favors a late start to sexual relationships and a strong orientation toward forming long-term comfort love relationships, whereas children raised in materially limited or emotionally violated environments tend to begin sexual relationships earlier and have a weaker ability to form a long-term relationship. Moreover, individuals who have fragmented early childhood attachment bonds often adopt an approach to love that is organized around a "hopeless romantic" posture, whereby they fall quickly in and out of love or remain aloof and coldly objective and thus never "fall in love" (Chisholm 1995, 1999).

Is Passionate Love Universal?

At the close of the twentieth century social scientists reached a consensus as to the vitality, importance, and universality of attachment love. This has not been the case, however, for romantic love. Until the publication of the cross-cultural study that Fischer and Jankowiak undertook on the romantic love (1992), the conventional wisdom held passionate love to be a by-product of particular kinds of social configurations. It was thought that romantic love could be found only in stratified societies that had a leisure class with a rich literary tradition (Stone 1988), or it could be found in smaller-scale societies that encouraged mobility and individual decision making (Lindholm 1998). Fischer and Jankowiak (1992) found romantic love in 146 of 166 sampled cultures. Since that study was published, five additional cultures—Inuit (formerly, the Copper Eskimo), Shavante, Canala, Huron, and Chagga—have been reclassified from an inconclusive (or not clear) to the positively identified (or love present) category. The addition of these five cultures raises the number of positive confirmations to 151 of 166 cultures, or 91 percent. This finding stands in direct contradiction to the popular idea that romantic love is essentially limited to, or the product of, Western culture or is found only in smaller, highly mobile, and socially fragmented societies. Moreover, it suggests that passionate love constitutes a human universal, or at the least a near universal (Brown 1992).

Charles Lindholm, an insightful and highly productive anthropologist, has taken exception to our finding. He argues against romantic love's being a human universal. For Lindholm romantic love requires a special kind of social situation that encourages frequent mobility, weak social networks, and few alternatives for finding intimacy. In this setting individuals should "attempt to escape from certain types of social contradictions and structural tensions through the transcendental love of another person" (1998:258), thereby ensuring romantic love is the stronger and more salient reality. In contrast, romantic love will be absent whenever individuals are embedded in a rich web of intimacies that prevent the formation of an all-exclusive passionate love bond. In this setting, Lindholm contends, individuals are less likely to need, value, or desire to become involved in a romantic entanglement. From this perspective romantic love's appearance is closely linked to the social contradictions that arise from living in a particular kind of society. It follows, therefore, that romantic attraction should be unknown in relatively stable societies that are organized around forms of intimacies other than the pair bond.

There are three difficulties with Lindholm's position. First, his primary interest is exploring the relationship between structural factors and the emergence of a particular cultural ethos. His analytical interest ensures that his investigative eye focuses more on macro structures than on individual variation (Lindholm 1988b:244).Consequently, contexts outside his analytical framework are ignored. In the case of romantic love his approach cannot account for the presence of a particular emotional state in one context, its absence in another, and its denial, despite its presence, in yet another (see discussion in Schlegel 1990). The second, and in many ways more fundamental, problem is empirical. Numerous cultures are organized around large extended families, with dense social networks and stable social organizations that also value the pair-bond relationship (see appendix for listed cultures).[2] For example, Shanshan Du points out in chapter 4 that among the Lahu intimacy, marriage, and romance are interlocked, which defies the suggestion that romance leads to marriage only under the sociostructural conditions typical of the industrialized West. The Lahu highly value the husband-wife bond as the ultimate manifestation of the ideal form of intimacy. The Lahu emphasis on the pair bond is typical of other highland societies (e.g., Miao, Dai) in Southeast Asia. Finally, Lindholm's model of the mind is a blend of psychoanalytical and cognitive models that tend to regard emotion as a cultural construction, or at least a force deeply influenced by culture. Our disagreement lies in the meaning of "deeply influenced by culture."

Our position is closer to that of Robert Levy (1973), who believed that "underlying emotions are similar from one culture to another; what differs is the extent to which a culture emphasized or valued an emotion" (Reddy 2001:37). Levy classified cultures as falling along a continuum of emotional expressiveness that ranged from the "hypercognized" (i.e., emotions are "emphasized and consciously rehearsed, expressed, and discussed" [Reddy 2001:37]) to the "hypocognized" (i.e., emotions are "not named, denied, and concealed" [37]). This analytical distinction is useful. In the end the essential difference between cultures that separate sexual gratification from passionate love may not be the absence of the experience as much as a restriction of the contexts deemed appropriate for the expression of sexual gratification and passionate love.

Levy's position has received strong support from the emerging and rich research in neurobiology of affiliation (Dupre and Morrone-Strupinsky 2005). In the case of passionate love this research found that attachment and romantic love "share a common neural mechanism" (Bartels and Zeki 2004:1155). This suggests the existence of a neurophysiological substrate conducive for the development and maintenance of a pair-bond relationship (Porges 1988, 1998:838; also see Esch and Stefano 2005). Porges (1998) thinks this neurophysiological state is essential to induce the emotional response necessary to the formation of the pair bond. It also implies that humans with and without a culture's instruction are neurologically oriented to "fall in love" (see overview in Gray and Ellison in press).

Recent research on brain-wave patterning lends further support to the universality of passionate love. This research discovered that different areas of the brain are activated when an individual feels sexual desire and passionate love (Aron et al. 2005). Because humans share similar biological underpinnings, their experiences of sexual arousal, deep attachment, and romantic love are remarkably similar (Aron et al. 2005). If humans were completely culturally constructed beings, passionate love would have no neurological basis. This suggests that passionate love arises from forces within the hominid brain that are independent of the socially constructed mind. From this perspective passionate love is a universal, and it should be present, albeit not necessarily valued, in every culture.

Bonnie Hewlett and Barry Hewlett (chapter 2) believe that much of the disagreement between the evolutionary psychologists and many cultural anthropologists stems from the failure of both disciplines to recognize or accept that there can be different approaches to investigating a phenomenon. In the case of passionate or romantic love, they write in chapter 2, "Jankowiak (1995) uses an evolutionary psychology approach and focuses on understanding the universal and biologically based components of intimacy, while Lindholm (1998, 2001) uses evolutionary cultural anthropology (niche construction, in particular) to explain how sociocultural structures contribute to dramatic differences in human intimacy." They add, "The different approaches have different aims: evolutionary psychology is trying to explain human universals/nature, whereas evolutionary ecology and evolutionary cultural anthropology are trying to explain human diversity."

Sociological configurations can and do influence the formation of a culture's ethical ideals and emotional ethos. That passionate love is an experience that can surprise individuals in every society does not explain why some societies value it whereas others deny its existence.[3] Because researchers have rarely studied the relative frequency with which a person falls in and out of love, it is not clear whether passionate love is experienced with less frequency in those cultures that deny or disapprove of the emotional experience. The relative frequency with which members of a community experience passionate love may very well depend upon that culture's social structure, degree of social fluidity, and ideological orientation. Thus a greater proportion of Americans than Makassarese (see chapter 6) or Murik (Lipset 2004) may experience passionate love. I suspect this is the case. However, until this is substantiated through further field research, it remains only a hypothesis, as untested today as it was in 1992.[4]

Recently, Victor De Munck and Andrey Korotoyev's cross-cultural study of the relationship between romantic love and sexual equality (1999) lent a qualification to Lindholm's social structure (or niche construction) thesis. Their analysis centers on identifying the specific societal contexts or niche constructions that promote what they term "strong or weak love cultures" (1999:267). De Munck and Korotoyev found romantic love weakly correlated as a basis for marriage when a "double standard" tolerates the participation of only one sex (presumably men) in premarital sex and/or extramarital sex. On the other hand, when premarital sex and extramarital sex are prohibited for both sexes, romantic love is perceived as a more positive value. Weak love societies may provide other forms of belonging or avenues to intimacy (e.g., brother-sister relationships, same gender associations) that are equally or more satisfying than the sexually charged pair bond. In weak love societies passionate love should be present but in a more muted form, whereas in strong love cultures romantic love should readily be evident in a society's official ideology and in ordinary behavior.[5] This distinction may provide a way of synthesizing Lindholm's insights into the relationship between social structure and emotional expression

(1988a, 1988b) and the work of other anthropologists with different analytical lenses (see Padilla et al. in press).

SEXUAL DESIRE AND LOVE: IDEAL TYPES

Every sexual encounter need not be about the desire for some kind of transcendental merging with another. Some people desire nothing more than physical gratification or "release from arousal without emotional entanglements" (Abramson and Pickerton 1995:9). Simply put, sex, as the use or objectification of another, can be an act of pleasure. However, the norms, guidelines, and regulations regarding its conduct may not be successful, while the regulations themselves can be—at least in terms of influencing an individual to change her or his behavior. For individuals interested exclusively in uncomplicated sexual gratification, the ideal partner is anyone belonging to the individual's preferred sex orientation who is willing, available, and nonjudgmental. In this way sexual desire, in its most objectified form, is a total pursuit of physical pleasure. This perspective was captured in Henry Miller's *Tropic of Capricorn,* with its numerous depictions of graphic acts of sexual intercourse, or in his words: "It was fucking *Paradise* and I knew it, and I was ready and willing to fuck my brains away" (Miller 1962:182, cited in Mayne 1993:72). For Miller and many men sexual intercourse can be, at least some of the time, only about heightened physical sensation. Other times, however, the motivation for seeking sex can be more complicated. Bonnie Hewlett and Barry Hewlett point out in chapter 2 that the Aka foragers' pursuit of sexual pleasure is intertwined with another, more important value—reproduction. For the Aka, sexual intercourse is a pleasurable experience that is secondary to their primary goal, which is to have a child. Or, in the words of a young Aka woman, "Love is the work of the night; love and play are nice together if it makes a pregnancy." For the Aka, unlike many contemporary Americans and urban Chinese, reproduction, not erotic satisfaction, is the higher value.

Presently, there is a lively discussion in both scholarly and popular literature about the origins of gender-linked differences in the criteria used by men and women to select short-term and long-term partners (Townsend 1998; Small 1995).Despite, or perhaps because of, this discourse, a consensus is emerging that holds that women, in certain contexts, are as open as men to casual sexual encounters (see chapters 7 and 10, also Berscheid and Regan

1999; Cai Hua 2001; Hrdy 1999). The debate has now shifted to the meaning of "certain contexts." Whatever the eventual outcome of these discussions, it is clear that sexual monogamy does not come easily to mammals (including humans) or birds (Barash and Lipman 2001). If the pursuit of sexual fulfillment often results in individuals' seeking novelty, the love impulse, in both its passionate and comfort form, engenders an opposite inclination: to find intimacy with familiarity. Unlike sexual gratification, love cannot be bought (or, for that matter, arranged, anticipated, or outlawed). If passionate love is bought, it is invalidated. In contrast, sexual release and thus satiation, in the absence of a love bond, can result in an immediate disinterest in the other (Porges 1998). People in a state of passionate love discover that sexual gratification does not lessen but intensifies interest in the other.

The human sex urge, as Kingsley Davis (1976:223) observes, is often about more than simply achieving an orgasm. It can be about the desire for tactile contact and intimate communication with another person. However, sexual orgasm can give rise to stronger feelings of emotional involvement, even when there was little or no earlier interest. The desire for physical intimacy (i.e., close physical and emotional relationship) brings erotic interests into social relations, thereby linking eroticism with such interpersonal emotions as affection, trust, insecurity, and jealousy (Davis 1976:223). Héctor Carrillo, in an important study of the relationship between passion and sexuality in Mexico (2002), repeatedly found couples losing themselves and all rationality as their union dissolved into an emotional, transcendent ecstasy through their sexual interactions. In this way the pursuit of a "good risk" of an intense emotional entanglement may lead to a "bad risk" in sexual behavior (i.e., the loss of "safe sexual practice") (David Suggs, personal communication, 2007).

The tensions, quandaries, and perplexities in balancing love and sex are evident in the way Nevada prostitutes, working in legalized brothels, interact with their customers. Studies of prostitutes in San Francisco, Stockholm, and Amsterdam found that a high percentage of male customers expected the woman to demonstrate an interest and concern for their well-being (Bernstein 2007). For these customers the illusion of emotional intimacy is just as important as, and maybe more important than, being sexually satisfied. A similar pattern is apparent among some male customers at urban strip clubs. In a setting celebrating the objectification of a woman's body, regular customers often strove to develop a "relationship" with a particular stripper who, for her part, pretended to care about them (Frank

2002). Chapters 8, 9, and 10 report that even the domain of the extramarital tryst can quickly transcend the sexual to include the emotional. These and other examples reveal that emotional intimacy can and does arise from a highly sexually charged atmosphere. This is the central finding in Nicole Constable's 2003 study of mail-order brides: whatever men's and women's initial motivations for entering into correspondence, most felt, or sought to develop, emotional bonds with each other in the process of courtship.

PASSIONATE LOVE'S UNIVERSAL ATTRIBUTES

"Passionate love" refers to any intense attraction that involves the intrusive thinking about one person within an erotic context with the expectation that the feeling will endure for some time into the future. Helen Fisher (2004:416–17) lists the thirteen psychophysiological characteristics often associated with being in passionate love (also see Harris 1995:86). De Munck reports in chapter 3 that these characteristics are "(1) thinking that the beloved is unique; (2) paying attention to the positive qualities of the beloved"; (3) feelings of "exhilaration," "increased energy," "heart pounding," and intense emotional arousal induced by being in contact with or thinking of the beloved; (4) feeling even more connected to the beloved in times of adversity; (5) "intrusive thinking"; (6) feeling possessive and dependent on the beloved; (7) "desiring 'union' with the beloved; (8) having a strong sense of altruism and concern for the beloved; (9) reordering one's priorities to favor the beloved; (10) feeling sexual attraction for the beloved"; (11) ranking "emotional union" as taking "precedence over sexual desire." In addition, those feeling passionate love find that the feeling of passionate love is "involuntary" and not controllable and that passionate love is generally temporary (i.e., it can "range from a few days to a few years; but the limited duration is one distinguishing feature from companionship love" [Steve Meyers, personal communication, 2007]).

These emotional states may also be manifested behaviorally as "labile psychophysical responses to the loved person, including exhilaration, euphoria, buoyancy, spiritual feelings, increased energy, sleeplessness, loss of appetite, shyness, awkwardness . . . flushing, stammering, gazing, prolonged eye contact, dilated pupils . . . accelerated breathing, anxiety . . . in the presence of the loved person" (Fisher 1998:32). The presence of similar neurological mechanisms and brain patterns may account for the ability to readily identify when someone is romantically involved or erotically excited (Fisher 1998:32; Fisher 1995).

These traits also contribute to the formulation of a psychological configuration in which people in love believe the other person is not replaceable. People in love also experience a heightened sense of egalitarianism that transcends social status (De Munck and Korotayev 1999). For example, in a state of passionate love the emperor of China was not superior to his lover, whom he treated, however momentarily, as an equal (see Hinsch 1990 for historical cases). This, then, is one of love's most defining properties: the capacity for individuals to form a pair bond anchored in emotional exclusivity. It is difficult, perhaps nearly impossible, to love more than one person at any one time.

American psychological studies that investigated this phenomenon reported that about 25 percent of the undergraduates surveyed acknowledged that, at one time or another, they had been "in love" with more than one person. Most who acknowledged loving more than one person at the same time also acknowledged that they had not enjoyed the experience and were relieved when it ended. In an unpublished study Helen Gerth and Jankowiak found that some individuals who acknowledged being emotionally intertwined with two partners often preferred one to the other. For instance, the closer love was not the first one to call to say "good night" but was the love chosen to accompany the individual to a much anticipated event or the love who was dreamed about more often. Other individuals, however, were adamant that they could love two people at the same time. Our in-depth interviews revealed that all participants made an immediate and clear distinction between two types of love: comfort and passionate love. Significantly, no one in our sample admitted to being in a state of excited or passionate love with two or more individuals, nor did anyone acknowledge being involved in a comfort love relationship with two different individuals. Everyone acknowledged being involved in a comfort love relationship with one partner and a passionate love entanglement with a different partner. When we asked the participants if they could imagine themselves in love with three or more people at the same time, they expressed surprise and negative exasperation at what such an arrangement would involve. In fact, no one interviewed thought the experience of being in love with two people simultaneously was a pleasant or satisfying experience. Everyone we interviewed ($n = 27$) agreed strongly that being involved with concurrent loves is, in the words of a thirty-six-year-old woman, "a terrible, exasperating experience."

Further support for the inability to passionately love more than one person at a time comes from studies of polygynous societies in which the impulse to form an exclusive or passionate love bond is a powerful and, at times, overwhelming desire (see chapter 5, and Jankowiak, Sudakov, and Wilreker 2005; Jankowiak 2006). This research strongly suggests that although humans are not sexually monogamous, they are emotionally monogamous.

Passionate love interest starts with an attraction, a simple psychological state. One finds another person appealing, likable, good looking, charming, or sexy, or some combination of attractive traits. Attraction can be mild or strong, immediate or slow burning. It is embryonic and can grow or not. Attraction can lead to infatuation, a more absorbing and intense phase but also a more problematic state. As soon as the person is perceived to be a personality, we can say that love has arrived. Or, as Joseph Campbell wrote to his wife-to-be, Jean Erdman, in the early stages of their relationship: "My powers of criticism are paralyzed so far as you are concerned. It is, in fact, difficult to distinguish my condition from that of a person hypnotized" (1990:147). Although sexual attraction is possible without infatuation, attraction always accompanies infatuation. In fact, sexual attraction is the very essence of infatuation.

In ordinary life sexual desire and passionate love are two urges that form a complex that enables one proclivity to flow into the other and vice versa. Instead of thinking of them as two diametrically opposed feelings, it is more fruitful to view them as two intertwining, albeit separate, domains that can easily and readily become intermingled. From a biochemical perspective this makes sense: sexuality and emotional bonding are mutually reinforcing. Research has found that a sexual orgasm (combined with prolonged physical caressing) can trigger an oxytocin release that further serves to strengthen personal memory and attachment and thus contribute to sustaining a romantic (and also a companionate) love bond (Porges 1998). Clearly, passionate love and sex are separate domains. What is striking, however, is how easily they merge into one another.

Here we are in a qualified disagreement with Lindholm (2001), who argues that erotic attraction is not an essential aspect of romantic passion. For him, passionate love is asexual idealization or it is not love but lust. Lindholm's explanation of how idealization and transcendence are independent of eroticism is insightful. It is one thing, however, to note the presence of chaste love as an ideal, as it was in a medieval courtly setting, and another to infer that sexual desire is entirely absent. He offers two case studies (e.g., medieval European troubadour society and the Marri Baluch) in support of his position that passionate love can be a chaste form of love. In medieval Europe courtly ladies were well aware of sexual banter and the importance of erotic attraction. It was not unknown, as James Reston points out, "for poets to entertain the court with verses about unfaithful women who had victimized [a fellow] and left him loveless" (2001:30). The new discourse of asexual love must be understood against the backdrop of sexual frankness. The gradual replacement of the sexually raunchy with a new asexual discourse appealed to many aristocratic women (Reston 2001:30; Robertson 1969). This did not mean that sexual desire was absent. Rather, it only changed the conditions and settings in which the emotions were expressed. In time, the new "courtly style" became an institutionalized form of flirting that resulted, in some instances, in sexual seduction.

The second example of a chaste love society is the Marri Baluch. In this Afghanistan society men express their "love" for a married woman (a dangerous act) while denying their sexual interest. This may arise from the Marri Baluch men's truly lacking sexual interest, or it could simply be a convenient trope for denying sexual interest. Shanshan Du (2002) found chaste love, a form of comfort love, voiced as a high ideal among the Lahu (of southwest China). It is not unknown for married women and men to sing love songs about someone else. These love songs are devoid of erotic content. Expressing erotic feelings would be deemed rude and vulgar. Du reports in chapter 4, however, that it is clear that "the absence of erotic expressions in Lahu love songs and formal courtship is rooted in ambiguous cultural representations of sexual desire, rather than the absence of erotic feelings among the individuals." For the Lahu and the Miao extramarital love discourse (or institutionalized flirting) is restricted by ethical norms of propriety more than by the absence of erotic feelings. We suspect that a more complete investigation of Marri Baluch culture would find a remarkable similarity to the Lahu in domains of sex and love.

What is striking about these ethnographic cases is what they tell us about an individual in passionate love. Once emotionally involved, it is difficult not to become sexually involved. Equally striking, with the exception of a few unisexual religious communities (e.g., Trappist monks, Catholic convents), few societies are able to maintain an idealized version of chaste love. Certainly this speaks to the immense difficulties in separating sexual desire from an idealized version of chaste love.

This difficulty arises from passionate love's ability to heighten all our senses and thus our entire consciousness. Emotional and sexual passion is at its peak. The lovers are greedy for each other's presence. They feed on it, energizing each other; the intoxication is full of adrenaline, the senses are open full bore. The possibilities of erotic expression are wide open, restricted only by the lover's imagination. This phase has an unmistakable feeling that the experience may not end. Of course, lovers often realize that it will. But from within the experience, the sense is overwhelmingly the opposite. As Lord Byron once said, "My heart leaps up." There is the sensation of leaping, of being high, off the ground, in the clouds. Ecstasy, the apotheosis of love: mind and body identified with each other. In effect, an oceanic feeling.

At the individual level the ability to personalize the love object is what makes it so special yet so dangerous. This accounts for one of the most perplexing of passionate love's many paradoxes—its one-sidedness. This feeling is encapsulated in William Carlos Williams's words to his beloved: "I cannot say / that I have gone to hell / for your love / but often / found myself there / in your pursuit" (1955:17). The attempt to construct a public forum in which to reexperience a private grief is found in a Northwest Coast Indian song, "Menmenlequelas," in which a man, upon discovering that his lover has deserted him, laments:

> You are cruel to me, you are cruel to me, my dear.
> You are hard-hearted against me, you are hard-hearted against me, my love.
> You are surprisingly cruel, you are surprisingly cruel against me, for whom you pined. . . .
> Don't pretend too much that you are indifferent of the love that I hold for you, my dear.
> Else you may be too indifferent of the love that I hold for you, my dear!
> My dear, you are too indifferent to the love that I hold for you, my dear   (Boas 1898:108)

The worst obsession of all, resulting in the bitterest pain, may come from an encounter with a seducer or seductress; those sometimes enchanting, yet always dangerous, individuals are universally recognized as a Don Juan or femme fatale. These male and female seducers are found in tales around the globe. The seducers seem to be incapable of love, or they willfully use the love experience to manipulate and dominate their lover or lovers.

For the culture at large the seducer is often in opposition to social mores and norms. Few cultures formally condone the hostile manipulation of its members' emotional and sexual needs. In this way a femme fatale figure is a challenge to the culture, an outlaw who manipulates the conventions of love for her own ends. Ultimately, the seducer is the worst danger of all. The irony is that, frequently, the seducer will use the scent of danger as an erotic enticement to draw her or his victims forward and into the emotional web of dependency, for humans find risk and danger thrilling and stimulating despite our best judgments to the contrary. In other words, a romantic entanglement, an emotional snare, may be created out of erotic attraction.

Because men are prone to idealize female beauty, they can develop a love crush for a woman who is completely uninterested in them. This is the point of the cautionary femme fatale tales: they are warnings to men not to become emotionally involved with a pretty woman whom they do not know. A cross-cultural study of the femme fatale motif (Jankowiak and Ramsey 2000) found it present in 73 of 78, or 94 percent, of the sample cultures.[6] Because the seducer tales revealed anxiety, anticipation, expectation, and conflict as recurrent themes, they are more warnings against becoming ensnared in a sudden emotional involvement or "falling in love" than they are evidence of a culture's fear of sexual pollution.

"Sexual beliefs and practices are varying solutions to relatively invariant problems of human life" (Suggs and Miracle 1993:488). Societies appear to be compelled to account for, justify, and control their members' sexual behavior and affectionate displays. The primary means to accomplish this end is to develop a system of norms that reflect the society's highest ideals, which always deal with issues of family formation and biocultural continuity, albeit in different ways (Davis 1976). That is why cultures define what are proper and improper sexual displays and practices. Cultures recognize the dreadful danger of an encounter with a seducer as it can result in personal destruction as well as social chaos.

Our premise is simple: from the stew that is our genetically based and chemically driven biological urge for sex and emotional affiliation come the psychological experiences that have been variously dubbed, defined, and distinguished as infatuation, limerence, romantic love, or passionate love. When the two experiences occur at the same time, an aesthetic unity is formed. However, whenever sexual desire and loving intimacy are at odds with one another, a competition occurs. This competition is accompanied by important implications for understanding the difficulty that cultures encounter in balancing and regulating sexuality, both as private experience and as a mode of social behavior.

Culture's Response to the Dilemma

Cultural attitudes toward sexuality range anywhere from a deep apprehension or fear to an open, naturalistic approach and to what can be perceived as permissive or promiscuous. More often than not, a culture's attitude is mixed. Most cultures, in fact, exhibit ambivalence toward sex and love, an ambivalence that bears a compelling resemblance to the multiple confusions and anxieties common in the West today and that are particularly acute in the United States. At the social level cultures are cognizant of how human desire leads to various forms of behavior between the sexes (and between members of the same sex) that must be regulated, guided, channeled, and restricted.

To guard against the formation of unexpected and unplanned love bonds, cultures have developed a multitude of forms of social regulation (Collins and Gregor 1995) that can include "harem polygamy . . . seclusion of women and chaperonage, obsession with virginity, descent systems that create primary allegiances to parents rather than spouses, clitoridectomy, the men's house complex, association of women with impurity and contamination . . . and patterns of sexual promiscuity that undermine enduring relationships" (Gregor 1995:338). Cultures that adopt these strategies of direction strive to uncouple passionate love bonds from feelings of sexual satisfaction. The senior generation in most cultures, Alice Schlegel reminds us, seeks to "control the young through control over their future sexual [love] lives" (1995:186). In these societies, the passionate love bond is held to be a potential rival to other, more important, nondyadic loyalties (Schlegel and Barry 1991). It is further understood that feelings of sexual attraction can lead to deeper relationships of human feeling that in turn can develop into full-scale resistance to parental authority. In the case of passionate love, parental guidance is often one of definition: Is it supposed to exist? If so, when and how should it be expressed (Person 1988)?

The devaluation of passionate love did not mean companionate love was equally devalued. The idealization of companionate love, as a publicly

stated and valued element for the making of the good marriage, is a relatively recent development (Hirsch and Wardlow 2006). This new global
phenomenon should not obscure companionate love's presence in numerous societies, and thus marriages, before the elevation of companionate to
official ideal in the local cosmology. Until this occurred, companionate love
remained an unvoiced, albeit immensely gratifying (from the perspective
of individuals involved), emotional state. The ethnographic and historical literature contains a wealth of cases that demonstrate the presence of
intimate or comfort love within societies that made a fetish of duty and
honor (Jankowiak, Sudakov, and Wilreker 2005). The transformation of
the world's economies that has resulted in the replacement of the extended
family with the conjugal family did not create the feeling state of companionate love as much as it transplanted comfort love from the private
domain into the dominion of cultural expectation.

Although there are different ways to integrate sexual desire and passionate (and comfort) love, one pattern stands out: the endorsement of one desire or form of love often results in the diffusion of the other. This pattern
can be found in the study of rural Chinese and Korean suicide patterns. In
both societies female suicide is clustered around two different age cohorts:
early twenties and late forties. The plight of young wives in patrilineal societies is well known; not well known is the plight of middle-aged women,
who also have a high rate of suicide (Wolf and Witke 1975). The cluster of
suicidal women in their late forties arises from a real or imagined shift in
emotional loyalty between a mother and her son. Because rural Chinese
and Korean mothers develop intensely close emotional bonds with their
sons (Wolf and Witke 1975), these women can become acutely paranoid,
believing that their son's new wife will monopolize his time, attention, and,
in the end, love. The reasons for suicide among middle-aged Chinese or
Korean women stem from their perception of being emotionally replaced
by their daughter-in-law as their son's primary source of affection. Believing their son's affection and loyalty have diminished, some women lapse
into a depression that leads to suicide. The Chinese and Korean arranged
marriage cases demonstrate that out of prolonged sexual intimacy can
come emotional intimacy or comfort love.

The interrelationship of the sexual, procreational, and emotional domains is also evident in Samoans' ambivalence toward sex and love. This
ambivalence arises from a brother-sister intimacy bond, an asexual form of
love, that serves as the paradigmatic model for the ideal relationship. This

folk model, Brad Shore believes (1996:291–92), accounts for a deep-seated uneasiness that Samoans adopt toward the erotic. This uneasiness never goes away. Shore suggests that the "psychological complexities of forming erotic attachments may account for [the frequent] violence between lovers and spouses" (1996:292). In effect, Samoans often use violence to eroticize their marriage. How representative is the Samoan case? Is sexual ambivalence toward the erotic typical of any culture (or individual) that idealizes the brother-sister relationship over the husband-wife bond? This holds for the Tamil Nadu of South India, where strong brother-sister intimacy competes with and undermines the husband-wife bond (Trawick 1990). It is also true for contemporary Hohhotian Chinese Muslims (Hui) who have close brother-sister ties, as well as a much greater frequency of spousal abuse than the local Mongol and Han Chinese communities (personal communication with Chinese researcher who prefers to remain anonymous, 2002). Further research may find that the high incidence of spousal abuse among rural Chinese spouses may result from Chinese men's striving to overcome their deep asexual love bond toward their mother. If so, the Chinese men use physical violence—much like the Samoans—as a way to transform an asexual love bond into an eroticized encounter. If this interpretation holds across cultures, it demonstrates that there are psychological costs to valuing the brother-sister bond more highly than the husband-wife bond.

THE METAPHORS OF SEX AND LOVE

How a culture understands the relationship between the many faces of love and sex determines which type of metaphor will be appropriate or inappropriate in conversation among and between members of the same and the opposite sex. The discontinuities between what we say with our voice and what we say with our body are one reason why cultural codes regulating sexual desire and emotional interest are so hard to enforce. This is also why, during intense social change, so many people are unsure of how to act in mixed company. In many instances they become intensely unsure of what signals they are sending or if, indeed, these signals are being received and understood.

Three distinct, albeit often overlapping, discourses are used to converse about feelings of love and sexual desire: deerotic, the polyerotic, and the uniromantic. Each discourse reflects a culture's synthesis of the meaning of love and sex. No matter what the culture's notion of an appropriate discourse, nonverbal expressions (particularly those that may contradict the verbal ones) are the source of confusion.

Perhaps the most common posture, the deerotic, prefers not to use explicit sexual metaphors in public conversation, deeming them crude and vulgar. This style is most commonly found in ranked or stratified societies that confine sexual topics to conversations among same-sex age-mates. On the other hand, the polyerotic style tends to accentuate sexual imagery in ordinary speech. For example, women in polyerotic cultures often respond to male sexual banter by asserting the value of their sexuality. For these women their sexuality is a source of pride and thus their dignity. Among the Tongan "discourse is humorous, with joking and teasing being frequently employed in conversation" (Morton 1996:176). Helen Morton typically found that Tongan women's response to men's sexual joking was to hit, punch, or push the men, albeit in good humor (see also Malinowski's *Sexual Life of Savages*). The polyerotic style is evident in the humorous putdowns ("playing the dozens") of late twentieth-century African American teenagers. As with any form of speech, the use of sexual imagery has numerous connotations and contexts. At times the banter can imply good-natured joking; other times it conveys intense sexual desire or hints at secret romantic desire or attachment. Occasionally, the banter disguises a troubling ambivalence toward the opposite sex. Significantly, with the exception of U.S. subcultures, societies that favor the polyerotic discourse pattern tend to disapprove of public expressions of romantic or affectionate love and displays of emotional intimacy. These behaviors are considered to be private matters and not open to public consumption.

Significantly, cultures that favor the Tongan pattern disapprove of public expressions of love and displays of emotional intimacy. These behaviors are considered to be private matters between individuals and not for public consumption. In contrast, the monogamous U.S. pattern is organized around the notion of idealized love, which approves and glorifies public displays of affection in speech and behavior, so long as such displays are not overtly sexual. Although romantic metaphors are the preferred language of courtship, it is understood, as it was in medieval court society, that the metaphors may range in meaning and implications from pure lust to unrequited affection. In looking back over the historical record, it is painfully obvious that ethnographers and explorers misunderstood or misperceived the numerous forms of affiliation that can exist inside and outside the "official" culture. The three competing discourse patterns represent the inability of the individual and the official culture to reconcile the two volatile emotions of sexual desire and passionate love. The ethnographic record shows a clear relationship between a gender's economic and political influence and the preference for a specific discourse or language pattern. This sex difference may account for the uniromantic discourse's pushing out the polyerotic in medieval European court society. When aristocratic women, the standard-bearers for eleventh- and twelfth-century European social manners, found uniromantic discourse more aesthetically satisfying than the polyerotic, a new style emerged. Whatever meaning courtly love held for the individual, this uniromantic style also served to establish social boundaries between the cultural elite and the peasantry. Whereas the peasantry enjoyed the crudities of sexual bantering, the elite, especially its women, preferred to deemphasize the erotic in favor of romantic imagery. In this way the earthy language of Eros, or what is conceptualized as the polyerotic pattern, was replaced by the high-flown language of romance and gentility, an idiom that is used in many strata across the United States today (Jankowiak 1999).

In our own era Kevin Birth and Morris Freilich's 1995 diachronic study of the transformation of Trinidadian gender relationships effectively documents the impact of disease, cultural diffusion, and social stratification on the change from the polyerotic pattern to a recognizably uniromantic pattern. In effect, Birth and Freilich found that romantic metaphors had replaced sexual metaphors as the preferred idiom, at least by men, for a male-female courtship and for public address. Previously, the preferred idiom was organized around sexual imagery that regularly disguised or diminished underlying implications of romantic passion. Birth and Freilich suggest that Trinidadian women's new economic independence enabled them to effect the change to romantic imagery, with its metaphors closely related to relationships, generosity, and family. Michael Angrosino (personal communication, 1994) found, during the late 1970s, that Trinidadians were careful to affirm the permissibility of speaking openly about sex but the need to touch privately on matters of the heart. Linda-Anne Rebhun (1995) also noted that nearby northeast Brazilians made a similar distinction. She found passionate love was always a possibility, though not necessarily an articulated fact of life, that customarily grew out of the sexual encounter.

Oscar Lewis (1966) made a similar observation in the 1950s when he found that Puerto Ricans had adopted a like-minded approach to matters of sex and matters of the heart.

EXPRESSING AND BEING IN LOVE: SEX DIFFERENCES?

The sex difference reported for men and women in more complex, state-level societies (see overview in Buss 1992; Symons 1979) may account, in part, for the phenomenon of instant attraction, or "love at first sight." If male erotic and romantic idealization of women is based on images of physical attraction, that would also account for men's ability to quickly shift between sexual fantasy and deep romantic affection. Customarily, women show more interest in assessing a man's social status or understanding his character. These criteria, in contrast to physical attractiveness, appear to be the more dominant for female mate selection and the formation of romantic fantasies. In China, for example, men often admit to "falling in love" with a good-looking woman whom they frequently encountered but seldom actually spoke to. In the words of one twenty-nine-year-old man, "I dreamed of someone like her last night. She was so beautiful. I knew I wanted to marry her" (Jankowiak 1993:219). The word *like* may be pivotal, for it suggests an image, not a particular person. This phenomenon is echoed in the Brazilian proverb "Born in a glance and matures in a smile" (Rehbun 1995:253). U.S. sociological research also has found that men tend to "fall in love" faster than women, who are correspondingly and consistently slower to make such emotional commitment (Canican 1987). In this way physical attraction, at least for men, might prove to be a primary catalyst for romantic idealization. Since it takes much longer to evaluate character than it does physical beauty, women may be slower to become romantically involved or to commit completely to a mate. Because no studies from small-scale societies focus on the speed at which men and women fall in love, it is difficult to determine whether Euro-American data is a cultural specific response or panhuman. This is less the case for studies of male and female sexual strategies.

Evolutionary psychological research (see overviews in Buss 2003, 2007; Batten 1992; Brizendine 2006) has consistently confirmed the reality of sex differences in the pursuit of short- and long-term sexual strategies around the globe. This research holds that men and women have innate sex differences in the qualities that attract them to a potential lover or mate; for men the qualities are youth, health, and physical attraction, whereas for women the qualities are ambition, social and economic success, and generosity (Symons 1979). Recently, female scholars (Ramsawh and Harris 2003) have noted that much of this research may be age biased: it focuses primarily on college students, or men and women in their reproductive prime. Left unexamined is the frequency with which a middle-aged woman is willing to adjust her short- and long-term sexual selection criteria. Ramsawh and Harris (2003) found evidence that mature women, in certain contexts, can benefit from modifying their selection criteria in short-term sexual encounters. In this way the differences in sexual selection criteria may disappear as women (but not necessarily men) age. This does not mean there are no innate sex differences. It does suggest that "cultural influences exaggerates [sic] basic differences that evolved under adaptive pressure" (Ramsawh and Harris 2003:1396; also see chapter 2).

The differences in male and female sexual strategies underlie much of the cultural tension that arises in trying to balance sexual desire and passionate love. Female sex choice is grounded in selecting a male whose accomplishments have the highest contextual value, while male choice is grounded more in physical attraction (Batten 1992). Because the value of a particular context can change, females are more able than males to rapidly adjust their mate selection criteria. The differences in sexual strategies can also result in male disappointment and anger at being rejected by someone they have idealized, albeit from afar. The sex differences in strategies can also be manifested in female bitterness and resistance whenever women perceive that their partner is wasting family resources. Because males and females often expect different things from each other, the sexual relationship can easily become filled with ambiguity, tension, conflict, and anger.

The cool objectivity found in mate selection criteria of different societies often quickly disappears whenever the discussion shifts to the meaning of love. For many, romantic entanglement is one of life's truly authentic and deeply moving experiences. It stands, as such, in direct opposition to the more instrumental and pragmatic values found in a culture's discourse on the ideal mate. The potential conflict found in their different reproductive interests ensures that men and women will often approach the domain of sexual pleasure with different expectations, ensures whenever men and women discuss the erotic, it will inevitably be with muffled ears. But as soon as the conversation shifts to the domain of love, the differences that were so explicit and raw in the sexual domain disappear. Men and women are united in the meaning and purpose of love.

The psychologist Dorothy Tennov (1979) maintains, with little evidence, that no difference exists between American men's and women's experience of passionate and comfort love. Although social factors are responsible for the cultural variation found in the expression of romantic passion, it remains to be seen, once a state of passionate love arises, whether both parties' experience is the same. Ethnographic evidence tends to support Tennov's position. For example, I found in the 1980s that urban Chinese women were somewhat more reserved and cautious than men during the initial stages of courtship (Jankowiak 1993). Susan Davis and David Davis (1995) also found a similar pattern among Moroccan women. However, we all reported that once a woman became emotionally involved, men and women evidenced no noticeable gender difference in the way they articulated or displayed the feeling state. Cathy Davidson (1992) drew a similar conclusion from her literary history of Western civilization's view of love. She reported that whenever she read an author's description of being in the state of love, she had immense difficulties determining the century in which the author lived. Tennov would, no doubt, think that Davidson would have trouble recognizing the gender of the writer as well. Recent neurobiological research (Marazziti and Canale 2004) is supportive of Tennov's position. This research examined the relationship between specific hormonal changes, sexual arousal, and emotional attachment and discovered that the levels of the hormones estradiol, progesterone, DHEAS, and androstenedione did not differ significantly between men and women in a state of passionate love (2004:934). The authors concluded that humans in a state of passionate love are remarkably androgynous, at least in their biochemical composition. If this research is confirmed by later studies, it would not be unreasonable to conclude that men and women in a state of passionate love (if not comfort love) are remarkably similar. It remains to be seen, however, whether this is also holds for men and women who are sexually aroused. To date, evolutionary psychologists have been relentless in documenting sex differences in the way the erotic is understood, pursued, and savored. The emerging research on comfort and passionate love is finding minor sex differences in the way love is experienced. If this finding proves to be representative, it may account for the perennial human dilemma: the push for sexual enjoyment often differs from the pull of affective involvement.

***

We contend that passionate (and comfort) love and sexual desire are three of the more powerful human sentiments. These three sentiments are organized around different cultural and psychological criteria, which puts them in direct competition with one another in several ways, and this competition raises important implications for understanding some of the turmoil often found in male-female relationships. The turmoil is not recent. The comparative story of love and sexuality is intertwined with the evolutionary story of hominid sexual dimorphism, which suggests that the pair bond arose about 1.8 million years ago (Fuentes 2002).Contemporary ethnographic research reported in this chapter and elsewhere (Ahearn 2001, 2003; Hirsch and Wardlow 2006; Rebhun 1999) finds that the love-sex conundrum exists everywhere, and, with it, the dilemma about how to satisfactorily reconcile these three often volatile and conflicting forces, especially for individuals in a given culture.

Sex and passionate (and comfort) love are fundamental experiences that often result in strong emotional bonds with which every community must deal. Parents realize that they must instruct their children about how to avoid romantic manipulation and, more important, how to recognize appropriate human affection. Cultural models are useful in that they provide an explanation of how to integrate the many facets of love and sex into a more unified whole. These models or explanations can be challenged by individuals and interest groups (e.g., Christian fundamentalists, libertines, and so forth; see Marazziti and Canale 2003) that offer alternative models for the proper relationship of the types of love and sex. But this raises a larger and more vexing issue: Is the dilemma for individual and culture between sexual desire and passionate love? Or is it between passionate love and comfort love? Or are we dealing with a triangular relationship? (Steve Meyer, personal correspondence, 2006). Certainly one can exist without the other—a disheartening fact in cultures in which the goal is to blend them—but this examination is primarily concerned with their universal tripartite relationship.

All these concerns are most vividly manifested in public discussions as well as in our private pathos, for it is the individual who must address, bracket, rationalize, and thus manage the perennial tensions between the facets of love and lust. Few achieve a lasting peace with it or are satisfied with their synthesis; most of us continue to combine in some fashion the push and pull of sexual attraction, delighting in passionate love and the stability that comes with a comfort love. The poet W. B. Yeats revealed his personal struggle with integrating these often dueling passions. Yeats noted that he had labored for nearly half his life under the cultural imperative of upholding the aristocratic conventions and refinements of high-brow comfort love but came to realize that this posture could be more distancing than any societal restraint. In the end Yeats understood that the conventional language of passionate love, the tradition that he inherited as a poet and, more important, as a man, had become an inbred, private language increasingly removed from true passion and real feeling. The volatile nature of contemporary life ensures that everyone around the world will continue, as observers and participants, to confront, in their own way, the meaning of Yeats's dilemma.

***

I would like to thank the following people for encouragement, suggestions, and revisions: Jim Bell, Vicki Burbank, Shanshan Du, Victor De Munck, Carol Ember, Ted Fischer; Helen Fisher, Vanessa Fong, Stacey Garretson, Elaine Hatfield, Barry Hewlett, Libby Hinson, Steve Meyers, Tom Gregor, Helen Gerth, Libby Hinson, Polly Kummel, Charles Lindholm, David Lipset, Anne Routon, Pam Stern; Alice Schlegel, David Suggs, Daniel Smith, Jennifer Thompson, and Holly Wardlow.

Notes

1. Recent neurobiological research lends further support to Bowlby's attachment theory. This research sought to document hormonal changes related to sexual arousal and emotional attachment. It repeatedly demonstrates the presence of an interrelationship of neurohypophyseal peptides such as oxytocin (a peptide originating in the hypothalamus within the brain), vasopressin, and the formation of distinct forms of affiliation manifested in monogamous union, mating, guarding, and paternal care (Hofer 1995; Unvas-Moberg 2003). In a related study Burnham and colleagues (2003) found a link between decreased levels of testosterone (T) in men in committed relationships. They write that the "long-term pair bond (and not just in the context of marriage) [is] an important predictor of male T levels" (2003:3). In effect, these hormones play an essential part in the evolution of social animal behavior (Gray et al. 2004; Gray in press).

2. Another objection comes from Bonnie Adrian (2003) in her book *Framing the Bride: Globalizing Beauty and Romance in Taiwan's Bridal Industry,* in which she notes in an endnote (263n4) that the 1992 cross-cultural survey is flawed as it is based on an erroneous assumption: that cultures exist as independent entities. This is a familiar criticism of cross-cultural research (often referred to as Galton's problem). Because cultures influence each other, it is difficult to determine cultural borders. Consequently, the migration of ideas, sentiments, and behaviors can result in a researcher's comparing cultures thought to be distinctive when they are in fact remarkably similar. Cross-cultural researchers seek to control for this problem by striving to keep the ethnographic time and social space as similar as possible (see discussion in De Munck 2000). Further, dismissing a study as erroneous because it "reifies culture" does not help us understand or account for the persistence of the behavioral trait across divergent linguistic communities or its presence within a range of belief systems and in different levels of social organizations.

In looking for evidence of a human universal, a researcher is less constrained by Galton's problem, or the issue of culture reification. Since the focus of the investigation is on individual behavior and not culture or its official ideology, even an extreme influence of one culture on another does not seriously distort the finding. If a human universal is present, it should be manifested in similar behavioral acts around the globe. This is what we found. Thus the objection that we "reified culture" is not applicable to any analysis of human universals, as the analytical focus is on the individual and not the community.

Adrian's second objection, based on research conducted by ethnopsychologists (e.g., Lutz 1988) who stress the relationship of cognition, emotion, and ethical choice, is conceptual. The position of ethnopsychologists is that emotions are social constructions, and thus there is no such thing as a basic emotion or human universal. This is Adrian's opinion, not Lutz's (1988:210); Lutz points out that there probably are universal emotional expressions (or basic emotions), because there are culturally constructed emotions. Lutz's qualification is consistent with the neurophysiological literature of emotions, mostly unread by strict cultural constructionists, who do not consider the neurophysiological literature relevant to understanding the factors that promote cultural variation.

3. It appears that Lindholm's cross-cultural study (1998, 2001) never developed criteria for dropping cultures from the sample. He used the entire Human Relations Area Files (HRAF) data set. This resulted in a distorted research design as the quality of ethnographic reporting is not similar for all cultures listed in HRAF. Therefore, a researcher cannot be confident that the data contained within his or her sample is equally comprehensive or of similar quality. It would not be until the 1980s when ethnographers (who were not working within the cultural and personality paradigm) began to study emotions, and with this area of investigation came an interest in the exploration of individuals' subjective lives (see overview in Lyons and Lyons 2004). The negative findings arise not because native populations did not

experience these emotions but rather because earlier ethnographers did not write about them. As Lew Langness noted in a 1986 conversation: "We were not supposed to write on these subjects." Given this limitation, any cross-cultural sample seeking to explore the presence or absence of a particular emotion must develop criteria in which to drop cultures that *do not contain* information about individual subjective feelings and behaviors. Failure to develop such criteria will result in a distortion of the validity and representativeness of the sample and therefore the analysis. Without examining a culture's folklore, we would not have found as many cases in which passionate love is present. In relying upon interviews (and folklore texts) we were able to overcome some gaps in conventional ethnographic accounts.

4. Our cross-cultural survey was designed, however, to see if there was evidence for romantic passion around the world, as evidenced in standardized behavioral acts and emotional expressions. Our survey was not designed to identify the cultural rules for expression of love in different societies. If everything is culturally constructed, how would a constructionist account for the presence of similar behavioral traits in so many different societies? Until cultural constructionists can provide a cultural explanation for the existence and persistence of behavioral attributes associated with people in love, the constructionists' objections to the analysis of evolutionary psychologists and behavioral ecologists can never be taken seriously.

5. Recently, David Lipset, in an important paper (2004) examines one component of our definition of passionate love and finds that idealization of the beloved is absent among the Murik (Papua New Guinea), at least as it is voiced during the Murik courtship process. In its place the ritualization of masculine expression has become the primary context for the assertion of masculine identity during courtship. As it was not the focus of the paper, he does not explore whether the Murik men are capable of idealizing their beloved in other contexts. He does note that it was not unknown for a woman to elope to another village to be with someone she chose, rather than follow her parents' wishes. Lew Langness (personal communication) also noted that Bema women often demonstrated a strong preference for someone other than the man selected by their parents. This resulted in friction, which was resolved after the woman ran away with her choice of marital partner. Lipset reported that a popular Murik folktale discusses how a man can use love spells to compel the woman of his choice to "look at no one but himself" (Lipset 2004:211). Lipset used this tale to make an important point: The Murik discourse on courtship and love does not privilege the self's merger with the beloved. However, the tale does reveal that the Murik behave as if love is about involvement best disclosed through a series of behavioral preferences that are organized around the creation and protection of sexual-emotional exclusivity. Thus the notion of emotional exclusivity for another does not seem foreign to Murik sensibilities. Their emotional preference is manifested behaviorally more than it is verbally. What is needed are more case studies, such as David Lipset's study of the Murik, in which

the ethnographer probes the subjective domain in order to understand the processes of love and sexual desire as they are manifested in daily life.

6. An early twentieth-century Inuit Eskimo tale is representative of the desire and fear surrounding female beauty. In the tale a hunter comes upon a dazzlingly hypnotic woman who sings: "Come, come, lonely hunter. Now I will embrace you, embrace you now." The hunter, overwhelmed by the singer's beauty, jumps into a frigid river and swims toward the woman, who begins to move slowly away, downstream. After extraordinary effort he finally reaches her, only to have the woman turn into a night owl and fly into the night, laughing. Exhausted from the ordeal, the hunter passes out and freezes to death (Boas 1969). A similar tale can be found in a story told by the Ibo of southern Nigeria that is aptly titled "A Pretty Stranger Who Killed a King." It deals with a man who falls in love with a strikingly pretty woman who is a witch in disguise; after he falls asleep, she cuts off his head (Bascom 1975:33).

REFERENCES

Abramson, P. and S. Pickerton, eds. 1995. *Sexual Nature and Sexual Culture.* Chicago: University of Chicago Press.

Adrian, B. 2003. *Framing the Bride: Globalizing Beauty and Romance in Taiwan's Bridal Industry.* Berkeley: University of California Press.

Ahearn, L. 2001. *Invitations to Love: Literacy, Love Letters, and Social Change in Nepal.* Ann Arbor: University of Michigan Press.

——. 2003. "Writing Desire in Nepali Love Letters." *Language and Communication* 23:107–22.

Aron, A., H. Fisher, D. Mashek, G.. Strong, Haifang Li, and L. Brown. 2005. "Reward, Motivation, and Emotion Systems Associated with Early-Stage Intense Passionate Love." *Journal of Neurophysiology* 94:327–37.

Barash, D. and J. Lipman. 2001. *The Myth of Monogamy.* New York: Freeman.

Bartels, A. and S. Zeki. 2004. "The Neural Correlates of Material and Passionate Love." *NeuroImage* 21:1155–66.

Bascom, W. 1975. *African Dilemma Tales.* Chicago: Mouton.

Batten, M. 1992. *Sexual Strategies: How Females Choose Their Mates.* New York: New York: G. P. Putnam's Sons.

Bernstein, E. 2007. *Temporarily Yours: Sexual Commerce in Post-Industrial Culture.* Chicago: University of Chicago Press.

Berscheid, E. and P. Regan. 1999. *Lust: What We Know about Human Sexual Desire.* Thousand Oaks, Calif.: Sage.

Birth, K. and M. Freilich. 1996. "Putting Romance into Systems of Sexuality: Changing Smart Rules in a Trinidadian Village." In Jankowiak, *Romantic Passion,* pp. 262–76.

Blum, D. 2002. *Love at Goon Park: Harry Harlow and the Science of Affection.* Cambridge, Mass.: Perseus.

Boas, F. 1898. *The Mythology of the Bella Bella Indians.* New York: American Museum of Natural History.

Bowlby, J. 1982. *Attachment.* New York: Basic Books.

Brennan, D. 2004. *What's Love Got to Do with It? Transnational Desires and Sex Tourism in the Dominican Republic.* Durham, N.C.: Duke University Press.

Brizendine, L. 2006. *The Female Brain.* New York: Morgan Road Books.

Brown, D. 1992. *Human Universals.* New York: McGraw Hill.

Buckley, K. 1989. *Mechanical Man: John Broadus Watson and the Beginnings of Behaviorism.* New York: Guilford.

Burnham, T.C., J.F. Chapman, P.B. Gray, M.H. McIntyre, S.F. Lipson, and P.T. Ellison. 2003. "Men in Committed, Romantic Relationships Have Lower Testosterone." *Hormones and Behavior* 44:119–22.

Buss, D. 2003. *The Evolution of Desire.* New York: Basic Books.

——. 2007. *Evolutionary Psychology: The New Science of the Mind.* 3d ed. New York: Allyn and Bacon.

Cai Hua. 2001. *A Society without Fathers or Husbands.* New York: Zone Publishers.

Campbell, J. 1990. *Hero's Journey: Joseph Campbell on His Life and Work.* New York: Harper and Row.

Canican, F. 1987. *Love in America.* Cambridge: Cambridge University Press.

Carrillo, H. 2002. *The Night Is Young: Sexuality in Mexico in the Time of AIDS.* Chicago: University of Chicago Press.

Chisholm, J. 1995. "Love's Contingencies: The Development Socioecology of Romantic Passion." In Jankowiak, *Romantic Passion,* pp. 42–56.

——. 1999. *Death, Hope and Sex.* Cambridge: Cambridge University Press.

Collins, J. and T. Gregor. 1995. "Boundaries of Love." In Jankowiak, *Romantic Passion,* pp. 72–92.

Constable, Nicole. 2003. *Romance of a Global Stage: Pen Pals, Virtual Ethnography, and "Mail Order" Marriages.* Berkeley: University of California Press.

Davidson, C. 1992. *The Book of Love: Writers and Their Love Letters.* New York: Simon and Schuster.

Davis, K. 1976. "Sexual Behavior." In R.K. Merton and R. Nisbet, eds., *Contemporary Social Problems,* pp. 219–38. New York: Harcourt Brace.

Davis, S. and D. Davis. 1995. "Possessed by Love: Gender and Romance in Morocco." In Jankowiak, *Romantic Passion,* pp. 219–38.

De Munck, V.C. 2000. "Introduction: Units for Describing and Analyzing Culture and Society." *Ethnology* 39 (4): 279–92.

De Munck, V.C. and A. Korotayev. 1999. "Sexual Equality and Passionate Love: A Re-Analysis of Rosenblatt's Study on the Function of Passionate Love." *Cross-Cultural Research* 33:265–77.

Du, S. 2002. "Chopsticks Only Work in Pairs": Gender Unity and Gender Equality among the Lahu of Southwest China. New York: Columbia University Press.

Dupre, R. and J. Morrone-Strupinsky. 2005. "A Neurobehavioral Model of Affiliative Bonding: Implications for Conceptualizing a Human Trait of Affiliation." *Behavioral and Brain Sciences* 28 (3): 313–50.

Esch, T. and G. Stefano. 2005. "The Neurobiology of Love." *Neuroendocrinology Letters* 26 (3): 175–92.

Fisher, H. 1995. "The Nature and Evolution of Romantic Love." In Jankowiak, *Romantic Passion*, pp. 23–41.

——. 1998. "Lust, Attraction and Attachment in Mammalian Reproduction." *Human Nature* 9 (1): 23–52.

——. 2004. *Why We Love: The Nature and Chemistry of Romantic Love.* New York: Owl Books.

Frank, K. 2002. *G-Strings and Sympathy: Strip Club Regulars and Male Desire.* Durham, N.C.: Duke University.

Fuentes, A. 2002. "Patterns and Trends in Primate Pair Bond." *International Journal of Primatology* 23 (5): 953–78.

Gray, P. In press. "Evolution and Endocrinology of Human Behavior." In M. Muehlenbein, ed., *Human Evolutionary Biology.* New York: Cambridge University Press.

Gray, P. and P. Ellison, eds. In press. *Endocrinology of Social Relationships.* Cambridge, Mass.: Harvard University Press.

Gray, P. B., J. Flynn Chapman, M. H. McIntyre, T. C. Burnham, S. F. Lipson, and P. T. Ellison. 2004. "Testosterone and Human Male Pair Bonding." *Human Nature* 15:119–31.

Gregor, T. 1995. "Sexuality and the Experience of Love." In Paul Abramson and Steven Pickerton, eds., *Sexual Nature and Sexual Culture,* pp. 72–92. Chicago: University of Chicago Press.

Hannan, P. 1988. *The Invention of Li Yu.* Cambridge: University of Cambridge Press.

Harlow, H. and R. R. Zimmerman. 1959. "Affectionate Responses in the Infant Monkey." *Science* 130:421–32.

Harris, H. 1995. "Rethinking Heterosexual Relationships in Polynesia: A Case Study of Mangaia, Cook Island." In Jankowiak, *Romantic Passion*, pp. 95–127.

Harvey, J. and Amy Wenzel. 2001. *Close Romantic Relationships: Maintenance and Enhancement.* Mahwah, N.J.: Lawrence Erlbaum.

Hatfield, E. 1988. "Passionate and Companionate Love." In R. Sternberg and M. Barnes, eds., *The Psychology of Love,* pp. 191–217. New Haven, Conn.: Yale University Press.

Hatfield, E. and R. Rapson. 1993. *Love, Sex, and Intimacy: Their Psychology, Biology, and History.* New York: HarperCollins.

———. 1996. *Love and Sex: Cross-Cultural Perspectives*. Needham Heights, Mass.: Allyn and Bacon.

Hinsch, B. 1990. *Passions of the Cut Sleeve: Male Homosexual Tradition in China*. Berkeley: University of California Press.

Hirsch, J. and H. Wardlow, eds. 2006. *Modern Loves: The Anthropology of Romantic Courtship and Companionship Marriage*. Ann Arbor: University of Michigan Press.

Hofer, M. 1995. "Hidden Regulators: Implications for a New Understanding of Attachment, Separation and Loss." In S. Goldberg, R. Muir, and J. Kerr, eds., *Attachment Theory: Social, Development and Clinical Perspective*, pp. 203–30. Hillsdale, N.J.: Analytic Press.

Hrdy, S. 1999. *Mother Nature: A History of Mothers, Infants, and Natural Selection*. New York: Pantheon.

Jankowiak, W. 1993. *Sex, Death, and Hierarchy in a Chinese City: An Anthropological Account*. New York: Columbia University Press.

———, ed. 1995. *Romantic Passion: A Universal Experience?* New York: Columbia University Press.

———. 1999. "Talking Love or Talking Sex: Culture's Dilemma. In David Suggs and Andrew Miracle, eds., *Culture, Biology and Sexuality*, pp. 49–63. Athens: University of Georgia Press.

———. 2006. "Illicit Monogamy in an American Polygamous Community." In Brigitt Röttger-Rössler, ed., *On the Culture and Nature of Love* (Zur Kultur und Natur der Liebe), pp. 99–128. Berlin: Mentis/Paderborn.

Jankowiak, W. and E. Fischer. 1992. "A Cross-Cultural Perspective on Romantic Love." *Ethnology* 31 (2): 149–55.

Jankowiak, W. and H. Gerth. n.d. "Are Humans Capable of Being Passionately in Love with Two People at the Same Time?" Unpublished research report.

Jankowiak, W. and A. Ramsey. 2000. "Femme Fatale and Status Fatale: A Cross-Cultural Perspective." *Cross Cultural Research* 34, no. 1 (February): 57–69.

Jankowiak, W., M. Sudakov, and B. Wilreker. 2005. "Co-wife Conflict and Cooperation." *Ethnology* 44 (1): 81–98.

Levy, R. 1973. *Tahitians: Mind and Experience in the Society Islands*. Chicago: University of Chicago Press.

Lewis, O. 1966. *La Vida: A Puerto Rican Family in the Culture of Poverty—San Juan and New York*. New York: Random House

Lindholm, C. 1988a. "Lover and Leaders: A Comparison of Social and Psychological Models of Romance and Charisma." *Social Science Information* 27:3–45.

———. 1988b. "The Social Structure of Emotional Constraint: The Court of Louis XIV and the Pukhtun of Northern Pakistan." *Ethos* 16:227–46.

———. 1998. "Love and Structure." *Theory, Culture and Society* 15 (3–4): 243–63.

———. 2001. *Culture and Identity: The History, Theory, and Practice of Psychological Anthropology*. Boston: McGraw Hill.

Lipset, D. 2004. "Modernity without Romance?" *American Ethnologist* 31 (2): 205–24.

Lutz, C. 1988. *Unnatural Emotions: Everyday Sentiments on a Micronesian Atoll and Their Challenge to Western Theory.* Chicago: University of Chicago Press.

Lyons, A. and H. Lyons. 2004. *Irregular Connections: A History of Anthropology and Sexuality.* Lincoln: University of Nebraska Press.

Marazziti, D. and D. Canale. 2003. "Hormonal Changes When Falling in Love." *Psychoneuroendocrinology* 29:931–36.

Mayne, G. 1993. *Eroticism in Georges Bataille and Henry Miller.* Birmingham, Ala.: Summa.

Miller, H. 1962. *Tropic of Capricorn.* New York: Grove.

Morton, H. 1996. *Becoming Tongan: An Ethnography of Childhood.* Honolulu: University of Hawaii Press.

Padilla, M., J. Hirsch, M. Munzo-Laboy, R. Sember, and R. Parker. In press. *Love and Globalization: Cross-Cultural Reflections on an Intimate Intersection.* New Brunswick, N.J.: Rutgers University Press.

Person, E. 1988. *Dreams of Love and Fateful Encounters: The Power of Romantic Passion.* New York: W.W. Norton.

Porges, S. 1988. "Love: An Emergent Property of the Mammalian Autonomic Nervous System." *Psychoneuroendocrinology* 23 (8): 837–61.

——. 1998. "Love: An Emergent Theory: Phylogenetic Substances of a Social Nervous System." *International Journal of Psychophysiology* 42:123–46.

Ramsawh, H. and C. Harris. 2003. "Women's Sexual Strategies: More Common (and Diverse) Than We Think?" Paper presented at the twenty-fifth annual meeting of the Cognitive Science Society, July 31 to August 2, Boston, available on line at www.ccm.ua.edu/pdfs/328.pdf.

Rebhun, Linda-Anne. 1995. "Language of Love in Northeast Brazil." In Jankowiak, *Romantic Passion*, pp. 239–61.

——. 1999. *The Heart Is Unknown Country: Love in the Changing Economy of Northeast Brazil.* Stanford, Calif.: Stanford University Press.

Reddy, W. 2001. *The Navigation of Feeling: A Framework for the History of Emotions.* New York: Cambridge University Press.

Reston, J. 2001. *Warriors of God.* London: Faber and Faber.

Robertson, D.W. 1969. "The Concept of Courtly Love as Impediment to the Understanding of Medieval Texts." In F.X. Newman, ed., *The Meaning of Courtly Love,* pp. 1–18. Albany: State University of New York Press.

Schlegel, A. 1990. "Gender Meanings: General and Specific." In Peggy Sanday and Ruth Goodenough, eds., *Beyond the Second Sex,* pp. 21–42. Philadelphia: University of Pennsylvania Press.

——. 1995. "The Cultural Management of Adolescent Sexuality." In Paul Abramson and Steven Pickerton, eds., *Sexual Nature and Sexual Culture,* pp. 177–94. Chicago: University of Chicago Press.

Schlegel, A. and H. Barry. 1991. *Adolescence: An Anthropological Inquiry.* New York: Free Press.

Shore, B. 1996. *Culture in Mind.* New York: Oxford University Press.

Skinner, B. F. 1974. *About Behaviorism.* New York: Vintage.

Small, M.. 1995. *What's Love Got to Do with It?* New York: Cornell University Press.

Stone, L. 1988. "Passionate Attachments in the West in Historical Perspective." In E. Gaylin and E. Person, eds., *Passionate Attachments,* pp. 15–26. New York.: Free Press.

Suggs, D. and A. Miracle, eds. 1993. *Culture and Sexuality.* Pacific Grove, Calif.: Brooks/Cole.

Symons, D. 1979. *The Evolution of Human Sexuality.* New York: Oxford University Press.

Tennov, D. 1979. *Love and Limerence: The Experience of Being in Love.* New York: Scarborough House.

Townsend, J. 1998. *What Women Want—What Men Want.* New York: Oxford University Press.

Trawick, M. 1990. *Notes on Love in a Tamil Family.* Berkeley: University of California Press.

Unvas-Moberg, K. 2003. *The Oxytocin Factor.* New York: Da Capo.

Wardlow, H. 2006. *Wayward Women: Sexuality and Agency in a New Guinea Society.* Berkeley: University of California Press.

Williams, Carlos Williams. 1955. *Journey to Love.* New York: Random House.

Wolf, M. and R. Witke, eds. 1975. *Women in Chinese Society.* Stanford, Calif.: Stanford University Press.

2. A Biocultural Approach to Sex, Love, and Intimacy in Central African Foragers and Farmers

Bonnie L. Hewlett and Barry S. Hewlett

Bembe created the earth. He created women. He then created men but he kept them away from the women. One day a man called Tole took all the men in his camp and started to hunt in the forest. They had no women with them, only calabashes they put on their chests to be like a woman. They hunted animals and ate them, all the men together. The next day Tole went alone into the forest, very early, and he listened and heard sounds he had not heard before. All the women were there. They had made a raft on the water and the women were playing on it. Now he hid and thought to himself, these are not men, but they are like men, only they have breasts. Something is wrong with their chests and they have no testicles, it is only flat. He crawled on his knees to catch one. The women were singing and playing on their raft and did not hear Tole. He tried to trap one, but they all ran to their hut. So the women went to their camp, and Tole went to his camp and told his friends, "I saw other people who have no testicles and have things pointing from their chests. Let's go and get them and find out what they are." It is because of Tole that men know women and women know men. —Aka story

This chapter examines sex, love, and intimacy in married couples in two central African ethnic groups—Aka foragers and Ngandu farmers. New data on love and jealousy emerged during life history interviews, and we summarize that sexual behavior data here. Our research is designed to begin to bridge critical gaps in the understanding of the daily lives, loves, marital relations, and sexual experiences of foraging and farming men and women in relatively egalitarian small-scale societies. Most of what we know about sociosexual relations within the marital union is based upon research in highly stratified cultures and nation-states. We present ethnographic data on Aka forager and Ngandu farmer sociosexual relations and then apply the data to our biocultural model. Our data and the heuristic evolutionary-based model illustrate the interactions of biology (sexual desire, attachment, compassion), ecology (political-economic setting), and culture (schema, ideas, cultural models about sex and love). Previous studies of sex and love usually relied upon one of two general approaches to explaining these aspects of human behavior—love and sex are universal and are biologically based behaviors or they are culturally or socially constructed human behaviors. We suggest that intimacy, sex, and love are best understood within an integrated biocultural approach.

THE STUDY

The data are based upon in-depth interviews with thirty-five Aka (17 women, 18 men) and twenty-one Ngandu (11 women and 10 men) married adults. More Aka were interviewed because the study originally focused on Aka foragers and the decision to include Ngandu farmers occurred late in the study. Approximately 40 percent of individuals in both groups were older than fifty, as we wanted to understand sexual behavior and marital histories through the life course. All individuals interviewed had been married at least once; most had been married several times. The interviews focused on men's and women's marital and sexual histories and their views of love, jealousy, sex, and fertility.

The questions about marital history that we explored included mate attraction, reasons given for divorce, reasons for bringing in a second wife (males) or accepting a second wife (females), sexual jealousy, and spousal violence.

The first author conducted interviews with Aka and Ngandu women; the second author interviewed Ngandu and Aka men. We conducted the interviews in Diaka and Dingandu, and we used male and female Ngandu research assistants for all interviews with Ngandu. We took the marital histories of the Aka, but Ngandu men or women who spoke Aka and French conducted the interviews with the Aka about their sexual ideologies. We obtained authorization to conduct the research at the national and local (e.g., village or camp) levels. We also obtained informed consent in the local language from each individual and emphasized confidentiality.

THE AKA AND NGANDU

The Aka foragers and Ngandu farmers in this study are neighbors in the tropical forest region of the Central African Republic. The population density is less than one person per square half-mile, and both groups have similar high mortality (child mortality of 35–45 percent) and high fertility (4–6 live births per woman).

The Aka and Ngandu have frequent social, economic, and religious interactions and see each other on a regular basis, yet they have distinct settlement patterns, modes of production, male-female relations, and patterns of child care (Hewlett 1991). Aka camps consist of 5 to 8 small (six feet in diameter) temporary houses with 25 to 35 individuals. The camp occupies an area of about 400 to 500 square feet. Ngandu villages consist of 50 to 400 individuals, and each house is at least 20 feet away from the next. The Aka are primarily net-hunting foragers, move their villages several times a year, have minimal political hierarchy (i.e., elders have little or no power over others), and have relatively high gender and intergenerational egalitarianism. The Ngandu are slash-and-burn farmers, live in the same house and work the same areas of land for most of their life, have strong chiefs, and have marked gender and intergenerational inequality. About 40 percent among the Ngandu and 15 percent of the Aka practice polygyny (Hewlett 1991).

The two groups are economically and socially interdependent. The Aka do not as a rule practice agriculture but rather obtain cultivated foods from the Ngandu through the exchange of forest game, wild vegetables (*coco*), and manual labor. Aka and Ngandu often belong to the same clan and share fictive kinship relationships.

Sharing among the Aka is substantially greater than among the Ngandu. The Aka share frequently (every day), with many individuals (most, if not all, of the camp), and share most of what they capture or collect. The Ngandu share food on a daily basis with members of the household, and they occasionally share food and labor with neighbors and clan members (i.e., cooperative labor a few times a year). Individuals who do not share and accumulate food or material items are suspected, or are targets, of sorcery, which is believed to cause illness or death. These beliefs and practices help maintain household equality and are deterrents to accumulation.

The Aka have one of the most egalitarian cultures in the ethnographic record. The egalitarian status of Aka men and women is in part related to their subsistence patterns of net hunting and gathering. Men and women contribute equal amounts of calories to the household diet. The contribution varies according to their seasonal movements. When the Aka are working in the villagers' fields and living in village camps, the women bring in more "village" foods, in the form of carbohydrates, as food is exchanged with other villagers for labor. The men's contribution increases once the couple and any children have moved back to their forest camp. Women frequently join in the net hunt (generally the whole family participates), and it is not uncommon to see a woman with a knife or spear in one hand and a baby in a sling in the other. Men join in the gathering of forest plants, tubers, and nuts. The women generally control the distribution of food sources, both meat and plant, although men and women have equal access to available resources. Aka men provide more direct care to infants than fathers in any other systematically studied culture (Hewlett 1991). The Aka are also characterized by extensive gender role flexibility. Women and men regularly switch subsistence and child-care roles.

Strong patriclan social organization among the Ngandu emphasizes deference and respect by women and children for elders, males, and ancestors; consequently, marked gender inequality exists. For example, men are expected to receive larger portions of food; women cannot touch hunting implements (guns and spears); women seldom occupy political positions, such as village chief. Violence against women is not unusual. The number and age of geographically close male kin are important (e.g., male-male alliances), because the Ngandu accumulate goods and property (e.g., planted crops) that must be guarded from others. Also intra- and intergroup hostilities in regard to women are not uncommon, as a little less than half of all marriages are polygynous, leaving many men without a spouse, which in turn often leads to conflict and violence.

Ngandu men and women have sharply delineated gender roles and status. Ngandu women are the primary providers of calories to the diet, in the form of carbohydrates obtained from the fields they have planted, weeded, and harvested throughout the year. Men's work tends to be more seasonal;

during the dry season the Ngandu men clear the fields for the women to plant. Men generally are involved in the weeding and harvesting of coffee crops, if the Ngandu family has coffee fields. Women take part in an informal market economy by selling their farm products, such as manioc, peanuts, corn, plantains, and palm oil, and forest products that they received in trade with the Aka. A few Ngandu women also distill and sell corn alcohol or they sell meat their husbands have obtained by trading for clothes, medicine, or manioc.

The Ngandu promote social unity and conformity, in contrast to the Aka, who encourage autonomy (Hewlett 1991).

These ethnographic backgrounds illustrate key differences in foundational schema of the Aka and Ngandu. Foundational schema are ideas, knowledge, and values that provide the foundation for cultural models (i.e., ways of thinking/explaining/anticipating the intentions and needs of others) in a variety of domains of cultural life. For instance, the U.S. foundational schema for independence shapes cultural models of child care, male-female relations, and religious beliefs. Foundational schema of the Aka include age and gender egalitarianism, an ideology of giving/sharing, flexibility of social roles, respect for the autonomy of individuals, and trust of others. The foundational schema of gender egalitarianism among the Aka shape cultural models regarding the sexual division of labor in subsistence and child-care activities, healing systems, and religious beliefs. Consistent with their egalitarian schema, the Aka avoid drawing attention to themselves, avoid ranking each other, and share extensively (Hewlett 1999). Foundational schema for Ngandu include age and gender hierarchy, deference to and respect for authority figures and older individuals (parents, older siblings), obligations to specific others (clan, lineage), a material basis for adult social relationships, and a general distrust of others (e.g., sorcery).

An Evolutionary Biocultural Model

Figure 2.1 shows the biocultural model we use to interpret our data. It is a heuristic, rather than a predictive, model—that is, it is used to generate discussion and hypotheses rather than make specific predictions, and it is based upon recent developments within evolutionary theory (E. Smith 2000). According to the model, male-female sociosexual relations can best

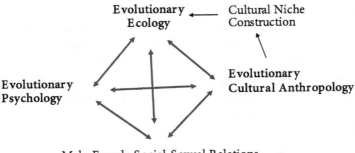

Male-Female Social-Sexual Relations

Figure 2.1   An Evolutionary Biocultural Model of Human Sociosexual Relations

be understood as the result of interactions of biology, culture, and ecology. Each evolutionary approach has distinct properties that need to be understood on their own, but most human behaviors are the consequence of interactions of these features.

Evolutionary psychology is the branch of evolutionary theory that has attracted the most attention and controversy, in part because this approach focuses on identifying biological (i.e., genetic) behaviors of humans. Most this research centers on understanding "human nature" and universals that evolved during the environment(s) of evolutionary adaptation, the hunting-gathering lifestyle that characterized more than 90 percent of human history. Evolutionary psychologists are interested in identifying biologically based human behaviors that evolved in order to solve recurring problems in environment(s) of evolutionary adaptation. Some behaviors may have evolved in the environment of evolutionary adaptation, but others may be part of our phylogenetic history. For instance, humans share a phylogenetic history with mammals and primates, and this shared history contributes to biologically based propensities and an "evolved psychology."

In order to understand the topics of this chapter—male-female sex, love, and anger—it is essential to have a background in human evolutionary psychology and genetically based behaviors such as sexual desire, attraction to specific mates, attachment, and sexual jealousy. Sexual desire and mate attraction to specific others are common to many sexually reproducing organisms (Fisher 2006), whereas attachment is often associated with the evolution of the limbic system (e.g., emotions) in mammals and is especially pronounced in Old World primates (the Catarrines). Sexual jealousy is particularly common in pair-bonded species in which male parental investment is high (Fisher 1992). While humans share sexual desire, attraction to specific mates, attachment, and sexual jealousy with other animals, humans have characteristics that are unique in the animal world: the ability empathize and to read the intentions of others, and the ability to acquire cumulative behaviors and knowledge (i.e., culture) (Hrdy 1999; Tomasello 1999). In our opinion, these human characteristics contributed to new configurations of sexual desire, mate attraction, attachment, and sexual jealousy. Romantic passion emerged through interactions between mammalian systems of sexual desire and mate attraction, and human abilities to empathize and idealize others. Romantic passion is a human universal as Jankowiak (1993) suggests, but it results from interactions of emergent human characteristics and is not an adaptation to a specific recurring problem in the environment(s) of evolutionary adaptation. Along the same lines, "love," and attachment to specific others, may be especially strong in humans, in part because we have the evolved cognitive and emotional structures to take on the feelings of others.

Another part of understanding the evolved biological basis of human behavior is ontogenetic development. Human biology changes with age, and this biology influences human behavior. This chapter focuses on adult patterns of sex and love; a study of children's sex and love would be very different, mostly because of ontogenetic changes in biology. In short, evolutionary psychology emphasizes the importance of understanding biologically based universal features of human behavior.

Evolutionary ecologists are different from evolutionary psychologists in that they view the human brain as a general purpose mechanism that allows humans to adapt to varied and diverse natural and social environments. Evolutionary ecologists are interested in explaining human behavioral diversity rather than biologically based human universals. Evolutionary ecology considers how organisms adapt to their environment through their interactions with members of their own species (and other species) as well as the physical environment; evolutionary ecology examines the selective pressures imposed by the environment and the evolutionary response to these pressures (Bulmer 1994). From this perspective humans try to optimize or maximize their reproductive fitness within particular social, demographic, or political environments. Few studies of human sex and love by evolutionary ecologists exist, but the evolutionary ecology research by

Belsky (1999) and Chisholm (1995) suggest that a child's rearing environment (e.g., the family's access to material and natural resources) predicts when the child will start sexual activity and how long her or his pair bonds will last. Children raised in rich environments will develop a reproductive strategy in which sexual relationships start late and male-female relationships last a relatively long time, while children raised in materially limited environments start their sexual relationships earlier and these relationships are relatively short term. Factors such as parasite loads, access to resources, and number of potential marriage partners in the area are all examples that evolutionary ecologists may consider to explain human variation in sex and love experiences.

The final evolutionary approach shown in figure 2.1 is evolutionary cultural anthropology (Hewlett and Lamb 2002). Researchers in this field focus on the evolutionary nature of culture—how is it transmitted and acquired, how it changes, and how it influences human behavior. Evolutionary cultural anthropologists point out that culture has the characteristics required for natural selection: (1) production of cultural variants, (2) fitness effects of cultural variants, (3) inheritance (i.e., transmission) of cultural variants, and (4) accumulation of cultural modifications. Population geneticists have also influenced evolutionary cultural anthropology, asserting that just as an understanding of genetic transmission revolutionized genetics, so may an understanding of cultural transmission influence cultural anthropology. Humans have different mechanisms for learning skills and acquiring knowledge because it would be maladaptive to learn everything by trial and error. Learning from parents (which evolutionary cultural anthropologists call vertical transmission) , friends (horizontal transmission), leaders (one-many transmission, indirect bias), or from all those around you (conformist transmission) can be an efficient way to learn in particular contexts. Each transmission mechanism has specific properties. Some mechanisms lead to the conservation of culture (e.g., vertical and conformist), while other mechanisms (e.g., horizontal) lead to rapid culture change. Researchers in evolutionary cultural anthropology have shown that many cultural beliefs and behaviors, especially those associated with family and kinship, are seldom linked to natural ecology and are highly conserved because of the mechanisms of cultural transmission (Hewlett and Lamb 2002). In short, the evolutionary cultural anthropology perspective suggests that culture matters.

Another component of evolutionary cultural anthropology identified in figure 2.1 is cultural niche construction. The concept of niche construction (Odling-Smee, Laland, and Feldman 2003) is a recent conceptual contribution to evolutionary cultural anthropology. Some species, including humans, modify natural selection pressures within their environments by creating a niche (e.g., burrow, nest, house) that produces a separate constellation of selective pressures (the constructed niche creates its own set of problems), which may or not enhance the reproductive fitness of individuals. Over time the niches and the consequences of the selective pressures are inherited. This is a potentially important contribution to evolutionary cultural anthropology because culture increases the ability of humans to construct niches. Technology, house types, settlement patterns, how people make a living, and political-economic institutions are part of the culturally constructed niche to which humans try to adapt. This helps to explain how culture is "out there" in the environment as well as in our minds (e.g., knowledge, information).

The major works on human sex, love, and intimacy fall into different evolutionary approaches outlined in the evolutionary biocultural model. Jankowiak (1995) uses an evolutionary psychology approach and focuses on understanding the universal and biologically based components of intimacy, while Lindholm (1998, 2000) uses evolutionary cultural anthropology (niche construction, in particular) to explain how sociocultural structures contribute to dramatic differences in human intimacy. It is important to remember that the different approaches have different aims: evolutionary psychology is trying to explain human universals/nature, whereas evolutionary ecology and evolutionary cultural anthropology are trying to explain human diversity.

We advocate an integrated evolutionary approach to understanding human sex, love, and intimacy. The majority of human behaviors are influenced by *interactions* of biology, ecology, and culture; few human behaviors are shaped by biological or cultural factors alone.

How does the biocultural model help to explain Aka and Ngandu sex, intimacy, and love? Before applying the model, it is important to define a few terms. *Sex* in this chapter refers only to heterosexual intercourse, because, according to data obtained from our interviews, Aka and Ngandu do not have terms for, or practice, homosexuality, oral sex, or masturbation (although a few Ngandu said that homosexuality does exist but "only in the capital city"). *Love* refers to strong emotional bonds or attachment to particular others. *Intimacy* refers to a close physical and emotional relationship (physical intimacy in a marital relationship generally includes sexual intercourse, whereas in a parent-child relationship it refers to regular physical proximity).

SEXUAL DESIRE AND FREQUENCY OF SEX

Sexual desire is a human universal and an integral part of human nature in both males and females. It is part of our evolved psychology, an unconscious drive to reproduce, to spread our genes, and contribute to the survival of the species. But what motivates sexual desire? Many evolutionists say that pleasure motivates most animals to engage in sexual activity (Symons 1979; Turke 1988). Middle-class Euro-American cultural models of human sexuality are consistent with this "sex for pleasure" hypothesis as they emphasize the importance of experiencing and sharing sexual pleasure (see the human sexuality section of any major bookstore). The desire for children, or feelings about children, seldom motivate, or are linked to, sexual experiences. Euro-American cultural models of sexual activity also regard sex as play, a leisure-time, rather than work-time, activity (although sex as work might well describe the experiences of couples having difficulty conceiving a child) (Coates 1999; Francoeur 1999). While pleasure is clearly a motivating aspect of sexual desire, do Western cultural models influence evolutionists' hypotheses? How do peoples in small-scale cultures like the Aka and Ngandu view and explain their sexual behavior? If sexual desire is generated by recreational pleasure-seeking behavior, how often do most humans desire the pleasure of sexual intercourse?

Urban industrial studies measure the frequency of sex in terms of number of times per week or per month and assume that couples generally have sex only once per night or day. Most studies further show that younger (30–39) couples report having sex two to three times a week (T. Smith 1991). By comparison, our research has found that Aka and Ngandu couples have about three times as much sexual activity as do individuals in stratified cultures. Aka couples, for example, have sex three times per week, three times per night on average. Ngandu aged eighteen to fifty have sex approximately twice a week, two times per night on average. Laying to rest our initial suspicions of male bravado, both males and females in each ethnic group reported similar frequencies in separate interviews. This frequency of sex per night declined slightly by age, but age explained only 6 percent of the variability. A comparison of frequency of sex-by-age data for U.S., Aka, and Ngandu married couples shows that U.S. couples aged thirty to thirty-nine have sex 86 times per year, Ngandu 228 times per year, and Aka 439 times per year. The question then becomes why such a marked difference in the frequency of sexual intercourse exists between the U.S. and Central African couples.

SEX: WORK OR PLEASURE?

Bila na bongedi (sexual desire is work).   —*Aka man*

I am old and no longer have desire; when I was younger I liked it; when I was young I had pleasure. I had sex for kids and pleasure. I do not like sex now but if I refuse to sleep with him, I have to pay money to his family.
—*Fifty-eight-year-old Ngandu woman, senior wife in polygynous marriage*

Love is the work of the night; love and play are nice together if it makes a pregnancy.   —*Young Aka woman*

Both Aka and Ngandu have terms for sexual desire (*bongide* among Aka, and *elebe* among Ngandu), and both men and women report experiencing feelings of desire in relatively equal frequencies, but among the Aka and Ngandu, sexual desire and expression appear to be substantially different from their expression in stratified nation-states. Aka and Ngandu believe that sexual desire, coupled with sexual activity, is the "work of the night," less arduous and more pleasurable than the "work of the day" but work nonetheless; as one Aka male succinctly put it, "The work of the penis is the work to find a child." Another Aka male and female shared similar views; the man said, "I am always looking for a child, it is pleasurable, but it is a big work," and the young woman noted, "It is fun to have sex, but it is to look for a child." Several informants compared the work of getting food to the work of searching for a child: "Getting food is more difficult, but both are lots of work. Sex life is not as tiring as work during day; the work at night is easier because you can make love, then sleep." Sex is the work of "searching for children." Both societies place a high value on children, in terms of wanting many, and while neither is a "child-focused" society, children are highly desired, and adults spend much time and energy "looking" or "working" for children.

The Aka were the most emphatic on these points. One young Aka male explained, "I am now doing it five times a night to search for a child; if I do not do it five times, my wife will not be happy because she wants children quickly." One woman said, "I have sex with him to get infants, not for pleasure, and to show that I love him." Forty to 50 percent of the population of Aka and Ngandu is composed of children younger than fifteen. While the two cultures are not, as noted, child focused, children are in many ways the life of the village and camps. However, Aka men were the only people to mention that they wanted to have frequent sex and many children in order to build a camp. "My father is dead, and I need to make a big family. My first wife found my second wife, who was looking to have many children," one man told us. He was thirty-five, had two wives, and reported having sex three to four times a night with two days of rest in between. A twenty-five-year-old man said that "it is work to find children and get children to make a large camp like my father." He reported having sex four to five times a night. That is not to say, however, that sexual activity is directed only with procreation in mind. Sex is at times an expression of desire and of love. One postmenopausal Aka woman explained to us that she is still interested in sexual activity for *bongide,* or sexual desire, "not for children," and also because she "loves him."

Ngandu males and females expressed the same sentiment, that sex is "to search for children"; however, among the Ngandu, both males and females complained frequently of the tiredness that they felt during the work of the night: "Sex is a work, when I give sperm it is a work, I get tired after sex." One Ngandu man was particularly emphatic that "having sex three times a night is to look for a child, *not* for pleasure." More women of both Aka and Ngandu explained to us that, while sex was "work" and sometimes pleasurable, the "infant is the most important." A few women also expressed the idea that sexual activity was also a "sign of love."

Why do both Aka and Ngandu have such frequent sexual encounters per night, once their hard "work" of the night has paid off and they have "found" a child, that is, the wife has become pregnant? Our findings suggest that both Aka and Ngandu believe that frequent sex is linked to pregnancy and fetal development, as a Ngandu man explained: "Since my wife is just pregnant, I need to have sex more often, two-three times a night, but then I take a three to four days' rest." The Aka emphasized the importance of male contributions to fetal development; 87 percent of informants said male sperm is essential to pregnancy and fetal development, whereas Ngandu informants said that both men and women contributed fluid to make a pregnancy and promote fetal growth. Individual variation exists among the Ngandu in the extent to which they think that the woman contributes to the development of the fetus. Some suggested that women also ejaculate "sperm" during orgasm, which aids in the physical development of the baby, but the Ngandu women said they did not have to climax each time during a night but that when women were excited or had an orgasm, they contributed substance. That is, the male sperm creates and "builds" the baby in utero, but it is possible for the woman to contribute also. Birth defects and/or miscarriages are the result of infrequent sexual (sperm) contributions by the father.

One Ngandu male also explained to us, "Both men and women have sperm or substances; that is the reason why SIDA [AIDS] is transmitted between a male and female; both combine to make a child," but he added that "both men and women contribute *malima;* if one spouse is sick, a pregnancy will not happen." The word *malima* is used to describe both male and female secretions during intercourse. While Ngandu hold various theories about how babies are created and "formed," they mostly agree that "women have *malima* as well as men, and it takes two sperms to create a baby . . . [I] do not know how the female gives, but I think it is necessary for a woman to reach climax sometimes, but not each time, to create a baby." Ngandu females expressed a similar view: "The *malima* of woman contributes to baby development, that is why it is necessary to continue with sex during pregnancy." Another Ngandu woman explained, "The two sperm join to create the baby, and the woman needs to be excited to give substances, but she does not need to climax each time to make the baby."

The Aka, as noted, hold a similar understanding, that it takes the "sperm" of both partners to create the new life; however, more Aka seemed to feel that the sperm of the father is primarily what creates the child: "Only men have *mamboli* [sperm] and make the baby; women say they cannot get pregnant without men, so it is men's sperm that makes the baby." Another Aka man told us that "women do not give much to the baby; it is men, especially at first, that give good development of the baby, [so sexual activity continues] twice every night until the baby is very big [about six months]; you then have to slow to once a night." It is the cumulative "sperm" throughout the pregnancy that creates the child, not conception that occurs on one night; that is, a new life is conceived and "built" over repeated encounters throughout the duration of the pregnancy.

While sex is viewed as pleasurable, that pleasure is secondary or tertiary to working for, and "building," a child or to demonstrate love for a mate. Ngandu men and women were somewhat more likely than Aka to mention pleasure as an important part of sex life. Ngandu women often related that "sex is pleasure, work, a sign of love, and necessary for infant growth" and "sex is for pleasure and for work to find children." Thus Aka and Ngandu cultural models emphasize procreation and the "work" of sex. Sexual pleasure as somewhat of a postscript to the sexual experience is in marked contrast to contemporary middle-class Euro-American cultural models, which emphasize the recreational and pleasurable aspects of sexual intercourse.

The biocultural model is essential for understanding sexual desire and the frequency of sex. Both Aka and Ngandu have sexual desire, but their cultural models dramatically influence their motivation for sex and how often they express sexual desire in intimate relationships. These data demonstrate the complexity of the issue of sexual activity for "work," pleasure, love, or some combination of all. Our basic physiologic makeup may control sexual drive, but our emotions and cultural models certainly influence the expression of sexual desire and sexual activity, which may also be affected by particular ecological conditions, such as high child mortality rates and a diversity of infectious and parasitic diseases.

LOVE AND INTIMACY

> My first sexual experience was with my husband, I had just begun my periods, when we were together. I lived in a small hut, when he began to come and visit. When he and I were young, I chose to marry him because he caught a lot of meat and he was very handsome and nice. Once he brought a pig to my camp and gave me some, and after a time I wanted to marry him. He was strong and worked hard, and he became good in my heart. He shared a lot of his meat with other people. I loved him a lot and wanted children with no other. My mother taught me [that] if you marry him, [if] he is good and nice and brave, if he asks for sex, do not refuse him. I never refused my husband, and if I had *elebe* [desire], I waited for him and then asked for the sex. We made

love for the infants and to show I loved him. When I was young, he said I was beautiful. We were always together, walking in the forest. He never hit me; other men hit their wives, but he never did. We lived together and worked together for many years, but he died. After he died, I had no relations with other men. I lived in a little hut and suffered a lot because I loved him so much in my heart. I wanted no other man. I lived alone with my children and I was still strong and young. They married and found others, and now I am alone. When I am alone at night, I think of him and cry, even now, after so long [she was seventy when interviewed].
                                                                —Aka woman

If sexual activity is "work," the night's work of "searching for a child," does love, then, merely reflect procreative and parenting efforts? Is love simply a universal means of ensuring that couples bond, mate, reproduce, and care for their children? Love has been long thought to be a Western cultural notion that does not extend beyond Euro-American borders (Wright 1994), but attachment to, and love for, particular others is part of our phylogenetic history, evolved psychology, and human nature. Attachment is an essential component of survival and well-being in Old World monkeys, apes, and humans (Konner 2005). Offspring that are not attached to a specific adult may not survive, and offspring that are not securely attached (i.e., provided with consistent and appropriate responses) may suffer socially and emotionally later in life, which in turn influences their reproductive potential. As Bowlby (1972) suggests, attachment probably evolved in parent-infant relationships; infants attached to particular others were more likely to survive, which enhanced the reproductive success of both infant and the mother or other biologically related caregivers. But love in humans can be particularly strong, in part because of the additional evolved propensity in humans to be able to empathize with others—the ability to read the needs of others, to identify with and understand another's feelings or difficulties (Tomasello 1999). The attachment process and the ability to empathize and feel compassion for others influenced relatively (in comparison with other higher primates) strong dyadic or multiple bonds in humans. We all know how strong our feelings can be for others, even if they are not present, or when we have never met them (e.g., human responses to victims of natural disasters, wars, or epidemics).

While love and compassion are universal and part of our evolved psychology, how love and compassion are experienced in intimate relationships varies dramatically. Both Aka and Ngandu identify love (*bondingo*) as an important component of marital relations. One Aka woman said, "I show I love my husband when we are together and I touch him and stay close to him." An Ngandu woman whose husband died several years previously told us: "Love is most important, and children will come later. I never looked outside of marriage for a lover; I do not desire other men because I want my husband—I have love in my heart for my husband. He was nice and respectful to me."

An Ngandu man also expressed his love for his wife, who could not have children: "I love my first wife the most, she is closest to my heart. She helps me and gives me food and respects me. We did not have children together; she was not able to. Now she does not menstruate, and we no longer have sex. I have sex with my second wife, to take care of the desire, but it is the first wife I love the most."

Both Aka and Ngandu men and women expressed love as part of their intimate relationship with their spouse, but how they experienced and demonstrated love varied substantially. Many middle-class Euro-Americans would describe Ngandu husband-wife relations as distant and perfunctory and Aka husband-wife relations as intimate, close, and giving. Ngandu husband and wife do not eat together, do not always sleep in the same bed, and share few activities, Ngandu men contribute little to subsistence or child care. By comparison, Aka husband and wife spend considerable time together during the day in a variety of subsistence tasks, including the net hunt; they eat together and sleep in the same bed (but not necessarily next to each other). As we mentioned earlier, husband and wife contribute relatively equally to subsistence, and Aka fathers provide regular child care. Husbands and wives in both groups do not publicly demonstrate affection, such as hand holding, hugging, or kissing. How is love expressed and measured? Both Aka and Ngandu mentioned having sex on a regular basis as a sign of love, but for Aka men and women, working hard and physical proximity were key measures of spousal love. Ngandu women occasionally mentioned that gifts of cloth or jewelry from their husband were signs of love. Ngandu men felt that their spouse's love was demonstrated by her respect for his demands and authority within the household and by such tasks as serving him a meal, washing his clothes, and giving him money. In addition, for the Aka and Ngandu, to speak of love is to speak of desire, and part of that desire is a desire for children. The biocultural model is useful for understanding the experiences of the Aka and Ngandu. Attachment ability, to be empathetic to the needs of others, to "read" their minds, is a part of our evolved psychology. At the same time Aka and Ngandu foundational schema regarding gender hierarchy and their different culturally constructed niches (e.g., sedentary versus mobile lifestyles) contribute to the diverse ways in which the two cultures experience and express love, desire, and sexuality.

Anger and Divorce

If I do not give him food or wash his clothes, he hits me.   —Ngandu woman

I hit my wives when they do not obey or listen to my requests. —Ngandu man

When he took another wife I hit him, but when she and I worked together, then it was OK.   —Aka woman

Conflicts arise in marital relationships and at times result in anger and physical violence. In preliminary discussions with Aka about marital relationships, several informants mentioned slapping or hitting their spouse. Our impression was that domestic aggression was rare among the Aka, and we had observed only occasional acts of a wife's yelling or slapping a husband. Ngandu spousal violence appeared to be frequent. A Ngandu woman showed up for an interview with a swollen eye and missing tooth after an argument with her spouse. Also, three Ngandu women arrived and wanted to speak of "brutal sex," essentially what turned out to be marital rape. We decided to ask informants about physical violence in their relationships.

Aka rarely hit their spouse (few times, if ever, during their relationship), but when it does occur, women were slightly more likely to initiate the hitting (9 of 17 incidents reported by men and 7 of 10 incidents reported by women). As one Aka woman explained, "I hit him when he forgot how many days he had been with the other wife." Two Aka men detailed their experiences with their angry wife: "My wife is very brave; she hits me, but I do not hit her. She hits me because I was walking in the forest and visiting other camps, and she thinks it is to find another woman," one man said, and the other man reported, "I hit my wife because she found another man, so she took a log and hit me. We are divorced." A characteristic feature of Aka hitting is that if a husband hits his wife, she is likely to hit him back. The reasons Aka husbands or wives gave for hitting their spouse were similar: the husband or wife was "walking about" (*tambula*) too long, that is, being away too long and potentially looking for and finding another partner. A few Aka women mentioned that they hit their husband when he simply proposed the idea a second wife. One older Aka man summed up his experiences with spousal violence: "I hit her because I was jealous and I was afraid I would lose her love. She hit me also when I was walking too long."

Hitting in response to the fear of loosing a mate was a common theme among the Aka. A young Aka woman expressed her concerns about her new husband's walking around: "If he finds another woman, I will hit him, and if I know the woman, I will beat her, too. I am afraid if he leaves me and the baby for another woman. I am afraid he will abandon us." Another Aka man said that his wife attacked him twice because he forgot the number of days he had slept with his other wife.

In contrast, the Ngandu women were less likely to initiate violence toward their spouse as a result of jealousy or fear of abandonment. Spousal violence among the Ngandu is regular, (i.e., several times a year), generally initiated by men, and seldom involves a wife's hitting her husband in response to his attack. The most common reason given by our male Ngandu informants was that their wife did not respect or follow their requests. She did not wash his clothes, give him food, or, as one man complained, "When I asked for something to eat, she ignored me and eventually I hit her." Invariably, their stated reasons for violence had to do with their wife's lack of obedience and respect: "I hit my wives when they do not obey or listen to my requests." As several men reported, "I hit only when she does not respect my requests"; "Only twice when I asked her to wash my clothes or give me food and she refused. She stopped giving me food for four days." Another common reason given was for refusal not only of household service but of sex: "I only hit her when she refuses sex with me." Indeed, members of one particular group of Ngandu women shared that each feared her husband because of what the women termed "brutal sex." One woman related this incident: "I am afraid of him when he comes home from being away. He always wants sex, and he forces me. It is brutal sex and afterward I am hurt and bleeding. I cry because I hurt so badly. If I refuse, he beats me. For women here life is very difficult, we work hard during the day, and at night with our husbands the sex is brutal, and we cry and bleed."

One Ngandu man explained that he became angry at what he saw as negligent maternal care: "My wife went outside, left oil in pot on the fire in house, and my daughter went to the pot and burned her hands. I was angry that she neglected to watch the child better and hit her." A small number of Ngandu men reported that sometimes their wife would hit them when the men were giving more things to a cowife (e.g., money, clothes) or if a wife caught a husband with another woman. In one case the wife stopped giving her husband food for three or four days to make sure the new relationship stopped.

Ngandu women said their husbands also resorted to physical violence if they thought a wife was looking to have a sexual affair with another man (putting on nice clothes, staying away at another village for a long time) or when a wife did not show public respect to her husband—one woman was hit when she spoke at church without his permission.

Aka and Ngandu patterns of anger and violence illustrate influences of both biology (evolutionary psychology) and culture (evolutionary cultural anthropology). The violence seen among Aka men and women and among Ngandu women, and their explanations for hitting—their spouse was sleeping or developing a relationship with somebody else—are grounded in the evolved propensity for sexual jealousy. Violence is a response to the loss or perceived loss of a loved one and the resources the loved one provided. It is also potentially a mate-retention strategy. The influence of culture is evident in the explanations given by Ngandu men and women for violence—that is, the lack of respect and deference shown for the male head of the household.

Divorce

Men do not understand the sense of marriage. It is very dangerous to take other wives. I will leave and find another. It does not work; many wives divorce because of it. It is very mean to take another wife. Men depend upon their women for their life, for clothes, and food and to take care of their children.
—Ngandu woman

My first husband found another wife, and I was mad and jealous and fought with him and said this is not possible, so I divorced him.   *—Aka woman*

We also asked Aka and Ngandu about their marital history and found that divorce is a common feature of married life. The most common cause for divorce in both groups was the spouse's sleeping with, searching for, or finding another mate (56 percent of all divorces) but was a more frequent reason among the Aka (64 percent versus 38 percent among Ngandu). As one Aka man related, "I divorced my first wife, because she slept with others, and it hurt my heart because I loved her so much." An Aka woman explained, "My husband found another wife, and I was mad and said it is not possible, now we are finished, and I refused him and we divorced."

Ngandu men were more likely to divorce their wife because she did not respect him or "did not listen to me." Ngandu women, but no Aka women, mentioned that their husband left because they did not have any children. One Aka man said two of his wives left him because they did not get pregnant and they were having sex five times a night. The reasons for divorce and who initiated the divorce were quite varied.

A major difference between the two groups was which spouse left the marriage. Fifty-eight percent of Aka men said their wife left them, and 67 percent of Aka women said they left their husband. By contrast, 71 percent of Ngandu men said they left their wife, and 83 percent of women said their husband left them. Again, the biocultural model is useful for interpreting the cross-cultural variability. The most common cause in both groups, infidelity, is of course consistent with an evolved psychology. Men risk losing the certainty of paternity, whereas women risk losing access to resources or protection from other males. Love, attachment, and the betrayed feelings that so often accompany unfaithfulness are a part of our evolved psychology. Ngandu gender hierarchy and Aka egalitarianism also influenced the patterns of divorce, as Ngandu men were likely to cite lack of respect as a cause of divorce, and generally Ngandu men left their wives. Among the Aka the reasons for divorce were varied, and men were not the primary initiators of divorce.

OTHER INTIMATE RELATIONSHIPS

Thus far we have focused on Aka and Ngandu marital relationships because our original study focused on understanding sexual behavior, but we want to briefly mention the nature of same-sex and parent-child relationships because they illustrate the diversity of intimacies within cultures and provide more clues about the nature of intimate human relations. Intimate same-sex relationships are common to both Aka and Ngandu. They are not sexual relationships and are never described as homosexual relationships, but they are intimate relationships in that the individuals are both physically and emotionally close. They may sleep together, spend much of the day together, and, unlike marriage relationships, show public affection toward each other, such as holding hands. These intimate relationships are particularly common in adolescence but can occur in late childhood or adulthood. Relationships such as these are common with adult men in both groups but are rare with adult women. For instance, it is not unusual to see two adult Ngandu males walking down the street holding hands. Individuals are also emotionally close and talk about special emotional bonds. We suggest that infatuation and idealization (key features of romantic love) also occur in these relationships, as individuals are excited about being together, seek each other out, and are emotionally intimate.

Parent-child relationships are also intimate, especially among the Aka. In both groups all children younger than seven, and even older adolescents, sleep with their mothers and other adults. Aka infants are held or are within arm's reach of an adult during all daylight hours, and children and adolescents spend a good portion of every day with their parents. After age two or three, Ngandu children are placed under the care of older children in the village while their mothers go work in the fields. Aka children tend to have equally strong feelings and love for both mother and father, while Ngandu children tend to have especially strong emotional feelings toward their mothers.

Discussion

A Biosocial Evolutionary Framework for Understanding Sex, Love, and Violence

In an effort to explain universal as well as particularistic results of this study, we consider psychological, ecological, and cultural interactions that shape behavior. Three cultural-ecological factors are important for understanding the particularistic themes: the nature of patrilineal descent and social organization, the nature of social relations, and the political-economic setting.

Strong patriclan social organization among the Ngandu provides a mechanism for defending and protecting material (e.g., land and crops) and reproductive (e.g., spousal) resources. Consequently, the number, age, and sex of geographically close kin, especially males, are important (e.g., male-male alliances). The Ngandu accumulate goods and property (e.g., planted crops) that must be guarded from mobile Aka and other farmers. In addition, more wives (and children) mean not only prestige and status but increased wealth. Wives are essentially the breadwinners: they work in the fields, herd livestock, and sell produce from their farms in the market. They bring more wealth and food not only to their own nuclear family but to the larger extended family as well. Therefore intra- and intergroup hostilities about women are not uncommon, polygyny is practiced by about 40 percent (Hewlett 1991), and many men do not have spouses, which leads to conflict and violence. Gender inequality is strongly conserved, and violence against women within this setting is frequent. By comparison, Aka are mobile, and intra- and intergroup hostilities are infrequent, so clan organization is weak. Strong patriclan organization among the Ngandu leads to dependency upon strong alliances, a greater number of clan members, and a culturally transmitted ideology of male deference, obedience, and respect, as male clan members are important for resource defense. Aka, on the other hand, are dependent on both men and women from both sides of the family, because it is important for them to be flexible in response to the availability of wild food resources. For the Aka the number, age, and sex of geographically close biological kin, specifically, male kin, is of less importance, because they have little need for resource defense (accumulated goods, property holdings) and male-male alliances. Therefore the Aka promote and culturally conserve gender and age egalitarianism, not deference to either elders or men. Violence, particularly violence against women, is not common.

The Aka have "immediate return" values and social organization (Woodburn 1982:205). This means that their activities are oriented directly to the present, and they labor to obtain food and other resources consumed or used that day or immediately thereafter. They have minimal investment in accumulating, in long-term debts or obligations, or in binding commitments to specific kin. Therefore the nature of violence has to do with protecting the commitment between spouses, not with protecting accumulated resources, spouses, and an ideology of male deference and authority built around clan obligation and alliances needed for that protection.

The nature of culture and social reproduction is important in understanding the diversity of responses within the marital bond. We emphasize the importance of understanding such factors as the conservative nature of patrilineal clan ideology and the material basis of social relations (i.e., Ngandu men often show their love for their children and wives by giving them gifts). Many aspects of culture are transmitted though conservative transmission mechanisms (e.g., vertical and group effect mechanisms), and some aspects of conservative transmission may not be linked to adaptation. The social transmission of patrilineal ideology among the Ngandu seems to be an adaptive aspect of culture. Ngandu children acquire this strong patrilineal ideology not through trial and error but through mechanisms that enable the rapid acquisition of culture. This strong ideology emphasizes deference and respect for elders, males, and ancestors. For the Ngandu social relations have to do with maintaining a gendered hierarchy of commitment and obligation, respect, and obedience. Disregard for this established hierarchy signals a potential threat, as it can lead to social disruption and reorganization. Therefore male deference, commitment, and respect for authority figures must be maintained. Intergenerational transmission of property and social status is crucial, because the interests of the group are dependent upon maintaining the interests of the clan, that is, male-male alliances. Economic activity, social continuity, delayed production and consumption, long-term planning, and concern are bound by the patrilineal lineages, social commitments, and the importance of remembering those to whom you must show deference and obedience, the group to which you are bound and committed.

A third cultural difference between the two groups is the material versus emotional basis of social relations. Several scholars have written about the material basis of social relations in Bantu-speaking central Africans (Levine 1977; Giovanna and Palloni 2006). Social relations cannot continue without a material exchange. For the Ngandu the love for and commitment to a loved one not only is tied to the maintenance of formal hierarchy and obligation but is expressed through gift giving (male to female as noted earlier) and to the "service" of female to male. For the Aka their love seems to be bound more directly to their relationship, which was not expressed as a provisioning one.

Diversity exists in the experiences and expression of love, sex, and violence, but, as we have noted, there are also several commonalities. Evolutionary psychologists are interested in identifying genetic or biologically based universals that evolved during the environments of evolutionary adaptation (i.e., long periods of human hunting and gathering) in response to recurrent adaptive problems. One recurrent problem faced by humans was the ability to not simply enter into a bond with another but to maintain that union. Earlier we listed several common patterns found in the data from the study of Aka and Ngandu (frequency of sex, love as a part of the marital bond, jealousy or divorce in response to a straying partner). Given the adaptive problem of responding to natural selection's pull to form sexual alliances, which are jeopardized by the seemingly naturally conflicting sexual strategies of men and women, one could hypothesize that psychology would evolve to deal with this discordance. The response of jealousy and anger to the potential loss of a loved one and the resources he or she provides, and the cross-cultural commonalities of the Ngandu and Aka, suggest that jealousy and violence as a mate-retention strategy are the flip side of the attachment or proximity module developed in the environment(s) of evolutionary adaptation as described by Bowlby (1972). In much the same way perhaps the expressions of anger and conflict represent an evolved psychology for communicating distress at the loss or potential loss of an individual who enhanced survival (and the resources she or he provided).

Aka and Ngandu patterns of anger and violence illustrate influences of both biology (the evolutionary psychology perspective) and culture (the evolutionary cultural anthropology perspective). The violence reported by Aka men and women and Ngandu women, and their explanations for hitting—that their spouse was sleeping or developing a relationship with somebody else—are grounded in the evolved propensity for sexual jealousy. As we noted earlier, jealousy is part of our evolutionary programming. Sexual desire and passion breed wariness: early in human history men who did not react jealously had mates who "walked too long" and were impregnated by other men, thereby passing on someone else's genes to future generations. On the other hand, women who did not react to a spouse's straying were left to raise their offspring without help. Evolutionary psychology focuses on how we are pulled into sexual unions of love and marriage that are then jeopardized by the conflicting sexual strategies of men and women: men to make the most of their abundance of genetic seed and women to satisfy their desire to partner up with the genetically favored man best able to invest in the care of her offspring. Jealousy is also a response to the threat and conflict of the differing reproductive interests of men and women (Konner 1983). Therefore violence is not only a response to the loss or perceived loss of a loved one and resources but also a mate-

retention strategy. The influence of culture is also evident in the explanations of Ngandu men and women for violence—that is, the lack of respect
and deference shown to the male head of the household.

In addition, both Aka and Ngandu couples expressed the importance
of intimacy and love within the marital bond. The combination of genetic
and cultural evolution—wherein selection favored a species-specific type
of intelligence and expressed empathy (and certainly other variables)—are
what makes us human. This articulated empathy, the ability to feel and understand what others are experiencing and expressing, and through these
qualities the ability to understand the needs of others—to respond to them,
for example, by daily sharing, by a compassionate response to need—makes
us different in distinct ways from our ape relatives. The compassion of our
ancestors from our evolutionary past, who took care of each other and felt
empathy for others, was the source of our emotionally charged behaviors
of adaptation necessary for survival—love, intimacy, desire, and jealousy
(Hrdy 1999:392).

***

In looking at models of sex and marriage, Quinn (1996) suggests that the
cultural ideal of a Euro-American marriage is that it should be fulfilling,
and each partner must make an effort to figure out the other's needs in
order to fulfill them and must sacrifice his or her own needs in order to
do so. Both partners have to work at creating and maintaining a successful
marriage—this is their cultural task solution. This may be in part because
generally there are no close kin or clan to help fulfill this task of encouraging the couple to work it out. Nuclear families are often not living near
their extended network of kin. Couples are dependent upon each other;
their relationship is primary, because they are without the alliances and
close help of a large extended family. Shweder's study (2003) of cosleep-
ing among the U.S. middle class highlights the "sacred" husband-wife relationship because, unlike spouses in other cultures, parents always sleep
together in the same bed, regardless of the number of rooms in a house.
Aka and Ngandu husband-wife relations differ in that the "cultural niche"
they have built within a similar ecological setting differs dramatically and
has a profound impact on their "models of marriage." The Ngandu live in
compounds of clans, and neighbors are close by and undoubtedly related.
Each home, however, is separate and private. Wives within a polygynous

household have their own rooms (at the very least), although they more often inhabit separate (but joined) homes. The Aka live in such proximity to their nuclear family and extended kin that their life is lived in public and open to censorship. Husband and wife are emotionally intimate, but they are not dependent on each other for social-emotional support, as is often the case in the United States. Individual autonomy is highly valued and encouraged, even within the marital bond, and this culture is conserved. As our data demonstrate, the Aka have other cultural models of marriage and ways of fulfilling marital task solutions. Topics of intimacy, sexual desire, jealousy, and anger are complicated and need stronger attention than what they have been accorded by scholars.

In addition, we have an evolved universal human psychology, but we have to be careful of developing interpretations of human nature based upon limited or biased data (e.g., Western notions of sexuality and ideal husband-wife relations). Human sex, love, and intimacy can only be understood as interactions of evolutionary psychology (biology), evolutionary ecology (ecology), and evolutionary cultural anthropology (culture). Human biology (genes) and culture have their own properties and need to be examined in detail, but they also interact in ways that pattern human behaviors. An integrated evolutionary model is a heuristic tool for thinking about these interactions and can help to generate testable hypotheses.

REFERENCES

Belsky, J. 1997. "Attachment, Mating, and Parenting: An Evolutionary Interpretation." *Human Nature* 8 (4): 361–81.
———. 1999. "Infant-Parent Attachment." In L. Balter and C. S. Tamis-LeMonda, eds., *Child Psychology: A Handbook of Contemporary Issues*, pp. 45–63. Philadelphia: Psychology Press/Taylor and Francis.
Bowlby, John. 1969/1972. *Attachment*. Vol. 1. Middlesex, U.K.: Penguin.
Bulmer, Michael. 1994. *Theoretical Evolutionary Ecology*. Sunderland, Mass.: Sinauer Associates.
Chisholm, J. S. 1993. "Death, Hope, and Sex: Life-History Theory and the Development of Reproductive Strategies." *Current Anthropology* 34, no. 1 (February): 1–24
Coates, R. 1999. "Australia." In R. Francoeur, ed., *International Encyclopedia of Sexuality*, pp. 87–115. New York: Continuum.
Fisher, Helen E. 1992. *The Anatomy of Love: The Natural History of Monogamy, Adultery, and Divorce*. New York: W. W. Norton.

———. 2006. *The Psychology of Love.* 2nd ed. Edited by J.R. Sternberg and M.L. Barnes. New Haven, Conn.: Yale University Press.

Francoeur, Robert T. 1999. *International Encyclopedia of Sexuality.* 2 vols. New York: Continuum.

Giovanna, M. and Palloni, A. 2006. "Aging the HIV/AIDS Epidemic, Kin Relations, Living Arrangements, and the African Elderly in South Africa." In Committee on Population, National Research Council of the National Academies, *Aging in Sub-Saharan Africa: Recommendations for Furthering Research,* pp. 117–23. Washington, D.C.: National Academies Press.

Hewlett, Barry S. 1991. *Intimate Fathers: The Nature and Context of Aka Pygmy Paternal Infant Care.* Ann Arbor: University of Michigan Press.

Hewlett, Barry S. and Michael E. Lamb. 2002. "Integrating Evolution, Culture and Developmental Psychology: Explaining Caregiver-Infant Proximity and Responsiveness in Central Africa and the United States of America." In H. Keller, Y.H. Poortinga, and A. Schölmerich, eds., *Between Culture and Biology: Perspectives on Ontogenetic Development,* pp. 241–69. London: Cambridge University Press.

Hrdy, Sarah Blaffer. 1999. *Mother Nature: A History of Mothers, Infants and Natural Selection.* New York: Pantheon.

Jankowiak, William. 1993. *Sex, Death and Hierarchy in a Chinese City: An Anthropological Account.* New York: Columbia University Press.

———, ed. 1995. *Romantic Passion: A Universal Experience?* New York: Columbia University Press.

Konner, Melvin. 1983. *The Tangled Wing: Biological Constraints on the Human Spirit.* New York: Harper and Row.

———. 2005. "Hunter-Gatherer Infancy and Childhood: The !Kung and Others." In B.S. Hewlett and M.E. Lamb, eds., *Hunter-Gatherer Childhoods: Evolutionary, Developmental, and Cultural Perspectives,* pp. 19–64. New York: Aldine Transaction.

Levine, Robert A. 1977. "Child Rearing as Cultural Adaptation." In P.H. Leiderman, S.R. Tulkin, and A. Rosenfeld, eds., *Culture and Infancy,* pp. 15–77. New York: Academic.

Lindholm, C. 1998. "Love and Structure." *Theory, Culture and Society* 15 (3–4): 243–63.

———. 2000. *Cultural Identity.* New York: McGraw Hill.

Odling-Smee, F.J., K.N. Laland, and M.W. Feldman. 2003. *Niche Construction: The Neglected Process in Evolution.* Monographs in Population Biology 37. Princeton, N.J.: Princeton University Press.

Quinn, Naomi. 1996. "Culture and Contradiction: The Case of Americans Reasoning about Marriage." *Ethos* 24 (3): 391–425.

Shweder, Richard A. 2003. *Why Do Men Barbecue? Recipes for Cultural Psychology.* Cambridge, Mass.: Harvard University Press.

Smith, E. A. 2000. "Three Styles in the Evolutionary Analysis of Human Behavior." In N. A. Chagnon and W. Irons, eds., *Evolutionary Biology and Human Social Behavior,* pp. 545–56. North Scituate, Mass.: Duxbury Press.

Smith, T. 1991. "Adult Sexual Behavior in 1989: Number of Partners, Frequency of Intercourse and Risk of AIDS." *Family Planning Perspectives* 23:102–7.

Symons, Donald. 1979. *The Evolution of Human Sexuality.* New York: Oxford University Press.

Tomasello, M. 1999. *The Cultural Origins of Human Cognition.* Cambridge, Mass.: Harvard University Press.

Turke, Paul. 1988. "'Helpers at the Nest': Childcare networks on Ifaluk." In L. Betzig, M. Borgherhoff Mulder, and P. Turke, eds., *Human Reproductive Behaviour: A Darwinian Perspective,* pp. 173–88. Cambridge: Cambridge University Press.

Woodburn, James. 1982. "Egalitarian Societies." *Man* 17:431–51.

Wright, Robert. 1994. *The Moral Animal.* New York: Pantheon.

3. Self, Other, and the Love Dyad in Lithuania
Romantic Love as Fantasy and Reality (Or, When Culture Does and Doesn't Matter)

Victor C. De Munck

This chapter describes Lithuanian conceptions of love and how they work in reality. Romantic love is not an isolated cultural model but is always linked to other cultural concepts and practices; thus I describe how the Lithuanians whom I interviewed used, altered, or ignored notions of romantic love in their life (particularly, but not exclusively, in terms of sex and marriage choices).

I also have two theoretical axes to grind. I assume that the Lithuanian normative model of romantic love and its relation to sex and marriage corresponds with—indeed, may be virtually identical to—a normative Western model of romantic love. Thus I will show what features of romantic love Lithuanians share with the West and which ones they do not. Also, I hope to demonstrate that, just because two (or more) national cultures share virtually the same model of romantic love, does not mean that members of those cultures will act on this model in the same way. There is more to culture and to human behavior than sharing one or more cultural models. Also important is how a cultural model of romantic love is linked to other models and whether romantic love, its network of linkages, and the behavioral outcomes of these linkages are culturally endorsed. Thus my key theoretical contribution here will be to show explicitly how culture really does matter in issues of love.[1]

In 1992 Jankowiak and Fischer conducted a cross-cultural survey to determine whether romantic love was a cross-cultural universal. They looked at the ethnographic records of 166 societies to see whether anthropologists recorded evidence of romantic love in them. Jankowiak and Fischer found evidence of romantic love in 147 of those societies; where they found no data on romantic love, they concluded that the ethnographer's eye probably was elsewhere. Their findings provide strong evidence that romantic love is a cultural universal. The next step in understanding romantic love cross-culturally is to discover and describe universal features of romantic love. This is what Helen Fisher and her colleagues (2002) attempted to do. They combed the cross-cultural and psychological literature to find evidence of universal emotion-motivation characteristics associated with romantic love. They found thirteen "psycho-physiological characteristics" that are "commonly associated with romantic attraction" (2002:415).

A theory of romantic love that is less hard science and more humanistic is the Platonic theory of romantic love, which is more than two thousand years old. It is an influential, if not the dominant, theoretical perspective of more humanistic research on love (e.g., Soble 1990; Singer 1966, 1994; Brehm 1988; Kövécses 1988). The core component of this theory (as I see it) is that a striving for unity is the "master motive" of romantic love. The importance of this criterion is underscored by Kövécses, who concluded that unity was the "dominant metaphor" for romantic love in American culture (1988:18). Combining classical and modern Platonic approaches to love, I produced a list of ten criteria associated with the Platonic theory of romantic love.

I will aggregate the ethnographic, psychophysiological (which refers to the "reality" of romantic love), and philosophical-Platonic criteria, which refer to the ideals associated with romantic love, into a list of criteria that reflects people's ideas and expressions of romantic love (see table 3.1). I will then use this list to evaluate Lithuanian conceptions of romantic love as elicited by free-list (a list of qualities compiled through free association) surveys and general discussions with students and other Lithuanians (see table 3.2). I assume that Lithuanian understandings of romantic love will include most of the criteria in the aggregated list of romantic love characteristics. I expect that some characteristics will be unique to Lithuania or to the Lithuanian cultural area (i.e., the Baltics and northeastern Europe). Thus one question I will seek to answer is to what extent the Lithuanian cultural model of romantic love is culturally distinctive.

Table 3.1 Aggregate List of Characteristics of Romantic Love

1. Thinking that the beloved is unique (or incommensurable)—empirical and idealist
2. Desiring union—empirical and idealist
3. Paying attention to the positive qualities of the beloved—empirical and idealist
4. Putting the beloved first (altruism)—empirical and idealist
5. Finding that "emotional union" takes "precedence over sexual desire"— empirical and idealist
6. Declaring the relationship to be monogamous—empirical and idealist
7. Realizing that feeling connected to the beloved is magnified in adverse times—empirical (idealist implied)
8. Finding that contact or thought of the beloved induces a physiological feeling of exhilaration—empirical (idealist implied)
9. Noting that the feeling of romantic love is not controllable—empirical
10. Experiencing "intrusive thinking—empirical
11. Feeling emotionally dependent—empirical
12. Feeling sexual attraction—empirical
13. Finding that romantic love is generally temporary—empirical
14. Striving for unity—idealist
15. Realizing that romantic love is not definable in terms of attributes or quantity—idealist
16. Understanding that romantic love is not measurable—idealist
17. Believing that romantic love is forever—idealist
18. Recognizing that romantic love is independent of sex—idealist

Note: Empirical refers to a characteristic that the empirically minded researcher would find to be an observable and hence quantifiable ingredient of the "whole" (i.e., romantic love); the idealist regards any characteristic as a symptomatic manifestation of the whole and considers the empirical aim misguided because at best it describes symptoms of romantic love and at worst confounds the symptoms for the essence of romantic love. For more on the empirical perspective see Fisher and colleagues (2002); for the idealist perspective see Aristotle (1956).

In this chapter I will discuss the features of the two lists—the Platonic and free lists—and present an aggregate list of romantic love characteristics; then I will compare the two lists. Next, I develop a Lithuanian cultural model of romantic love from the free-list materials and, more important, from written commentaries about romantic love provided by informants. I also use interviews from four Lithuanian informants to evaluate the extent to which the cultural model I developed can help explain their love lives. I conclude by addressing the question of how culture matters, particularly in

Table 3.2 Lithuanian Free List of Terms Associated with Romantic Love (sorted by frequency)

TERM	FREQUENCY*	PERCENT**	AVG. RANK***
Being together	40	50.0	4.850
Joyousness	16	20.0	3.813
Walking together	14	17.5	3.500
Feeling an emotional upsurge	14	17.5	3.786
Happiness	13	16.25	5.077
Kissing	12	15.0	4.083
Doing things together	9	11.25	4.889
Feeling that love is temporary	9	11.25	5.111
Desiring sex	9	11.25	3.444
Paying attention to one another	8	10.00	4.250
Engaging in love talk	8	10.00	5.375
Surprising the beloved	8	10.00	3.400
Feeling passion	7	8.75	3.286
Going to the movies	7	8.75	2.857
Traveling together	7	8.75	4.286
Having tender feelings	7	8.75	3.857
Feeling of attachment	7	8.75	2.714
Holding hands	7	8.75	3.000
Recognizing mutuality of feelings	6	7.50	4.000
Trusting one another	6	7.50	1.500
Seeing love as a dream	6	7.50	7.333
Feeling admiration for the beloved	6	7.50	3.500
Giving little presents	6	7.50	6.167
Being honest	5	6.25	5.600
Feeling impractical	5	6.25	5.800
Having candlelight dinners	5	6.25	2.800
Being in the initial stage of love	5	6.25	2.800
Caring for the beloved	4	5.00	4.500
Feeling a physical upsurge	4	5.00	3.750
Feeling strong	4	5.00	3.000
Longing for one another	4	5.00	2.500
Feeling self-confident	4	5.00	6.750
Feeling of oneness	4	5.00	8.750
Feeling carefree	4	5.00	7.250
Feeling doubt	4	5.00	10.750
Feeling that love is not enduring	4	5.00	2.500
Bringing flowers	4	5.00	2.750

TOTAL   292†

Frequency refers to the number of people who mentioned an item.

**Percentage* refers to the percentage of informants who mentioned a term. Thus "being together" was mentioned by forty people, or 50 percent, of those who filled out the survey.

***Average rank* refers to where in a free association a term was usually mentioned (first, second, third, and so on). A high average rank means that people who mentioned a term did so quickly and before other terms.

†The total is the total number of responses provided by the eighty informants.

relation to any analysis of universal features of romantic love. I conducted my field research in the small rural town of Telsiai and in Vilnius with the aid of two assistants. We collected free lists and commentaries from eighty Lithuanians, forty from each field site. We conducted three one-hour interviews with each of twenty-seven Lithuanians.

ROMANTIC LOVE ATTRIBUTES

Fisher and colleagues found thirteen psychophysiological characteristics that are associated with romantic love:

1. Thinking that the beloved is unique.
2. Paying attention to the positive qualities of the beloved.
3. Finding that contact or thought of the beloved induces feelings of "exhilaration," "increased energy," "heart pounding," and intense emotional arousal.
4. Realizing that feeling connected to the beloved is magnified in adverse times.
5. Experiencing "intrusive thinking."
6. Feeling possessive of and dependent on the beloved.
7. Desiring "union" with the beloved.
8. Having a strong sense of altruism and concern for the beloved.
9. Reordering one's priorities to favor the beloved.
10. Feeling sexual attraction for the beloved.
11. Finding that "emotional union" takes "precedence over sexual desire."
12. Noting that the feeling of romantic love is "involuntary" and not controllable.
13. Finding that romantic love is generally temporary.

(2002:416–17)

These thirteen indicators all reflect psychological states of the individual.

I put together a second list of characteristics by using the Platonic theory of love, which has a twenty-four-hundred-year history and many avatars in philosophy and the social sciences (e.g., Brehm 1988; Kövécses 1988; Lindholm 1990, 1995, 1998; Singer 1966; Soble 1990; Swidler 2001).[2] Key to the Platonic model is that romantic love is a transcendent "striving for unity," which is in turn motivated by the desire for "perfection" or "wholeness" or "possessing perpetually the absolute good." In the Platonic approach love is in the eye of the beholder, and the lover appraises his beloved as "perfect," "unique," "the one and only" and bestows love on only that person. Love is not completely removed from sexuality, because Plato uses the metaphor of the white horse (the nobler form of love) and the black horse (sexual desire, a lower form of love) to describe human nature. In Plato's metaphor of the horses both horses symbolize inherent and necessary drives or characteristics of humans.

The Platonic theory deals, of course, with idealistic expectations for romantic love, whereas Fisher and colleagues focus on the more pragmatic aspects of romantic love, those that are observable and measurable. Nonetheless, the two models overlap, especially in regard to the concept of unity. However, the concept of unity has different connotations. For Fisher and colleagues it is a "craving for emotional union" (2002:415), but in the "higher" Platonic sense union (I am using *union* and *unity* synonymously) leads to an absence of any emotional feeling because the two are now permanently indivisible (hence romantic love lasts forever), so there is no reason to "crave" union. Alan Soble, whom I place in the Platonic camp, states that unity is a "transcendent feeling . . . that cannot be broken down into attributes" (1990:38). This position is also advocated by Lindholm (1995, 1998), Brehm (1988), and Kövecses (1988) and is one that Swidler (2001) ascribes as central to "romantic love mythology."[3] In the Platonic theory love is an absolute that one seeks "perpetual possession of." It follows that union, in a looser, neo-Platonic sense, can be defined as a striving to be together or declaring the relationship to be monogamous.

Thus I identify the following attributes with a modernized neo-Platonic theory of love:

1. Romantic love is goal directed.
2. The goal is to find one's perfect mate and to unite into a whole being with the beloved.
3. Romantic love is in the eye of the beholder.
4. The beloved is conceived as "one's other half."
5. The beloved is irreplaceable.
6. Romantic love is, but need not be, independent of sex.
7. Romantic love is monogamous.

8. Romantic love is an absolute, not definable in terms of attributes or quantity.

9. Romantic love lasts forever.

The first six features all deal with the lover's attitude toward the beloved in order to attain and maintain a monogamous bond. Sexual desire is ambiguous, and perhaps the most problematic feature of any universal model of romantic love, because by itself it implies commensurability; that is, sexual desire can be satisfied by various partners. But the desire for unity implies some sort of sexual union as well. Thus sexual desire may, from the Platonic perspective, be a consequence of romantic love but not a core feature of romantic love. Clearly, then, the items in a list of characteristics can vary in importance across culture, time, and individuals. Such variation is likely for many other such attributes as well. In the next section I discuss the data gathered from eighty Lithuanian informants.

LITHUANIAN FREE-LIST DATA

Forty Lithuanians from a small rural town, Telsiai, and forty from Vilnius, the largest city and capital of Lithuania, were asked, "What do you associate with romantic love?"[4] The respondents were between twenty and forty years of age; forty-six were female and thirty-four were male. The responses of the rural and urban Lithuanians showed no obvious differences, so I do not differentiate between them in this discussion. Gender differences were minor and not differentiated in the analysis of the free-list data. The initial free list contained 336 Lithuanian terms. My two assistants and I culled the number of items by combining responses that we considered to be synonymous; longer commentaries were reduced to a phrase. This effort generated a second list of 189 terms; listed here are only those terms that the Lithuanians mentioned four or more times and that my assistants and I translated into English. (To save space I have omitted the Lithuanian terms but will supply them to readers who wish to have them.)[5]

"Being together" (1) subsumes various terms that refer to a state of being or wanting to be together; included were statements such as "wanting to be together," "spending time together," and the like. We considered "doing things together" (7) to be a second concept because it does not necessarily imply seeking a "state of togetherness." "Oneness" (33) was also kept as a separate category, because it is a strong version of the Platonic concept of unity. "Attachment" (17) and "longing" (31) are also terms indicative of a "striving after unity." These five phrases—"being together," "do things together," "one," "attachment," and "longing"—cumulatively constitute 22 percent of the terminology and indicate that "unity," or the striving for unity, is probably the dominant theme of any Lithuanian cultural model of romantic love.

"Joyousness" (2), "feeling an emotional upsurge (*emocinis-pakilimas*)" (5), "happiness" (6), and "feeling carefree" (34) all speak to a general sense of "feeling good" that is derived from being in love; these phrases are more or less equivalent to Fisher and colleagues' criterion of "exhilaration."

"Devoting attention" (10), "love talk" (11), "trust" (20), "honesty" (24), and "caring" (28) refer to relationship-maintenance and -enhancing activities. This idea was presented by a thirty-four-year-old female informant from Telsiai, who wrote, "If it [romantic love] happens, it means that partners pay a 'big attention' to each other and that they talk to each other honestly, lovingly, and trust each other very much; in this way they become even more open to each other." Honesty, attention, and love talk lead to trust, and all three are perceived as means to open up to each other and, in that sense, to know the other as one knows oneself. Thus the combination of these terms can be seen as related to a striving for unity because this unity is achieved by gaining mutual psychological transparency, which itself is gained by practicing honesty, care, attention, and love talk.

Six informants deemed that the "mutuality" of feelings of love (*abipuses*) (19) is a requirement for a lasting romantic love relationship. A twenty-three-year-old man from Vilnius wrote that romantic love "must be mutual if it is to last. The couple should live . . . one life and plan their future as if they are going to spend their whole life together." For these informants "mutuality" is an important bridge concept in that it directly connects the concept of unity with the dynamics of a relationship.

"Mutuality" was also used as a means to talk about a relationship's becoming stronger and overcoming obstacles. For instance, a twenty-year-old man from Vilnius wrote, "When people feel romantic love for each other, they become closer. Through mutual expression of feelings, the couple feels that they can overcome any barrier that separates them. . . . Romantic feelings have to be mutual and need to be confirmed by both parties. Once mutual love is declared, there are no more doubts and no more uncertainty."

In that same vein a twenty-three-year-old Vilnius woman said that even though the couple may have to "hide their relationship from their parents ... they don't care. They will give and take from each other in equal measure." "Lovers," she continued, "become very honest with each other; they always try to strengthen their relationship by meeting each other's mutual expectations, being supportive and positive, and listening." The responses of this woman and the twenty-three-year-old Vilnius man provide evidence for Fisher and colleagues' criterion that "adverse times can intensify the feeling of connectedness." The key to such effort is that it is mutual and honest. "Meeting each other's expectations" and "being supportive and positive" also refer to the love criteria of "attention to positive qualities" (3), "altruism" (4), and "emotional union" (5). Though direct expressions of "monogamy" were infrequently expressed in the free-list terms, it is clearly a default assumption in the statements made by the informants and in the concepts related to "being together."

Informants mentioned other positive aspects of love that are not closely associated with the Platonic ideal of love but that do fit with the criteria for romantic love assembled by Fisher and colleagues. For instance, Lithuanians recognized a physical sexual component to romantic love: "kissing" (7), "sex" (9), "passion" (13), "holding hands" (18), and "feeling of physical upsurge" (29) are terms that either refer to or imply sexual contact between the couple. In another free-list question—"What activities do you associate with romantic love?"—"sex" (which included "making love" and "intercourse") was the overwhelming first choice of activities, mentioned by 66 percent of Lithuanian informants. In the free-list question analyzed here—"What do you associate with romantic love?"—only nine of the eighty informants (11 percent) mentioned sex. Thus sex is a commonly cited activity associated with romantic love, but it is not among the most significant aspects of romantic love. This finding provides strong supporting evidence for the fifth criterion for love—that "emotional union" takes "precedence over sexual desire."

The most common activities associated with romantic love are: "walking" (4), "surprises" (12), "going to the movies" (14), "traveling together" (15), "holding hands" (18), "little presents" (23), "candlelight dinners" (26), and "flowers" (37). "Flowers," "surprises," and "little presents" might reasonably be combined and aggregated into one category—"gifts." Informant discussions of gift giving and holding hands centered on giving attention (*demesys*) to their partner, and they said that gifts symbolized that the two were a couple, or what I call a "love dyad." A thirty-year-old woman wrote, "Unexpected presents, frequent calls, memorable dates in unusual places, going to interesting places, and simple presents are ways to express your feelings and to give special attention to your second half (*antroji puse*)." Gift giving and males' offering food to a female are court-ship behaviors that have been observed in other species, including fruit flies (Fisher 1992:34–35).

For Lithuanians "walking" was the most common activity, and it was usually mentioned in conjunction with a particular context such as a walk in the moonlight, by the seashore, in a forest, on a deserted street, and so on. For Americans walking is almost always associated with holding hands and with no particular context except, for some, a beach. In discussing with Lithuanians the importance of walking, we found the consensus was that walking is a romantic way to get to places and that Vilnius has many parks and interesting places where couples can walk. Walking is seen as an intimate activity in itself. One woman said, "When you walk, time goes slowly, and you feel like you are doing something intimate; sitting is too intense, especially when you are getting to know one another, but walking is both a distraction, a means to dissipate nervous energy, and a way to be together."

Another important activity for Lithuanians was "going to the movies" (14, or 9 percent), which was mentioned only once in the eighty American free lists. My guess is that going to the movies in Lithuania is still regarded as a special event, whereas in the United States it has ceased to be a special event because people either go in large groups or watch a video or DVD at home.

In summary, the free-list items and this discussion show, or at least strongly imply, that the first eight cross-cultural features are present and salient in Lithuanian conceptions of romantic love. That other terms did not appear on the free lists does not mean they are not part of a Lithu-anian model of romance; they may be tacit or taken-for-granted aspects of the model or best elicited through other methods. I did find it interesting that "mutuality" was a significant term and, in fact, judging from the com-mentaries, seems to be a key component of the Lithuanian cultural model of romantic love. *Mutuality* is an interesting word because it implies that an equality of status is an important factor for romantic love. What I had not considered earlier is that "mutuality" indicates that many informants interpreted love from the perspective of the relationship (or "love dyad") as a whole, rather than from their own or their beloved's perspective. As a result I began to think of love as a relational system with its own particular systemic processes and properties, rather than as a feeling. Thus the unit for analysis of romantic love may very well be the couple rather than the individual.

A LITHUANIAN CULTURAL MODEL OF ROMANTIC LOVE

Unfortunately, an analysis of a list of characteristics cannot capture the dynamics of the relationship that exists between the attributes. In their commentaries informants described love as a dynamic process, shifting their frame of reference from the self to the other to the relationship itself (i.e., the love dyad). In the commentaries the path of romantic love oscillates among three reference points—ego, other, and couple—with informants filling in the various obligations, strengths, weaknesses, and requirements they associate with each reference point. Key to these efforts is the attempt to reflect on the couple as a love dyad with mutual rights and obligations; thus there is a narrative of unity, but it is rarely one that involves merging or condensing into a "one."

This dyadic social dynamic is nicely illustrated by a twenty-one-year-old Vilnius woman who wrote, "Couples [in love] unconsciously obligate themselves to each other; they become responsible for each other, they are responsible for their partner's happiness, and they try to prevent some actions from hurting each other. You feel happiness and joy that you are loved and not alone in the world; when you are loved, you are not in this world alone . . . there is someone who cares about you, and who misses you." This woman described love in terms of unity but with a twist. For her unity is not only a goal to strive for, but, even more important, it is a means to ward off loneliness and to acquire a special (that is, incommensurable) status. Though the informant begins with the socially altruistic sense of "responsibility" and "obligation," in the second half of her statement she refers to the benefits of being loved. By virtue of being a member of a love dyad, the individual is protected from feeling lonely and ordinary. The Platonic notion of "unity" is reformulated and is conceptualized by the Lithuanian informants as less transcendent than many neo-Platonians would have it (Lindholm 1998, 2001; Kövécses 1988). Informants do wax poetic about unity, but rarely do they see it as a merging of two into one; rather, they see it as a merging into a social unit, the love dyad, in which each has particular rights and obligations, just as in any other social relationship.

The Lithuanian cultural model of romantic love, provided by the free list and, more important, the responses of the informants, could be formulated as follows: Romantic love refers to a social dyad that entails certain mutual responsibilities: honesty, protection, happiness, openness, and expressions of love. All these increase trust, which, like gravity, holds the couple together.

Thus far I have described three different frames for romantic love: the first is the ego frame, which is an evaluation of the benefits that ego derives from love; the second is the altruistic, or bestowal, frame in which one evaluates how one is obligated to the beloved and what one desires to give to the object of one's love; and the third is the dyad, which is the expected functions of the couple as a social group and the strength and sense of being a unique social unit, a unity, that is derived from participation in this dyad. All three frames operate in romantic love relationships. But the Lithuanian cultural mode of romantic love has more to it.

The Lithuanian respondents used such phrases as "temporary" (8), "dream" (21), "not pragmatic" (25), "initial stage of love" (27), and "doubt" (33) to refer to the idea that romantic love is not enduring and is at best a temporary phase that may lead to a more "mature" love. This more skeptical approach to romantic love represents, I believe, an alternative way of framing one's understanding of romantic love. This idea of Lithuanians' possessing two contrary models of romantic love and moving between them is somewhat similar to Swidler's 2001 assertion that Americans hold two cultural models of romantic love—"real love" and the "myth of romantic love"—simultaneously. The "real love" narratives that Swidler describes are, as she explains, almost antiromantic love, muting strong affectionate feelings and casting the relationship in terms of the "mundane" and "ordinary" cycle of day-to-day activities. Thus these narratives are pragmatic and view romantic love as temporary or illusory and do not even refer to it as significant. Her depictions of the "myth of romantic love" fit well with the (neo) Platonic ideals of unity and the uniqueness of the individual, which were also expressed by the Lithuanians. Swidler explains that these two love narratives serve two different "institutional functions": the function of the "myth of romantic love" is to give people a reason for dating and for marrying; the function of "real love" is to keep the couple together after they are married.

There are differences between my Lithuanian informants and Swidler's informants. These differences may stem from the different age groups of our samples. Swidler dealt primarily with people who were already married, and many of her informants were in their forties and fifties. I dealt primarily with people who were not married or who were recently married and in their twenties and thirties. Thus I was working with a sample that should adhere to the "myth of romantic love" model. Swidler explains that "when thinking about the choice of whether to marry or stay married people see love in mythic terms. Love is the choice of one right person whom one will or could marry. Therefore love is all-or-nothing, certain, exclusive, heroic, and enduring. . . . The institutional demands of marriage continually reproduce the outlines of the mythic love story" (2001:129).

But this was not the case with the Lithuanian informants, as many (if not most) who were in a romantic love relationship and unmarried doubted the reality of romantic love, perceiving it as a fantasy. One twenty-two-year-old rural woman who held this view wrote (with a twist of irony): "Romantic love is when both sides love each other, fulfill each other's desires, listen to romantic music, and go together for a walk. In a word—it's the love that one finds in TV soap operas. Romantic love can only exist between dreaming people."

In that same, though less wry, vein a twenty-four-year-old man wrote that "romantic love equals exaggerated feelings: exaggerated perceptions of the other; an exaggerated estimation of closeness, physical attraction, etc." And a female informant wrote that "romantic love can last only one or two years but not longer." Later, in a focus group discussion with twelve Lithuanian college students and in discussions with other Lithuanians, the verdict was virtually unanimous: romantic love was a fantasy, perhaps a delightful one, but it was not real. What is interesting and important here is that Lithuanians can have a romantic cultural model that is virtually the same as that of Americans (or whomever), with the important proviso that the Lithuanians can frame it as "real" or "not real." As we shall see, this has immense consequences for how their model of romantic love influences behavior and links with other cultural models (such as marriage, career choices, etc.).

The language my informants used to describe "real love" usually did not fit with either the "companionate love" model described by many American researchers of love or with Swidler's informants' version of "real love." The Lithuanian informants viewed "real love" as a more tempered, less intense, kind of romantic love. Like Swidler's informants, Lithuanians saw "real love" as fitting into everyday ordinary life, but in contrast to Swidler's informants, they usually saw it as *differentiated* rather than *undifferentiated* from ordinary life. In addition to distinguishing between "real" and "romantic love" models of romantic love, Lithuanians seem to typically frame romantic love as "play" or "not real," while Americans, especially those in love, do not use or are less likely to use such framing. Why the difference?

In perusing the American free-list data and comparing it with the Lithuanians' list, I noticed one startling difference: the Americans cited "friendship" (ranked 2nd; cited by 31 percent), "comfort" (ranked 7th; cited by 17 percent), "contentment" (ranked 14th; cited by 10 percent), and "security" (ranked 16th; cited by 9 percent). None of the Lithuanian informants mentioned any of these terms or used terms that connote themes of security or comfort. Not even in the commentaries on free-list responses did Lithuanian informants refer to security, comfort, or the like. I do not have enough data to significantly explore the reason for this difference; certainly many Lithuanians also feel comfortable, content, and secure with their lover, so it is not the absence of these feelings, but the lack of expression in association with romantic love is important. There could be two reasons for this. First, if romantic love is thought of as a fantasy, it is unlikely to be associated with feelings of comfort and the like, even when the romantic relationship is comfortable. Second, I think Lithuanians usually get their feelings of comfort and security from family and friendship networks. For the Americans these terms fit with Swidler's conception of "real love." "Comfort," "security," and "friendship" are precursors to and indexes for a successful marriage. Joining these comfort terms with romantic love helps frame romantic love as "real" and "substantial" and tones down its more flighty connotations. Such feelings, in conjunction with the feelings of romantic love, are perhaps necessary to determine whether one's "one and only" will also be a suitable spouse.

This discussion suggests that the American model of romantic live has a wider range of functions than does the Lithuanian model because the American model incorporates "real love" so that romantic love can be linked to marriage and other life choices. This, I suggest, is the reason why American cultural models of romantic love appear to be less romantic than Lithuanian models. The gap between models of romance and marriage is greater for Lithuanians than Americans in the sense that romantic loves is less likely to lead to marriage for Lithuanians than for Americans. As a result, in the context of romantic love, Lithuanians can permit unreality and fantasy to bloom relatively unburdened by the constraints of reality, whereas the American model, or "myth," of romantic love can be said to have the qualities of reality and enduringness injected into it.

This analysis led to a resolution of another apparent cultural difference that troubled me. In comparing Lithuanian and American free-list responses, I found that American informants gave short and unromantic answers, while the Lithuanian informants often wrote long explanations and provided poetic responses. Thus one of the most poetic American responses to the question about what you associate with romantic love was "surreal feeling," but more commonly the response might be "divine union," "warm fuzzy feeling," or "put partner first." In contrast, both Lithuanian women and men (who, according to my informants, have a reputation for being decidedly unromantic) would provide fine-grained details of what they mean, such as, "wet stars" (*šlapios žvaigždės?*), "wading in the marshes during a warm rain" (*braidymas po pelkes lyjant šiltam lietui*), "a flower's secret" (*gėlės paslaptis*), "the shadow of the moon's path on a lake as it moves to eternity" (*mėnulio tako į amžinybę šešėlis virš'ežero*), "the tranquility of a cigarette" (*cigaretės svaigulys*), "lyrical deviations" (*lyriniai nukrypimai*), "a photo of your lover instead of a pornographic picture" (*mylimojo nuotrauka vietoje pornigrafijos*), "torturing passion" ("*kankinanti aistra*"), or "the opposite of a mechanical life" ("*priešinga mechaniškam gyvenimui*").[6]

Why this difference? Informants were usually recruited the same way, at college campuses, neighborhood hangouts, friends of friends, or at parks. Informants were comparable in terms of age and social background. The only explanation that made sense to me was that Lithuanian informants typically (not always) saw love as fantasy and as an intense but bounded, temporary period of life so that they could wax poetic and, in a sense, throw caution to the wind and fully engage in the fantasy. Americans, on the other hand, were more inclined (though, again, not always) to view love as part of their life and not as a kind of separate fantasy world and therefore perceived it less poetically and more seriously.

Both Americans and Lithuanians can view romantic love as temporary, which accords with Fisher and colleagues' 2002 criterion of romantic love as temporary. But the difference is that for Americans the notion of romantic love as temporary comes from experiential evidence of its short duration, either because people split up or because they shifted to a "real love" model. As a result the temporary nature of romantic love is perceived not as an inherent quality but as a potential consequence of romantic love. For Lithuanians temporary and fantasy are inherent qualities of romantic love, and they not only expect but even wish for it to end, so that the relationship may progress into "real" or "mature" love. This was expressed by a twenty-five-year-old woman who wrote, "Mature love is different from romantic love; it is when people decide that they suit each other and then decide to become life partners." In other words, for this informant (and other Lithuanians) romantic love does not directly lead to marriage (as it does for Swidler's American informants), but if it is to end in marriage, it must first be transformed into "mature love," a condition in which individuals can make life choices. I hasten to add that I suspect this is a normative model that most Lithuanians subscribe to but do not necessarily heed.

Before I turn to the interview material, I want to summarize the major points thus far. First, the free list and commentaries by Lithuanians show—conclusively, I think—that the Lithuanian model of romantic love fits with the major criteria of love enumerated by Fisher and colleagues. However, I also have shown that such a list of characteristics misses some important features of romantic love that can be discovered only through the ethnographic semistructured free-list method and commentaries on the free lists. Through these methods we found out that Lithuanians consider romantic love to be a mutual positive feedback loop; that there are three points of reference—self, other, and the relationship; the data reveal a particular dynamic of romantic love in which couples are expected to pay "big" attention to each other, and this big attention consists of being honest, engaging in love talk, caring about the other person, sex, giving gifts, going on walks, and participating in various romantic activities; together, these activities lead to increasing trust and openness between the couple. It is important for the couple to be together and to establish a feedback cycle of obligations and responsibilities to make the other partner happy and to care for that person; as a result the person will gain in self-confidence and energy and be happier. Thus romantic love is perceived as a love dyad in which the couple creates a positive feedback loop between the partners.

In addition, most Lithuanians seem skeptical of the permanence and "reality" of love and view it as a fantasy, or temporary state. Thus they are doubtful that romantic love can last and that life decisions can be made on the basis of romantic love. In the interview material I will focus primarily on the way Lithuanians frame romantic love as "real" or "fantasy," "long-lasting" or "temporary," and how this influences life decisions.

Romantic Love in Reality

I use interview material from only four informants to demonstrate the way framing of romantic love as "true" or "false," "long-lasting" or "temporary" influences personal choices. If my argument about framing is correct, we should see the framing of love as "unreal" or "real" used as a culturally appropriate frame for interpreting life and love events.

Inga is a twenty-three-year-old university student. I interviewed her three times, mostly in English.[7] Here we will discuss two of her love relationships, her first one and her most recent one, as well as her sense of herself in a relationship, as she described it. She was raised in Telsiai; during the summer, as is typical of Lithuanians, she, her sister and brother, and their parents went to their cottage to garden and live in the countryside. There, one evening with a group of teenagers, she met a friend of her cousin's.

> *Inga:* At the moment when I met him I liked him. He was really nice and handsome. And I couldn't believe that . . . how could such a handsome guy—how could he look at me?
> *Victor:* Uh-huh, such an ugly girl as you (*said mockingly*).
> *Inga (laughing):* Uh-huh. I thought not very ugly, but I didn't consider myself a very special girl, either. I didn't believe that he could like me—I'm not so special. What's happening? What's going on here? It must be a dream or something like that.

What I find interesting here is her notion of herself as "not special," "not ugly," either, but it seemed to me a rational appraisal of her appearance. Note also that her description of her first feelings of romantic love are as a "dream," not as real. Of course, many American women are likely to recount their first crush in a similar manner. Nevertheless, she already seems adept at objectifying her own feelings and thus being skeptical of the reality of feelings of romantic love. The relationship begins to develop more; Inga describes their whirlwind romance (in English).

Inga: I offered to show him all the garden, and then we went to the river and it was like late evening [*laugh*], and all the stars were in the sky and we talked a lot. We liked each other. Then the second day, we went out to look at the stars again and he kissed me. The relationship was so, so fast. We talked of our love everyday and kissed. Nothing else. It was like our love lasted maybe two weeks. It was like a crush. It was very fast. We saw each other, we liked each other, and we would meet every day from the morning to the late evening, and after two weeks we got so bored with each other.

Victor: How did you feel when you were with him during those two weeks?

Inga: Those little trembles . . . *šiurpuliukai.* Your mouth gets dry, and you are trying to feel like "Oh, there's nothing special, you should feel comfortable, you should just relax" but you cannot. . . . I . . . I love that feeling very much, and that's why I love to get crushes often. You feel very good for a week or two weeks and then it's over.

This story of "first love" is typical of other male and female Lithuanians'. Inga describes what appears to me to be the development of the idea of romantic love as illusion, fantasy, a temporary but highly romantic affair. In her use of the word *fast* there is a sense of romantic love as being exhilarating, like a roller-coaster ride. It was so fast that it burned out in two weeks, when they became "so bored with each other." Next she describes the physiological sensations of love, much as they are described by Fisher (1992) and Fisher and colleagues (2002). Inga says that she enjoys this feeling and seeks such romantic encounters, but they are only "very good for a week or two weeks and then it's over." Again she seems to be evoking this notion of romantic love as a kind of "fantasy" or Batesonian "play" frame, a game to which you give yourself wholly but still retain a kind of rational detachment because you know that it is not serious. The break-ups do not seem sorrowful; they are brought on by mutual boredom.

I now describe her most recent love relationship, which she was involved in at the time of the interview. She met a Lithuanian American (I will call him Thomas) at a bar. They danced and talked (in English) for a long time. They kissed a little, and he then said he wanted a "serious relationship" and they should meet the next day, Sunday morning, at a bridge over a small creek in a park.

Inga: I thought it was really very romantic for him to ask me to meet him on the bridge like lovers and kiss on the bridge and walk. . . . It was very romantic—it was like a dream . . . it would never happen. He just . . . he just had some kind of possibility to make you feel very special, and I liked that feeling so much I could fall in love with that kind of guy, and he said that he wanted a serious relationship. If a Lithuanian guy would tell me that, I would know that he really wanted a serious relationship, but I knew that Americans . . . they always talk like that, and you can't . . . trust them. But I thought . . . maybe . . . could be . . . you never know, so I could miss a thing if I didn't go and meet him. . . . I went to that park on that bridge and I waited . . . but he never showed.

She equates romance with a dream, and though she knew that Americans weren't serious, or perhaps because she knew that, she went to the park in case he actually showed up. She then explains,

Inga: Thomas was like the man of my dreams or something like that, but I knew that it was a dream and I had to check. And I checked, and I went to that bridge but he wasn't there. I waited for an hour and then I went home.

All was not lost, however, for a mutual friend had given Thomas her e-mail address, and he wrote her. Apparently he had waited at another bridge. They started to meet regularly, and she quickly fell in love with him. In her words, "We are boyfriend and girlfriend. We are a couple now." They declared mutual love, and she began to stay over at his flat about three times per week. They also phoned and e-mailed daily. At the time of the interviews Thomas's parents were coming to visit for a week from the United States, and Thomas wanted Inga to meet them, but she said she couldn't.

Inga: I have other things to do and I have an exam. You know, always, my studies come first.
Victor: Uh-huh. So did he ask if you would meet them for one day?
Inga: I told him that I won't be able to meet him for a couple of days and then, after that, we can meet.
Victor: So you stayed home and worked.
Inga: All week I was working. Studying international law.

Victor: How'd you do?

Inga: Very good. I got a ten. I like that my personal life doesn't affect negatively on my studies—I am very happy about that. And it's even better that I have some guy.

Victor: Did he phone you?

Inga: Yes, he phoned me.

Victor: Was he irritated?

Inga: Yes. I don't know why. Even his mother phoned me up, Sunday. But I had to study. Friday I had my exam, and we met in the evening. We went out with his parents for dinner, and I spent Saturday with them as well. I liked very much [that] I felt like I was special because he bought me flowers and perfume for my exam. I love him. But I don't know him well. . . . I don't understand much about him.

Inga's romantic relationship with Thomas is contained and does not seep into the rest of her life. Thomas seems the prototype of a romantic male: he buys flowers, takes her out, makes her feel "special," wants to be with her, is a good dancer, financially successful and, to borrow her word, "perfect." They have declared mutual love for each other and have sexual relations. She thinks of him constantly, recalling small details about their previous interactions. Yet she was not willing to meet him during that week, even for a lunch engagement. When speaking of her exams, she shifts, as if she has pulled a mental switch, from attending to her love life to attending to her career. She talks of marriage and wanting children, even implying that she wouldn't mind if she was an unwed mother. Even so, she was not willing to consider marrying Thomas, although he had apparently told her he wanted her as a "life partner." She was not willing to sacrifice some hours of studying or sleep to meet Thomas and his parents.

If we assume that romantic love is indeed a master motive and that Inga is not lying, I don't think her behavior makes much sense. On the other hand, if we understand that she frames romantic love as false, or "like a dream," then it does make sense, for one does not risk one's future for a dream. Even if she wanted to follow her romantic inclinations, she knows that this would be foolish. Not only does she know this, as most Americans might, but she has framed the entire relationship as a "dream."

It is of course possible that some Lithuanian women would have sacrificed their exams and that some American women would have acted like Inga. That is not the point. The point is that in the interviews Inga portrays herself as simultaneously romantic and rational and that this portrayal follows logically from the free-list and commentary data. Inga's portrayal of herself would also be appropriate in the United States, but I think it would not be the norm. In any case, Inga's behavior is most easily explained by presuming that her framing of romantic love as a dream is a culturally endorsed frame for the cultural model of romantic love.

The second interview was with a twenty-seven-year-old woman, Gita, who lives in Vilnius. I am quoting her because in many ways she describes herself as highly romantic and thus seems the opposite of Inga. The interview was conducted in Lithuanian by a female assistant, Laura.

> *Laura:* As I understand it, love means a lot for you?
> *Gita:* Yes, a lot. It is one of the things without which I couldn't do anything. When I am in love, everything else stops—my interests become not so interesting, my principles, ambitions, aims about career, work, studies disappear. Everything disappears, stops, I become totally indifferent—I am afraid of myself. It is a universal engine—physically and spiritually.

For Inga love is controlled by reason; for Gita it is just the reverse: love controls everything, "everything stops . . . everything disappears." She makes similar remarks repeatedly in her interviews and considers herself highly romantic; romantic love is the master motive in her life. It seems that she is concerned about her own excessive romanticism when she states, "I am afraid of myself." She also frames romantic love as an uncontrollable natural force that sweeps over her. Thus she is not responsible for her behavior when she is in love. This is not so dissimilar to being in a dream where one is also not responsible for one's behavior. I quote her response to the question "Are sex and love connected?"

> *Gita:* There are three terms for me: sex, love, and making love. When there is love—there is making love. When there is physical attraction—then there is sex (*kada yra meileMyra mylejimasis, kada yra potraukis fizinisMyra seksas*). . . . Spiritually there is a very big difference.

She then goes on to enumerate her various love relations. An excerpt follows:

Gita: Last winter I was still deeply depressed over Raimis [her former lover, who left her] and there appeared a guy whom I had met two years ago. I liked him back then. He is studying to be a dentist, and he is a musician: romantic, clever, a strong personality, likable. . . . He fascinated me (*suzhavėjo*), not because he is handsome but because of his masculinity. . . . For me a man should be a little bit more handsome than a monkey but not much. But first of all I am fascinated by a man's masculinity. When I met this guy and we became lovers, I began to recover. He was from Kaunas. He restored me, I felt very good, I recovered, I started living again, because I fell in love. I trusted him, I did a lot of stupid things for him. I ignored all of my friends and hurt them. I devoted myself (*atsidaviau*) completely to him. Then, finally, when some school term started for him, some exams, I found out that he didn't care much about me (*jam ash ne tiek daug ir rupiu*). For him his studies, his career, are in first place. He told me he might not even stay in Kaunas and that he didn't see a future with me. Well, I became very depressed and began again to visit my friends. After him, my friends at work introduced me to someone also from the workplace. Now we are going out, and I am very happy because I met him. The previous relationship that hurt me so much now is in the past, thanks to him [her new lover].

What is interesting is that she seems to go through a cycle of romantic love, happiness, separation, depression, romantic love, happiness, separation. And she goes through this cycle psychologically unscathed, rebounding intact and jumping into the next relationship with equal fervor. For her romantic love seems to be more like a game, or some kind of adrenaline rush to which she is addicted, much as Ovid described ludic (i.e., playful, promiscuous) love. If Inga had held Gita's cultural model of romantic love, she undoubtedly would have visited Thomas and his parents; love, not success in her studies, would have been the dominant motive. But if we get beyond the apparent difference in the degree to which Inga and Gita feel romantic love as a driving force in their lives (that is, its "level of internalization"), we can see that they both frame romantic love as "unreal" or as an "illusion." Though Gita goes through all the highs and lows of romantic love, her psyche seems to be unaltered by it. If Gita perceived romantic love as real, it would be almost impossible to fathom her enthusiasm for jumping, with the same apparent eagerness and naïveté, into one relationship after another. Further, despite Gita's claim that for her "love is all," she is twenty-six, has a good job working for a tourist agency, has never been married, and does not have children. Thus she is able to keep her love life separate from her "real" life.

I now turn to two male narratives. The first is from an unmarried twenty-seven-year-old law student named Darius, the second from a married twenty-three-year-old, Vytis. My goal, as with the women, is to see if these men frame love as "unreal" and to get some sense of how they link their cultural model of romantic love to sex and to the rest of their life.

Darius is handsome and portrays himself as somewhat of a Don Juan, a man to whom women are attracted. He first had sex at thirteen and since then has had relations with many others, though, he said, "Sex is not important to me." Darius explains his philosophy of love and sex as follows:

> *Darius:* I've always put women first and only thereafter thought about myself. That's why women have liked me and why I have always had a lot of women, because first of all I think about them. I would say that this is especially appreciated among woman and so they talk about it, and their girlfriends then want to get to know me. Males do not talk about the performance itself, women do and share this knowledge. . . . As I told you, there have been a lot of women, and I somewhat know, though not perfectly, their psychology.

Darius said that he has been in love twice. The first time was romantic; he described it as a "special rapture" (*susižavejimas ypatingas*) and "dreamy" (*svajingas*). Darius describes his second romantic relationship as follows:

> *Darius:* The second love was the love of a mature man, there were no prickles in the belly (*dygčiojimai pilve*). There occurs . . . a desire to protect that person; you feel like a primitive man protecting his woman from all dangers. With her I began to think about the future and how to live together. This second love was of a much stronger color, not a pastel color. . . . There was a full understanding of our actions, and we held a serious attitude toward each other. We worried and took daily care (*buitinis rupinimasis*) of each other. We worried if the other was hungry, had clothes, and

so on. We already communicated like adults. The second love was stronger and wiser than the one before, because we didn't make mistakes like I did in the first love.

Darius could well be one of Ann Swidler's informants, distinguishing between romantic and mature or real love. On the other hand, there is a difference. Swidler insists that her informants held both the romantic and real love models of romantic love toward their partner simultaneously because each served a different function. The romantic love model dictates why one chooses another person, and the real love model functions to embed that relationship in the quotidian round of daily life. For Darius romantic love and mature love do not exist simultaneously. Romantic love is "a dream," and "mature love" occurs when you begin to take each other seriously. The two kinds of love do not complement one another, they oppose each other. This interpretation seems warranted from his response to the question "Can romantic love last?"

> *Darius:* I don't think so [he said this emphatically]. I know this for sure from my own experiences. . . . It always ends . . . that fairytale, it always has to end: happy or unhappy, and only then do you start looking at the world realistically.

Later he describes how romantic love can be choking and that the reason for the break-up of the second relationship was that the woman wanted the relationship to be more romantic.

> *Darius:* There was too much of each other; we were not teenagers who need to be together all the time. It began to suffocate. As an adult you have a big circle of friends with whom you want to spend time. Also, among males, when three males are talking, a woman is unnecessary. . . . The feeling of love remains but becomes friendly, not romantic.

This second, more mature love to which Darius refers lacks the poetry and fantasy that, I have argued, is associated with Lithuanian notions of romantic love. Indeed, Darius notes that while his sex life is satisfying, he hasn't been able to have a mature love relationship because women prefer romantic love and they criticize him for not being romantic. For Darius his career

as a budding lawyer and his circle of friends are more important than romantic love. He knows he should want a mature love relationship, but he is
uncertain whether he wants to make such a commitment at this time.

Darius's cultural model of romantic love is similar to that of Inga and
Gita; for him it is also a dream, not to be taken seriously. But unlike Inga
and Gita, Darius is, or so he says, not at all motivated by romantic love.
He views romantic love as something that takes time, money, and energy,
in other words, a fantasy that can still obstruct his career ambitions and
relationship with his friends. Darius also said that he doesn't want a serious relationship now because "it takes time, money, and moral obligations,
and I can't afford it yet." He doesn't have a great job, he doesn't earn much
money, he still feels too young and "open to the world," so he doesn't yet
want to feel "obligated" to another person; consequently, he prefers short
sexual encounters to a long-term relationship. It may be that Darius's rejec-
tion of a cultural model of romantic love and his decision to postpone the
search for mature love are more typical of males than females, particularly
since mature love is so strongly tied to the breadwinner role for males.

I conclude these interviews with an account from a man. Vytis is to
Darius as Gita is to Inga—he is a romantic, whereas Darius is not. Vytis
graduated from university and has a civil service job that provides him
with a reasonable middle-class income. He married his wife after gradua-
tion and recently bought an apartment in a new apartment building. The
discussion begins with his response to his break-up with his first girlfriend
when he was seventeen. The interview was conducted in Lithuanian by a
student assistant named Linas.

> *Vytis:* I think it always happens that, after separation, every person
> for about a month or two thinks that it's the end of everything,
> until he meets another person whom he falls in love with. I think
> it happens very often that after a separation a person misses "his
> second half." I began with two or three friends to go to a park or
> disco where we tried to pick up a girl ("*nukabinti mergina*"). Usu-
> ally at parks we would see some girls sitting on a bench. We would
> decide which one was for each of us, and then we would approach
> them. We would then ask them to go for a walk and try to talk
> with the girls separately. The first few times I would feel nervous
> (*jaudindavausi*), I would try to look cool [*kietas,* which actually
> means hard]. If in the beginning I would fail, I thought that it was

her fault and that she was stupid. Later I started learning from my failures, trying to correct things that girls didn't like. But in the beginning it wasn't serious, for example, I would get a phone number and never call that girl. It became more important to get a phone number. If a girl gave me her phone number, I would feel like Don Juan.

This account is reminiscent of Inga's, for, like her, Vytis consciously trains himself to become competent at sexual and romantic relationships. In this learning stage sex and love are connected, and it is not clear how or if they are separated. Vytis said he finally met a girl with whom he regularly had sex. He said that the relationship was important to him, but they never declared love. After a month she broke it off:

> *Vytis:* After that, sex didn't mean anything to me anymore. . . . I started devaluing girls; they were no longer important to me. Nevertheless, I still continued to have sex with women but never with the intention of having an enduring relationship.

Then, in his second year of college, he fell in love again, with the woman who would become his wife. But first, he said, she was his "best friend" (*geriause drauge*).

> *Vytis:* I didn't notice how we started to walk everywhere together. I didn't think it could be a serious relationship. I started meeting her at our trolley bus stop, by the dormitories, and we gradually began to go everywhere together, holding hands. After a week or two I tried to kiss her; I would bend my head down, but she would always turn away from me. And then one day, after about a week, I bent down and she lifted her head and we kissed. Then, I thought, with relief, "At last." The following day we pretended that nothing happened. But then again we started kissing.

They courted, and he waited to propose until after he graduated and found a job, because, he said, "I could not propose to her if I could not support a family." He defined their relationship as "real love" because "we can talk about everything and she can tell me everything." During the first four months of their romantic relationship, he wasn't sure if it was "serious" or "ephemeral." He described his love at the time as follows:

> *Vytis:* I had (and have) a big love (*didžioji meilė*) for her . . . [I asked what this means, and he said it] consists of romantic love and passionate love (*romantiška meilė ir aistringa meilė*). Romantic love is when you feel good with that person. You want to see her not because you want to make love with her (*pasimylėti*) but because you want to see her, to talk to her. You just hear her voice and you feel so good that you even feel a thrill (*virpėjimas*). There is such a feeling that when you hear a voice after a period of separation and you feel a shiver (*drebi*). It's so nice to feel that you are going to meet that person, to see her, to tell her things. Romantic love is when it is all-important to be with that person.

Vytis uses a Platonic model of romantic love more than the others, perhaps because he married the first woman with whom he had a romantic love relationship. Also, unlike the other three informants, Vytis does not frame romantic love as "unreal" or as "fantasy." In fact, his model is more akin to that of the American normative model of romantic love. His relationship with his wife began as best friends, and it transformed itself into a romantic relationship. Though he doesn't talk about their being comfortable together, he does appear to frame the relationship as one that is comfortable and secure.

Like Darius, Vytis perceived marriage as distinct from romantic love and more connected to the contingencies of everyday reality. He felt he could not ask his girlfriend to become his wife until he could become a breadwinner. After that goal was accomplished, however, he proposed. Thus his sense of romantic love fits with my earlier description of Lithuanian "true love" as still differentiated from, but adapted to, ordinary life, that is, as a tempered-down version of romantic love.

The critical difference between Vytis's cultural model and that of the three other Lithuanians interviewed is that he does not frame it as unreal. I think this is because he made the decision to marry his wife while he was still in a romantic love relationship. Therefore he could not frame it as unreal. In order to make a decision while in a romantic love relationship, he had to frame it as "real," and to justify framing it as "real," he had to scale down his model. In having done so, he shows that, unlike Gita, romantic love for him was not an uncontrollable force, because he could wait until a more economically realistic time to propose to his girlfriend. Also, the relationship consisted of being "best friends" first, so he incorporated or connected a companionate love with a romantic love model. By connecting his romantic love model with marriage and career, and also with a companionate love model, Vytis was able to frame romantic love as real and as a suitable basis for proposing marriage.

CONCLUSION: HOW CULTURE MATTERS

Culture both matters and is irrelevant. It doesn't matter in the sense that romantic love is a cultural universal, as Jankowiak and Fischer showed (1992), and also is probably comprised in all cultures of criteria presented in the Platonic model and in the list of attributes compiled by Fisher and colleagues (2002). Thus romantic love has to be an evolutionary requirement of Homo sapiens, at least as foragers. On the other hand, the way the characteristics of romantic love are thought about and expressed, as well as how they configure behavior, does depend on culture, history, circumstances, and individual disposition. This chapter examined the way culture and individual dispositions shape Lithuanian understandings of romantic love and how these are enacted in love relationships. I argued that, regardless of individual disposition, people understand love through a normative cultural model that, by itself, does not have any kind of hegemonic control over individuals' choices; people are free to abide by or modify this model as they see fit. But they cannot ignore it.

I have shown that lists of characteristics, particularly those based on extensive research, are useful for establishing the attributes associated with romantic love and for cross-cultural comparison. But such lists are insufficient for understanding the relationship between romantic love and other cultural models, or for understanding how love works in reality. Nevertheless, such lists are a beginning and do reflect what probably are the core universal features of romantic love.

Ann Swidler showed how culture matters in the United States, describing two cultural models of romantic love that serve different social and psychological functions. Similarly, I have described two Lithuanian models of love: romantic and real, or "mature," love. In addition, I have shown that

Lithuanians often frame romantic love as "not real," "temporary," or "fantasy" and that this framing has behavioral consequences. This is not to say that members of other cultures, including Americans, don't do the same, but my data suggest that this is a normative framing device for Lithuanians and appears to be more typical for them than for Americans. I have suggested that this framing of romantic love also has a social function, directing the lovers to recognize their own excessive romanticism and realize that they should not make real life decisions when "in love."

The four case studies illustrated how informants, regardless of their romantic dispositions, used, rejected, or modified what I have described as the normative model of romantic love. Three of the four informants explicitly demarcated and isolated romantic love as "unreal" as opposed to everyday life and real love.

Vytis provides an interesting contrast to the other three informants because he does not refer to romantic love as fantasy but uses a "real love" model of "romantic love," one that is similar to the American model. Indeed, I claim that logically he had to do so, because he went directly from love to marriage. Considering Vytis's case leads to a revision of labeling models as purely American or Lithuanian and suggests that models of romantic love are relativized to the situation. The case of Vytis shows clearly how the Lithuanian model of romantic love can be modified by an agent (i.e., Vytis and his wife) so that it can be adapted to the cultural model for marriage.

In conclusion, models are not etched in stone. They are used by individuals, who use them or modify them to fit their circumstances and interests. The next step in the cultural research on romantic love will be to elaborate on the specific historic and developmental processes that shape cultural models of romantic love and, second, to explain how these models influence behavior and are constrained by universal psychophysiological human needs and desires (see chapter 1, and Buss 1994).

NOTES

1. "Culture matters" is taken from the subtitle of Ann Swidler's book *Love Talk: How Culture Matters* (2001).

2. Swidler's "romantic love mythology" is neo-Platonic; I identify as Platonic those approaches that regard notions of love as ineffable, transcendent, and the like.

3. Ann Swidler discusses romantic love mythology, mostly in chapter 6, "Love and Marriage," in *Talk of Love;* she argues that romantic love functions as the primary motivation to marry.

4. Five other free-list questions were asked but of different populations.

5. I can be reached at Victor@bestweb.net.

6. The Russian free-list responses were even more poetic than the Lithuanian ones.

7. Inga, like many students, had gone to the United States for a summer job at a park in the Northwest. Her English was essentially fluent. Most of the younger generation, who are university students, speak English well.

REFERENCES

Aristotle. 1956. *Ethica Nicomachea.* In W. D. Ross, trans., *The Student's Oxford Aristotle.* Oxford: Oxford University Press.

Brehm, Susan S. 1988. "Passionate Love." In R. J. Sternberg and M. L. Barnes, eds., *The Psychology of Love,* pp. 232–63. New Haven, Conn.: Yale University Press.

Buss, David. 1994. *The Evolution of Desire.* New York: Basic Books.

Fisher, Helen E. 1992. *The Anatomy of Love: The Natural History of Monogamy, Adultery, and Divorce.* New York: Fawcett Columbine.

Fisher, Helen E., Arthur Aron, Debra Mashek, Haifang Li, and Lucy L. Brown. 2002. "Defining the Brain Systems of Lust, Romantic Attraction, and Attachment." *Archives of Sexual Behavior* 31 (5): 413–19..

Jankowiak, William R., and Edward F. Fischer. 1992. "A Cross-Cultural Perspective on Romantic Love." *Ethnology* 31 (2): 149–55.

Kövecses, Zoltán. 1988. *The Language of Love.* Lewisburg, Pa.: Bucknell University Press.

Lindholm, Charles. 1990. *Charisma.* Oxford: Basil Blackwell.

——. 1995. "Love as an Experience of Transcendence." In William Jankowiak, ed., *Romantic Love: A Universal Experience?* pp. 57–71. New York: Columbia University Press.

——. 1998. "The Future of Love." In V. De Munck, ed., *Romantic Love and Sexual Behavior,* pp. 17–32. Westport, Conn.: Praeger.

Singer, Irving. 1966. *The Nature of Love.* New York: Random House.

——. 1994. *The Pursuit of Love.* Baltimore: John Hopkins University Press.

Soble, Alan. 1990. *The Structure of Love.* New Haven, Conn.: Yale University Press.

Swidler, Ann. 2001. *Talk of Love: How Culture Matters.* Chicago: University of Chicago Press.

4. "With One Word and One Strength"
Intimacy Among the Lahu of Southwest China

Shanshan Du

Cal Lad: Your aunt and I have been married for more than forty
years, and we have always been with one word and one strength.
That was what brought us through the many hardships in many
years. It was most difficult when the children were young because
we worked so hard but still did not have enough to eat.

Author: What does one word and one strength really feel like to you?

Cal Lad: If a couple really live their lives with one word and one
strength, their hearts are warm and merry when they are together,
even at times when life is hard. But if they are not with each other,
neither of them can have a merry heart even if they are on joyful
occasions. You saw your aunt and me dancing during the celebra-
tions of the last Lahu New Year, didn't you?

Although I could not see her, I knew she was dancing with
me, somewhere behind in the women's circle.[1] I felt that I could
hear her steps, although others in the outer circle were following
the same rhythm. I knew that she could distinguish between the
sounds of my gourd pipes and those of other men. I also knew
that she could hear the unique sounds of my foot stamping among
the crowds. So I blew the gourd pipes and stamped my feet with
greater and greater strength as the night went on. My heart was so

joyful that I could go on dancing the whole night. [*Pauses with a smile that glows with a sense of serene satisfaction*]

Your aunt was not strong enough to dance too long. When she had to go home to rest before midnight, she encouraged me to stay and have fun. I stayed, but the dancing was no longer enjoyable. Soon I got very bored and I returned home, too. You see, things are totally different when I am not with my old woman [an intimate term of reference]. For a young couple, they would say that their hearts become chilly and lonely when they are apart.

This excerpt of my conversation in 1996 with Cal Lad, a sixty-year-old man and one of my fictive Lahu relatives, vividly illustrates some general characteristics of the ideal intimacy as delineated by the traditions of the Lahu people of southwest China. While providing an ethnographic example of a culture-specific form of intimacy, the Lahu constructions of intimacy also challenge some widespread Western biases that are explicit or implicit in the study of romantic love.[2]

THEORETICAL AND ETHNOGRAPHIC BACKGROUND

The designation of romance as axiomatic and exclusive to the European cultural heritage, especially that of the modern era, remained unchallenged in academia until the turn of the new millennium. After Jankowiak and Fischer's groundbreaking cross-cultural study (1992) demonstrated the near-universality of romance, the publication of *Romance Passion: A Universal Experience?* (Jankowiak 1995) marked anthropologists' first collective attempt to systematically explore human diversity and commonality in this emotional domain. Since then increasing numbers of ethnographic examinations of romantic expressions in particular sociocultural and historical contexts (e.g., Du 1995, 2004; Milani 1999; Moore 1998; Rebhun 1999; Smith 2001) have further undermined the Eurocentric presumptions embedded in the earlier studies of romantic love.

While these recent anthropological studies debunk the exclusive connection between romance and Western cultural roots and their influences, a significant debate has broken out concerning how widespread romance is across different cultures. Arguing against the position that romance is a near-universal human experience (as set forth in chapter 1; Jankowiak and Fischer 1992; Chisholm 1995; Fisher 1995; Jankowiak 1995), Lindholm (1995, 1998, 2001:350) considers romance a limited cultural phenomenon, existing only in a few types of societies. In particular Lindholm (1998:254–55; 2001:357) classifies two major types of romance and links them with two types of social structures. The first type of romance—which is extramarital, chaste, and courtly—is believed to correlate with societies that are closed, competitive, individualistic, highly structured, male dominated, and practicing arranged marriage. In contrast, the second kind of romance, which is intrinsically linked to sexuality and marriage, is associated with societies marked by openness, competition, individualism, fluidity, relative gender equality, and the practice of marriage of choice. According to Lindholm (2001:357), romance does not exist in nonindividualistic societies, except for the few whose unique institutions simultaneously encourage premarital sexual freedom and exercise strict control of marriages, which are expected to stay cool.

Notwithstanding the inspirations that Lindholm's comparative analyses bring to the anthropological study of romantic love, he appears to be unfamiliar with the emerging ethnographic research in Southeast Asian societies, leading him to consider individualism and competitiveness as essential sociocultural conditions for romantic love. My research among the Lahu reveals, however, that romantic love can flourish in a society characterized by cooperation, group orientation, and prohibition against premarital sex, features that are diametrically opposite those in his models. Exploring the Lahu constructions of intimacy offers a glimpse of the extraordinary richness and intensity of Lahu romantic tradition, which closely bonds to marriage yet ties ambiguously to sexuality.

The Lahu (Du 2003a) are a Tibeto-Burman–speaking people (Chang 1986:1; Matisoff 1988:11) who are divided into several subgroups with mutually intelligible dialects and slightly different subcultures, including the Lahu Na, Lahu Shi, Lahu Nyi, and Lahu Shehleh (Walker 1974). The Lahu people live in the mountainous region that constitutes a southerly extension of the Tibetan highlands along the border areas of the People's Republic of China, Myanmar (Burma), Laos, Thailand, and Vietnam. According to the 2000 census, the Lahu population in China was 453,705, which accounted for about two-thirds of the total Lahu population (Walker 1995:7).

The subsistence pattern of the Lahu is typically a mixture of farming, raising domestic animals, hunting and gathering, and fishing (Du 2003a). Intensive agriculture (irrigated wet rice) and the growth of cash crops have greatly increased in the last few decades. Households constitute the center of Lahu village life (Hill 1985; Du 2002) and serve as basic units for production and consumption. The Lahu people practice monogamy, and married couples tend to jointly own and manage their household. The Lahu kinship system is fundamentally bilateral, although there are varying degrees of matrilineal or patrilineal skewing in different regions or subgroups. Varying degrees of bilocal tendency mark the patterns of postmarital residence. Most Lahu villages traditionally lacked social stratification, and the only strict markers for hierarchical status are generation and age (Walker 1995; Du 2002). Similar beliefs in the supreme parental god Xeul Sha prevail in Lahu indigenous religion, which is also characterized by animism. Lahu of different regions have also been influenced to different degrees by a wide variety of externally introduced religions, including those of Mahayana and Theravada Buddhism, Protestant and Roman Catholic Christianity, and communist atheism (Du 1996). Radical sociocultural changes have been forcefully introduced to the Lahu in China since the Chinese Communist Party took over, especially during the Mao era (1949–76). Since the 1980s, although relaxed state policies have generated cultural revivals, the increasingly influential forces of market economy and globalization have challenged Lahu traditions.

In this chapter, which is divided into three major sections, I intend to elaborate cultural connotations of Lahu intimacy by exploring its relationship with marriage, romance, and sexual desire.[3] First, I will demonstrate the ways in which monogamous marriage is defined as the exclusive locus of intimacy, which is manifested by the harmonious function of the husband-wife team in sharing the various tasks and responsibilities of the household. Then I will demonstrate the idealizations of Lahu intimacy by examining the normative and idiosyncratic expressions of romance in the contexts of courtship and love suicide. In the third section I will illustrate the extreme social discouragement of any public display of sexual desire and the social and symbolic underpinnings of the strong ambiguity toward eroticism in Lahu culture. In conclusion I argue that this study can contribute to our understanding of the diverse manifestations of intimacy across societies by demonstrating a special cultural ideal in which intense romantic love is encapsulated within the idealization of marriage, which repels any public expressions of sexual desires.

MONOGAMOUS TEAM: THE ESSENCE OF INTIMACY

Intimacy, marriage, and romance are interlocked in Lahu society, defying Lindholm's suggestion (1995, 1998, 2001) that romance leads to marriage only under the sociostructural conditions that are typical of the industrialized West, especially competitiveness, individualism, and uncertainty that derive from the absence or triviality of a kinship network. As I will show in this section, Lahu cultural norms, which are structured around kinship networks and ethics that highly value cooperation and group orientation, identify intimacy exclusively with monogamous marriage, in which love is expressed as harmonious teamwork.

MONOGAMOUS MARRIAGE: THE LOCUS OF INTIMACY

While pair bonding's significant role in the emotional dynamics of intimacy is widespread across cultures, even those cultures that feature polygamous marriage systems (Jankowiak and Allen 1995; Jankowiak, Sudakov, and Wilreker 2005), its centrality to Lahu constructions of intimacy is extraordinary. Contrary to common assumption that individualism and social emphasis on marital union are connected (Hsu 1981; Jankowiak 1995:2; Lindholm 2001:347), monogamous marriage serves as a building block for Lahu social structures that are based on a strong kinship system (see chapter 5 in Du 2002).[4] On the one hand, the Lahu bilateral kinship system emphasizes marital pair bonding so strongly that the terminology that calculates kin relations does so from the perspective of a married couple. On the other hand, instead of isolating the couple from the rest of the community as an autonomous social entity, this principle of kinship terminology provides a categorical foundation for the couple to form circles of kin relations with other couples. In practice the head couple of a household is intricately connected to related head couples of other households in a village and a village cluster to form concentric circles of social relations accompanied by different rights, duties, and obligations. Consequently, the bilateral kinship

networks between household head couples regulate the forms and intensity of interhousehold reciprocity in both economic and ritual activities
(Du 2002:chap. 5). Kinship-based interdependence and cooperation are so
crucial to Lahu society that individualistic features such as competitiveness
and independence are considered "harsh" (*hie* in Lahu), which are the most
undesirable personality and social traits (Du 2002:73–74).

Just as it is central to Lahu social structure, the intimate pair bonding of a
monogamous marriage defines Lahu personhood throughout the life cycle
and beyond. The threshold for adulthood is the wedding, which unites two
socially immature individuals into a single social entity and transforms them
into full members of society (Du 2002:53–57). After the wedding ceremony
the bride and groom achieve the social rank of "adult" (*chaw mawd*) and are
expected to share responsibility, prestige, and authority as they go through the
life journey together. After fulfilling their joint responsibilities in life, a couple
is believed to be able to reunite in the afterlife. According to Lahu folk beliefs,
the deceased couple holds the honorable and authoritative position of "parental spirits" and together enjoy offerings and ritual respect from their children
and children-in-law. Since the presumed eternal bond between husband and
wife constitutes the essence of ideal human life, those who die before marriage
or before fulfilling marital responsibilities are considered the worst failures at
life and are believed to be marginalized as lone souls in the afterlife.

The extreme sociocultural emphasis on the bonding of the monogamous
marriage is congruent with Lahu cosmological order, which is rooted in the
Lahu concept of *awl cie* (pair), which refers to a single entity that is made
up of two similar yet distinguishable male and female components. I term
this Lahu conceptualization of pair bonding the "male-female dyad," which
is comparable to an organic compound that consists of two elements, neither of which has an essential nature of its own and therefore no internally
bounded identity. In other words, this concept highlights the harmonious
bonding between the two components, which identify with each other
through their shared membership and joint function in the whole. Lahu
cosmology portrays the world in terms of male-female dyads, as expressed
by their motto: "Everything comes in pairs, aloneness does not exist." Not
surprisingly, all the beings and entities in Lahu mythology form male-female
dyads, including the supreme god of creation (Xeul Sha), the Sun (female)
and the Moon (male), the earth (female) and the sky (male), as well as the
original ancestors of human beings. The dyadic order pervades Lahu culture
to such an extent that the Lahu in some areas have transformed the image of

the Buddha from a solitary male figure into a more culturally acceptable ideal of the divine couple. The appearance of a "married" Buddha is close linked to the arrival of Mahayana Buddhism in the Lahu territory. (Du 2003b).

HARMONIOUS TEAM: THE CONTENT OF INTIMACY

According to Lahu conventions, intimacy is manifested primarily in the harmonious function of a couple in their shared familial and social responsibilities, rather than in the private emotional attachment between the husband and wife. The depth of intimacy of a couple is thus measured mainly by the degree to which the monogamous team operates in accord. Such a functional connotation of intimacy is vividly expressed by the Lahu proverb "Chopsticks only work in pairs," which defines a couple as a single labor team that performs various tasks. Like the two parts of a pair of chopsticks, the husband and wife should coexist symbiotically and function harmoniously within their shared identity in the marriage.

Specifically, love is intrinsically associated with the joint roles of a couple in both child rearing and productive tasks, as expressed by the common sayings "Husband and wife doing it [tasks] together," "Not dividing between you and me," and "With one breath and one strength." Social ideals expect a married couple to jointly "work hard to eat" (*kheor cad*), a phrase that connotes all the tasks involved in feeding a household, from planting to weeding, harvesting, storing, pounding rice, cooking, fetching water and firewood, raising pigs and chickens, and gardening. As a result sexual division of labor characterizes only a few tasks, such as weaving and hunting. Defined as a dual parental team, a married couple are also expected to work together as much as possible in all child-related activities, including pregnancy, childbirth, child care, discipline, and moral and practical education, and make joint decisions on the children's behalf (Du 2000, 2002; Lei and Liu 1999:142–43). Most strikingly, many villagers of Lancang Lahu Autonomous County still adhere to their tradition of husband midwifery, which expects a husband to serve as the midwife with the assistance of all four of the couple's parents and other relatives (Du 2000, 2002). A couple usually carry the infant and/or young child to the field, taking caring of their child while working together. According to my surveys in 1996, the cultural ideal of gender sharing of both domestic and subsistent tasks is widely achieved in social practice in rural Lahu communities.

The joint roles of a couple, which define the intensity of their pair bonding, extend to the traditional institutions of male-female coleadership. In the rural Lahu area a household is typically headed by a couple that is collectively called *yiel shief phad*, which means "the master(s) of the household," "head couple," or "household co-heads" (Du 2002; Hill 2004). In addition to managing their own household, a head couple are also obliged to act as joint representatives of their household to participate in village-wide activities, including ritual reciprocity among their kin set as well as political activities in the village (Du 2002; Wang and He 1999:292). The male-female coheadship was also institutionalized in Lahu tradition at the level of village and village clusters until they were disrupted or eliminated after the Chinese Communist Party took over in 1949. In each individual village of the Fulqhat village cluster, one of the few places where such an institution was revived in the 1980s, there exist three pairs of traditional village leaders parallel to the state-appointed officials—the village head couple, the head couple of spiritual specialists, and the leading blacksmith couple. At the level of village cluster there is also a Buddhist monk couple, serving at the pair of Buddhist temples located at the center of the village cluster (Du 2002, 2003b).

Lahu mythology provides strong symbolic underpinnings for the intrinsic connection between the intimacy of a married couple and their joint roles in taking familial and social responsibilities. Lahu origin myths describe in great detail the ways in which the supreme gods Xeul Sha, who represent the primordial model for the perfect intimacy of the male-female dyad, acted as a single concordant entity throughout the entire process of creation (Du 2002:32–37). The manifestation of pair bonding in the social practice of male-female coheadship is also congruent with a wider cosmological order, as expressed by the common saying "A pair of male-female masters rules together." While the paired supreme god forms the top of the spiritual power framework that rules the universe (Du 1996), deities or spirits that are subservient to the paired supreme gods also operate in male-female units, including the paired spirits or deities of a household, village, and region.

ROMANTIC IDEALIZATION: POETIC EXPRESSIONS OF INTIMACY

Psychological studies of love generally agree upon the sharp distinction between passionate romance and calm attachment, which are marked, respectively, by the infatuating idealization of the love object and the secure companionship of a stabilized couple (see review by Diamond 2003:176). By examining the love songs of traditional Lahu courtship and the love-suicide songs sung both for entertainment and for star-crossed lovers making a life-and-death decision, I will show in the remainder of this section the complete immersion of romance and companionship in the ideal intimacy delineated by the Lahu norms. Specifically, while the mutual idealization of the love object lays the foundation for romance, the power and richness of romantic passion are expressed poetically through a couple's yearning to attain the perfect companionship in a marriage, in either the world of the living or that of the dead. In other words, by idealizing the companionship of a couple through their harmonious performance of joint roles in their marriage, Lahu romantic expressions serve as a forum in which the core meanings and values placed on intimacy are passionately reaffirmed.

COURTSHIP SONGS: PRELUDE TO MARITAL INTIMACY

Lahu tradition designates the period between the end of harvest and the beginning of planting season (roughly between October and February of the next year) for courtship and wedding ceremonies (Du 1995, 2004). At night during this season a small group of close friends and relatives of the same sex often gather to meet a group of the opposite sex outside the village. While a bonfire typically separates the two groups, men and women can converse and sing to each other casually or romantically, actions that are prohibited on other social occasions. In such a semipublic context the most desirable and appropriate form of courtship is for a young man and woman to sing love songs to each other, expressing their romantic interests to each other, and to discuss their intentions to marry. The friends of the couple will communicate the successful result of the singing courtship to their parents, who will start preparations for the marriage if they agree with their children's choice.

Grounded in the enormously abundant symbolism of Lahu mythology and rituals, Lahu love songs are framed within conventional styles and sung in poetic language and romantic melody. Nevertheless, the aesthetic and emotional power of the antiphonal singing of love songs derives as much from the singers' knowledge of Lahu singing tradition as from their spontaneity and originality, which add a personal and romantic touch to the symbolic repository of Lahu oral traditions. When a talented couple engage in singing courtship songs, a session can last until dawn, when social conventions demand the singers stop singing and return to the village. Following the couple and their unfolding romance, the same group often reunite on the following night to resume the singing session, a process that can last for many consecutive nights. While such a couple are deeply engrossed in their own romantic experiences, their antiphonal singing often enchants the entire audience, sometimes to such an extent that those gathered forget to tend the fire until they feel chilly.

A Lahu couple jointly create a rosy picture of a dreamy marriage when the lovers sing to each other courtship songs, which mingle passionate romance with secure attachment. The idealization of intimacy as a monogamous team is best exemplified by "Chasing Bees," a traditional Lahu song that consists of about five hundred verses (Cal Yawl 1989:225–47). When a couple sing "Chasing Bees" during courtship, sacred and aesthetic sentiments are intricately woven into the romance as the lovers are undertaking an imaginary joint journey to attain beeswax and other materials for the rituals that serve to seek blessings from Xeul Sha for their prospective marriage. Some tasks described in the song are purely imaginary, such as capturing and killing the python and dragon. As I show in the next section, the combination of the sacred and the heroic in the lovers' joint adventures dramatically heightens the romantic sentiments of the singers (Cal Yawl 1989:243):

You press the body of the python between the fire tongs
I string through the nose of the python with a cane
You press the body of the dragon between the fire tongs
I string through the nose of the python with a cane . . .
[You] skin the python to cover the female drum
[I] skin the dragon to make the male drum[5]

Meanwhile, many mundane tasks—such as cutting bamboo, collecting honey and beeswax, and transporting materials—are also associated with romantic sentiments and sacred values (Cal Yawl 1989:232–36):

You [intend to] take the bees' cakes
I [plan to] take the bees' wax
Looking through the cloud, [you] see no ladders
Seeing through the grasses, [I] find no ropes

[You] use the leaves of white *li* tree to make smoke
To drive away narrow-waisted bees
[I] use the leaves of yellow *li* tree to create smoke
To drive way broken-waisted bees

[After very vivid and detailed descriptions of the difficulties in reaching the bees' cakes and bees' wax, the song continues:]

You and I have one word and one strength
The high mountains and steep cliffs cannot deter us
You take a long knife on your right hand
I take a chopping ax on my left hand

[After more details of how to cut bamboo and make tools to reach bees' cakes and place them on baskets and bags, the song continues:]

You carry the bag on your back
I carry the basket on my head
Carrying the bag to the golden village of Nanben
Carrying the basket to the silver village of Baka.[6]

Many other love songs romanticize the couple's commitment to the tedious and demanding tasks in the singers' prospective marital life, just as "Chasing Bees" blends romance and teamwork. Expressed through both conventional styles and spontaneity, the poetic valorization of a couple's harmonious function covers almost all possible tasks in everyday village life, especially the choosing of a site for their dream house, building the house, working together in the field, raising children, and taking care of their parents on both sides. The poetic discussions about how a couple intend to work together during the woman's prospective pregnancy are perhaps the most vivid example of romanticizing the mundane chores (Du 2002:83):

When you carry a burden inside you
I am responsible for that burden.
When we weed the field
you only need to weed
Three handfuls of grasses at the top of the field,

Three handfuls of grasses at the end of the field,
Three handfuls of grasses at the left side of the field,
Three handfuls of grasses at the right side of the field.
You may take a rest afterward
I will finish weeding the rest.
After the weeding is finished
All the credit will be yours
Because you have weeded the field
At the top and the end
At the front and the rear
At the left and the right.
What I have done is just patching the details in the middle. . . .
At harvest time
You only need to carry the sickle,
I will carry the threshing stick and three pieces of mat
The mat I have spent three days weaving from bamboo strips.
You harvest at the top and the end of the field
The left and the right of the field,
You will harvest with such a little effort
As if you were merely counting the rows.
On our way home
You only need to carry the light pig food.
I will carry the grain on my back,
I will hold the gourd-and-pipe [a musical instrument] in my hands,
I will play the music while carrying home the grain [on my back].

In response to such a committed loving offer, the young woman assures her
lover of her commitment to work together as an inseparable pair even after
she becomes pregnant (Du 2002:83–84):

I will carry our child within me for ten months
Within these ten months
I will carry the child up to the mountains
Five months and ninety-nine times,
I will carry the child down to the rivers
Five months and seventy-seven times.
But I will not blame you for the arduous task,
The task to carry the child even before its birth.

Although my body will be heavy
I will be with you all the time
I will not separate from you in our work.

In brief, rather than representing romance through an infatuated ideal-ization of the love object, Lahu courtship songs express sentiment by ide-alizing the security, companionship, and teamwork of marital life itself. In this sense, centering on companionship and teamwork, Lahu romance defies the commonly assumed essential differences between passionate ro-mance and calm companionship.

LOVE SUICIDE: ULTIMATE SEARCH FOR INTIMACY

Some may argue that rather than bridging the chasm between romance and companionship, the great emphasis on harmonious teamwork in Lahu courtship songs merely suggests the lack of infatuating passion and thus the absence of romance itself in Lahu culture. But this argument falls apart because of the prevalence of love suicide, the most intense and dramatic expression of romantic passion; it abounds in Lahu oral literature and has taken many real lives.

Love suicide usually exists in the realm of literature and art; the best-known example is, of course, the tragedy of Romeo and Juliet. Among the Lahu in China love suicide is not only a subject in traditional folklore and the poetic form of oral literature but also a reality, as it has taken many young lives, especially as a result of the recent radical social changes. Since the 1950s love suicides have plagued rural Lahu who reside on the west side of the Lancang River in southwest China. The results of my surveys and interviews in Qhawqhat, a village cluster in Lancang that has a high suicide rate, showed seventy-two suicides resulting from love pacts between 1950 and 1996. The rate of love suicide was astoundingly high considering that the average population of Qhawqhat during this period was only about two thousand.

My research suggests that this phenomenon is primarily the result of a tragic clash between the Lahu tradition of monogamous pair bonding and the radical externally imposed social changes that have inadvertently eroded the institutional integrity and moral cohesion of Lahu marriage and family since 1949 (Du 1995, 2004). The familial and emotional tensions and crises generated by radical sociocultural transformations were particularly severe during the Mao era. One the one hand, the practice of collectivism and the political upheavals severely disrupted the indigenous institutions that promote cohesion in husband-wife dyads, resulting in a drastic increase in marital conflict and extramarital relationships. On the other hand, traditionally tight restrictions on divorce and severe punishment of those involved in illicit relationships both increased, trapping many Lahu youth in socioemotional dilemmas that led some to make life-and-death decisions.

Lahu star-crossed lovers are often forced to chose between life and love because neither elopement nor extramarital liaison constitutes a viable solution. On the surface this social phenomenon can be simply explained by the severe punishment of these actions in the customary laws of many Lahu regions. At a deeper level, however, the individuals' internalization of the exclusive cultural association of intimacy and marriage seems to also play a significant role. This is shown in the two major paths chosen by most star-crossed lovers to resolve their dilemma. The most common solution is to choose life over intimacy, of course. Rather than abruptly cut off the romantic attachment, however, the lovers re-create a compromised new dream of becoming in-laws, the closest legitimate relationship possible for the couple. As shown in the following verses, which are sung at the end of a fruitless courtship, the couple's aborted desire for complete intimacy is indirectly completed in the imagination by transferring their own romance to the prospective marriage of their children (Du 2004:248):

> You and I have discussed to this point [their dream marriage]
> You and I have developed deep affection and affinity
> Yet we are unable to become one family
> [Therefore,] the fruit of our discussions can only pass to our next
>   generation
> When your daughter grows as tall as you are
> When my son grows as tall as I am
> Our affections can be transferred to them
> They will be able to marry each other. . . .
> You and I will become in-laws

Rather than compromise the ideal intimacy for which they long, others choose love over life by committing double suicide. Instead of killing themselves out of desperation, these couples jointly take an extreme action in the belief that they will be married in the world of the dead. In this sense double suicide represents an ultimate pursuit of the Lahu ideal of intimacy, which resides in the vision of a marriage in which the couple has the perfect emotional union and oneness of thought and mind.

The decision to commit double suicide is often made through the antiphonal singing of love-suicide songs that seem to possess a mystical, sirenlike power to convince many to die for love. Love-suicide songs tend to follow the completion of the singing of love songs when the lovers face an insurmountable obstacle to their union. Typically, such songs begin with poetic expressions of desperation at the anticipated separation. As the verses that follow show, the singers declare that life is not worth living without each other (Du 2004:249–50):

> You and I, two of us
> Discuss with one mouth [as if we were of one mouth]
> You and I, two of us
> Talk with one breath [as if we were of one breath]
> You and I, two of us
> We are attached to each other so deeply
> You and I, we both have parents
> But they do not consider on our behalf [to approve our marriage]
> I may no longer see your beautiful appearance
> I may no longer see your splendid stature
> My heart is lonely and despaired
> Whenever I long for you
> I do not know what is to be done
> Whenever I long for you
> I feel lonely and despairing
> Let me die and keep hanging over your clothes
> Just as a bat hanging on a banana tree by the river

While the beginning of love-suicide songs provides the lovers with an opportunity to reassure each other of their mutual affection and commitment, the remainder of the song prepares them psychologically to commit suicide with confidence, hope, and peace. By elaborating the richness the world of the dead, a major portion of the singing helps to increase the confidence of the couple in the religious realm that they intend to enter by taking their own lives. Easing the lovers' agony and guilt at the moral and emotional consequences of their decision, another section of love-suicide songs details a series of imaginary occasions when their surviving and regretful parents benefit from the plants and trees on the grave of the lovers. Through poetic euphemism the lovers also discuss the strategies and methods of committing suicide. Either party can conclude the singing of suicide songs with a final stanza extolling the lovers' everlasting intimacy, which combines passion with companionship (Du 2004:253–54):

> I agree with what you just said
> I agree with what you just spoke
> You and I cannot attain [marriage] in the world of the living
> We will get it in the world of the dead
> We can only get it in the world of the dead. . . .
> [After we arrive there and marry]
> We will work together for numerous days
> We will labor together for countless days

The singing of love-suicide songs often lasts many nights, attended by the same audience, typically close friends of the couple. The dramatic idealization of the perfect intimacy in the real-life performance can be so emotionally and aesthetically overwhelming that some members of the audience can be so moved to follow the couple to the world of the dead (Du 1995, 2004). In recent years the most common method of suicide has shifted from taking a poisonous local plant to drinking pesticides. Admiring the talent of the singers and sympathizing with their misfortune, members of the audience tend to be loyal to the illicit couple and keep their secret, thus preventing the lovers from suffering enormous disgrace and public humiliation, regardless of their final decision about how to cope with the social and emotional dilemma.[7]

SEXUAL DESIRE: AN AMBIGUOUS COMPONENT OF INTIMACY

While fusing functional companionship and romantic passion within marital teamwork, the Lahu ideal of intimacy places sexual desire in a marginalized and ambiguous position. On the surface sexual desire is excluded from the ideal realm of intimacy, as manifested by its invisibility in romantic songs and association with shame in social norms and mythology. However, sexuality still constitutes an indispensable component of Lahu idealization of intimacy because such intimacy is rooted in the idealization of marriage itself. In this sense the Lahu ideal of intimacy differs from the asexual "chaste love" described by Lindholm (1995:65; 2001:351–53), although it is ambiguously connected with sexuality through the symbolism of shame.

Social Norms

The normative separation between eroticism and romance in Lahu cultural heritage is most conspicuously displayed by the absence of any direct sexual expression in the enormous reservoir of traditional love songs. Instead of bearing any hints of eroticism, the normative Lahu expressions of the admiration of the physical attractiveness of one's love object are purely aesthetic and asexual. Examples include "you are brighter than the brightest flower in the world that blossoms for three years and becomes brighter and brighter every night," "your skin is as white as silver, as shining as gold," and "your voice is as beautiful as the singing of a cicada." Interestingly, eroticism is not implied even in direct praise of the body, such as "your body is as straight as the best tree along the river bank" and "your calves (and arms) are as thick and solid as the base of a bamboo trunk." The reason is that such expressions of admiration, as with all other phrases used to idealize the love object, are used interchangeably for both sexes. In fact, one can identify the sex of the person being praised in Lahu courting songs only by the phrases "the good and soft young man" or "the good and soft young woman" (Du 1995, 2004).

Consistent with the cultural exclusion of eroticism in the poetic expressions of romance, any physical expression of sexual desire is forbidden in public. According to the conventions in most Lahu areas, physical contact between the lovers is prohibited in courtship, and premarital sexuality can bring shame to the entire family. Strikingly, any public expressions of physical intimacy, including hand holding, are considered shameless even for married couples. Instead of being "inseparable [in public] as dogs are," a respectable husband-wife pair should keep a few feet apart from each other, even when the spouses walk together to the field with their children.

The strong social disapproval of public displays of marital intimacy appears contradictory to the centrality of monogamous union in Lahu culture. From the point of view of Lahu social structure, however, this seemingly paradoxical phenomenon serves to balance pair bonding and collective solidarity. As Lindholm has correctly pointed out (1998:254), a conjugal couple constitutes an autonomous unit in industrialized Western societies and some simple societies, where the romantic and erotic bond of a couple serves as the only refugee for otherwise loosely bonded individuals in a competitive and unpredictable world. In contrast, Lahu monogamous union constitutes only a knot in a wide social net. Most important, the pair bonding of a Lahu couple is tightly and inseparably woven with the bonds with the lovers' parents, siblings, and the siblings' spouses. In this sense, notwithstanding its sociocultural significance, the husband-wife pair is subject to the collective orientation of Lahu society, especially to the moral authority of the couple's parents when they are alive and the spiritual authority after their death.

I have limited knowledge of the role that eroticism plays in the personal experiences of romantic interactions because I never initiated the sensitive subject out of respect for my Lahu informants and their culture, which also coincides with my own background as a Han Chinese woman. According to the voluntary confidences I have received on various private occasions, however, I find that the degrees of conformity to the normative dichotomy between eroticism and romance vary greatly at the individual level. One surviving lover of an attempted double suicide stated with genuine pride that the lovers never held hands before the tragedy. In contrast, another survivor implied both the commonality and secretiveness of sexual contacts between star-crossed lovers by remarking that there might have been lovers who had never touched each other before committing suicide together. While I was expressing my amazement at the pure love of the victims of love suicide, one survivor made a shocking remark, claiming that all illicit romance remained pure as long as the partners were not caught having sexual relationships. This seemingly sarcastic comment weighs heavily in our understanding of an extremely sensitive matter, given that this person survived the suicides of a lover and several close friends on different occasions. The existence of sexual desire and behavior in the intense romantic experiences of at least some Lahu individuals was evident when a fetus was exposed as the relatives were cremating the body of a young unmarried woman who had committed love suicide. In this way the Lahu understanding of the relations between love and sex is at odds with Lind-holm's (199:64) position that romantic love is asexual or "chaste." For the Lahu love is the idealization of another within an unstated, albeit assumed, erotic context.

MYTHOLOGICAL REPRESENTATIONS

The ambiguous relationship between intimacy and sexual desire in Lahu social norms is deeply grounded in symbolic representations of sexuality in Lahu mythology. At the level of Lahu cosmology the intimacy of a perfect male-female pair is primordial, eternal, and asexual. In contrast, Xeul Sha, the twin gods, created a love potion to inject sexual desire into the Sun and the Moon as a last resort to cope with the hopeless dysfunction of some male-female pairs and to make up for the imperfection of intimacy described in Lahu creation myths. My research suggests that the absence of erotic expressions in Lahu love songs and formal courtship is rooted in ambiguous cultural representations of sexual desire, rather than suggesting the absence of erotic feelings among the individuals (Lindholm 1995:64–66; 2001:351–53).

In the Lahu cosmos the supreme paired gods, commonly addressed by a single name, Xeul Sha, represent the perfect intimacy (Du 2002:31–37). The ideal union of Xeul Sha resembles neither the mother-infant symbiosis described by Shakespeare in his poem "The Phoenix and the Turtle" (Bock 1987:258) nor the perfect sexual union (the reunion of the two halved souls) elaborated by Aristophanes in Plato's *Symposium* (de Botton 1999:719). Instead, this perfect, eternal union in Lahu culture is represented by a pair of male-female twins, similar to those in Balinese mythology (Boon 1990; Errington 1987). According to Lahu mythological representations, the primordial pair bonding of Xeul Sha is so pervasive and transcendental that the twin gods share not only nearly identical features but their identities, especially sexual identities. While all knowledgeable Lahu elders with whom I spoke identified Xeul Sha as a male-female pair, the sexual identities of this god are barely distinguishable in Lahu creation myths without close examination through an academic magnifying glass. Strikingly, only a few verses of the most comprehensive version of Lahu origin myths reveal the sexual identities of the twin gods (Du 2002:35):

At the very beginning
At the very start,
There was no sky in the world
There was no earth in the world.
Xeul Yad came into being
Sha Yad came into existence.
At the time when Xeul Yad was born
At the moment when Sha Yad was born,
Xeul Yad was as thin as a hair
Sha Yad was as small as a leg hair.
Xeul Yad turned around and grew big
Sha Yad stretched out and grew tall.
Xeul Yad took the name of Cal Pul [male name]
Sha Yad took the name of Na Pul [female name].

Except for this introduction, the thousands of verses of Lahu creation myths address the paired gods by the gender-neutral names Xeul Yad and Sha Yad. In addition to the scarcity of descriptions that distinguish the sexual identities of the two gods, there is no trace of any morphological and reproductive difference between the halves of this primordial pair in Lahu oral literature. As shown throughout the complicated process of creating the universe and living beings, Xeul Sha formed such a perfectly harmonious team that the two halves are intrinsically linked with each other as one entity in thoughts, emotions, and actions. Neither of the paired gods demonstrates an internally bounded identity, and they are considered both "one" and "two" entities, depending on the linguistic context. Interestingly, although Xeul Sha were identified as parents of the male-female pair of demigods and the first human couple, Xeul Sha produced their "children" by using Xeul Sha's sloughed-off skin (scurf), thus involving no sexual encounters. In this sense neither romantic nor erotic attraction is relevant to this primordial and eternal pair, who exist as a two-in-one entity and function in perfect harmony in both creating and running the universe.

In stark contrast to the asexual nature of the twin gods Xeul Sha, sexual desire and romantic attractions, which were packaged in marriage, served as indispensable remedies for the functional deficiencies of two male-female pairs in Lahu origin myths, that is, the Sun (female) and the Moon (male) and the first human couple. Specifically, eroticism and romance glued together the functional cracks of these two imperfect unions.

The story of the Sun and the Moon constitutes an integral part of the enormous body of Lahu origin myths, and it is frequently sung during weddings and on festive occasions to explain the origin of marriage. According to the myth, although the Sun and the Moon were created for the purpose of providing the world with light, their teamwork remained dysfunctional until sexual desire was imposed on them by a love potion. When Xeul Sha first set them in motion, they were reluctant to carry on their mission through endless traveling. The Sun and the Moon resumed walking in the sky only after the Xeul Sha created tiger and frog to chase each of them. Nevertheless, the Sun and Moon soon stopped moving again because of intestinal and liver pains, and Xeul Sha had to create a pair of shamans to cure them. Years later the lovers simply refused to follow each other anymore. As the following song shows, Xeul Sha invented a love potion—a last resort to bring this dysfunctional couple together—that triggered both romantic and sexual attractions between this celestial couple. Consequently, they desire to marry each other:

Xeul Yad scrubbed off the scurf from the hands
Sha Yad scrubbed off the scurf from the feet
Xeul Yad made male aphrodisiac
Sha Yad made female aphrodisiac
[Under the influence of the Aphrodite]
The Moon was yearning for the Sun
The Sun was longing for the Moon
The Moon's heart chills by thinking of the Sun
Tears fell from the eyes of the Moon
A drop of his tear fell in front of where Xeul Sha lived
Where a plum tree grew
The Sun's heart became lonely by thinking of the Moon
Tears dropped from the Sun's eyes
A drop of her tear fell behind where Xeul Sha resided
Where a peach tree grew . . .
Because Xeul Yad put male aphrodisiac on the Sun
Because Sha Yad put female aphrodisiac on the Moon
The Moon began to follow the Sun
The Sun began to follow the Moon
The Sun of Xeul Yad desired their marriage
The Moon of Sha Yad wanted their wedding

In response, the paired gods created the morning star and the evening star to serve as the matchmakers for the Sun and the Moon and prepared for their wedding. The myth concludes by saying that the couple have been following each other with intimacy and affection ever since:

After the Sun of Xeul Yad married
After the Moon of Sha Yad became a pair
The Sun and the Moon follow each other joyfully
The Sun circulates around the sky
The Moon revolved around the earth
The Sun lightening the sky 360 days
The Moon shines on the earth for 360 nights

Likewise, Xeul Sha also created sexual desires for the first human beings, a pair of male-female twins called Only Man–Only Woman. Unlike the Sun and the Moon, however, the couple was imbued with sexual desire for the purpose of overcoming human mortality through sexual reproduction. As mortal beings without the divine creative power, sexual reproduction was essential for the first couple to assure human beings continued to function, that is, to produce rice and make offerings to their parental gods. As moral beings, whoever, sexuality between the human twins would violate incest taboos. In this sense Lahu origin myths make intrinsic associations between human sexuality and shame.

According to Lahu origin myths (Du 2002:41–43), it was Xeul Sha who suggested that Only Man–Only Woman marry each other so that they could produce children. Acting as a single moral being, the twins declined Xeul Sha's proposal, invoking their siblinghood. Attempting to inspire the only pair of human beings, Xeul Sha asked each twin to take one half of a grinder, consisting of two large round stone pieces that grind against each other to produce a powdered or liquefied substance, and roll it down a mountain. Although the male and female pieces of the grinder ended up in a conjoined position, the twins jointly claimed that siblings should not follow the example of the stone grinder. Failing in several other similar attempts to inspire and convince the human twins, Xeul Sha had to offer them an aphrodisiac drink without telling them its function. Compelled by the irresistible power of sexual desire caused by the drink, Only Man-Only Woman finally "stayed together" (a euphemism for intercourse).

Immediately after their incestuous actions, however, the couple jointly experienced such intense feelings of guilt and shame that they begged those who witnessed their actions (an eagle and a leopard) not to tell Xeul Sha, promising the animals the right to the livestock of the couple's prospective offspring.

In both cases sexual desire was identified as an externally generated and uncontrollable force used by the paired gods to forge a functional and long-enduring pair whose intimacy had innate imperfections. Specifically, while the aphrodisiac motivated the Sun and the Moon to chase each other in their endless journey, it tricked the first human couple to violate incest taboo and, consequently, assured that the human race would continue.

From a comparative perspective the symbolic representations of sexual desire in Lahu origin myths are extraordinarily negative, especially in the consistent and intense connection between sexual desire and the shame of incest. Whereas the union of the Only Man and the Only Woman constitutes a common theme in origin myths worldwide, many do not portray the couple as siblings and their sexual union as incest, for example, the Bible story of Adam and Eve and the first couple in the myth of the Dai people of southwest China (Yan, Wang, and Dao 1995:82). Whereas some myths indeed define the only man and woman as brother and sister, the couple end up reproducing human beings without violating incest taboos. According to the mythology of Yi (Wu 1999:118), for example, the couple felt too embarrassed to marry each other, so the sister was impregnated supernaturally by drinking water from a river and gave birth to a gourd from which different ethnic groups sprang. While the myths of the Lisu (Zuo 1999:83), the Hani (Wang 1990:59), Jinuo (Du Yuting1996:161), and Miao (Wu 1999:111) of southwest China share with the Lahu similar incestuous motifs of human origin, these other groups accepted the union of the first couple as necessary for reproducing human beings (Wu 1999:111; Du Yuting1996:161). Lahu myths are an exception because they explicitly attach negative moral judgment to the action and link the shame of original human sexuality with the loss of livestock to wild animals in contemporary village life.

Such extremely negative symbolic baggage attached to sexual desire may explain the exclusion of eroticism from Lahu love songs, which embody both the aesthetic and moral idealization and valorization of romantic intimacy. In this sense the absence of eroticism in Lahu normative romantic expressions reflects mainly the overwhelming influence of the ambiguity toward sexual desire in mainstream Lahu ideology, rather than suggesting the exclusion of sexual desire and intense romance at the level of individual experiences.

To conclude, while the monogamous couple forms the building block of the group-oriented Lahu society, the intimacy of the conjugal pair and its balance with kinship networks constitute the center of Lahu culture. The harmonious function of the husband-wife team is highly valued in social life and is romanticized as the ultimate manifestation of ideal intimacy. While romance and marriage are tightly bound together in defining the ideal intimacy, sexual desire is symbolically associated with the remedy for the imperfect male-female team. Accordingly, social norms prohibit public expressions of sexual desire in both courtship and marriage, serving as the structural underpinning to balance the intensity of the marital bond and the collective orientation of society at large. The extravagance, intensity, and complexity of Lahu sociocultural constructions of intimacy contribute to our general understanding of cultural diversity in human emotions and present a powerful challenge to the persistent Western biases in the studies of romantic love.

NOTES

1. In Lahu dance tradition, men occupy the inner circle, playing a musical instrument called gourd pipes and stamping their feet loudly and rhythmically. On the outer circle, women join their hands, slightly move their hands while stamping their feet according to the rhythm of the music.

2. During eighteen months of ethnographic fieldwork in both China and Thailand, I collected data by such methods as participant observation, formal and informal interviews, and household surveys. I would like to thank William Jankowiak for his insightful comments at several stages of the writing of this chapter.

3. Unless otherwise specified, I use the term *intimacy* here to mean the close union that is linked, explicitly or implicitly, to romance or sexuality.

4. For criticisms of this widespread notion, see Jankowiak (1993; 1995:166–83).

5. The drums presumably are the pair required for blessing rituals. All translations of song texts in this chapter are mine.

6. The village(s) are legendary destinations where the couple hold the imaginary rituals to seek blessings from the paired gods Xeul Sha.

7. In most Lahu areas traditional norms place great shame on both premarital and extramarital relationships, especially extramarital ones.

REFERENCES

Bock, Philip K. 1987. "'Neither Two nor One': Dual Unity in 'The Phoenix and the Turtle.'" *Journal of Psychoanalytic Anthropology* 10 (3): 251–67.

Boon, James A. 1990. "Balinese Twins Times Two: Gender, Birth Order, and 'Household' Indonesia/Indo-Europe." In Jane Monnig Atkinson and Shelly Errington, eds., *Power and Difference: Gender in Island Southeast Asia*, pp. 209–33. Stanford, Calif.: Stanford University Press.

Cal Yawl. 1989. *Ladhol Qameul Lirdaw* (A Collection of Lahu Folksongs). Edited by Zhiqing Peng and Zheng-fang Liu. Kunming, China: Yunnan Nationalities Publishing.

Chang Hong-En, ed. 1986. *Lahu Yu Jian Zhi* (The Concise Annals of the Lahu Language). Beijing: Nationalities Publishing House.

Chisholm, James S. 1995. "Love's Contingencies: The Development Socioecology of Romantic Passion." In Jankowiak, *Romantic Passion*, pp. 57–71.

de Botton, Alain, ed. 1999. *The Essential Plato*. Translated by Benjamin Jowett with M. J. Knight. New York: Quality Paperback Book Club.

Diamond, Lisa. 2003. "What Does Sexual Orientation Orient? A Biobehavioral Model Distinguishing Romance Love and Sexual Desire." *Psychological Review* 110 (1): 173–92.

Du, Shanshan. 1995. "The Aesthetic Axis in the Construction of Emotions and Decisions: Love-Pact Suicide among the Lahu Na of Southwest China." In Michael Flaherty and Carolyn Ellis, eds., *Social Perspectives on Emotion*, 3:199–221. Greenwich, Conn.: JAI Press,

——. 1996. "Cosmic and Social Exchanges: Blessings among the Lahu of Southwest China and the Feast-of-Merit Complex in Highland Southeast Asia." In Cornelia Ann Kammerer and Nicola Tanenbaum, eds., *Merit and Blessing in Mainland Southeast Asia*, pp. 52–78. New Haven, Conn.: Yale University Southeast Asia Monograph Series.

——. 2000. "'Husband and Wife Do It Together': Sex/Gender Allocation of Labor among the Qhawqhat Lahu of Lancang, Southwest China." *American Anthropologist* 102 (3): 520–37.

——. 2002. *"Chopsticks Only Work in Pairs": Gender Unity and Gender Equality among the Lahu of Southwest China.* New York: Columbia University Press.

——. 2003a. "The Lahu." In Melvin Ember and Carol Ember, eds., *The Encyclopedia of Sex and Gender: Men and Women in the World's Cultures*, pp. 600–7. The Human Relations Area Files Encyclopedia Series. Hingham, Mass.: Kluwer/ Plenum.

——. 2003b. "Is Buddha a Couple? The Lahu Gender-Unitary Perspectives of Buddhism." *Ethnology* 42 (3): 253–71.

——. 2004. "Choosing between Love and Life: Negotiating Dyadic Gender Ideals among the Lahu of Southwest China." *Critical Asian Studies* 36 (2): 239–63.

Du Yuting. 1996. *Jinuozu Wenxue Jianshi* (Concise History of Jinuo Literature). Kunming, China: Yunnan Nationalities' Publishing House.

Errington, Shelly. 1987. "Incestuous Twins and the House Societies of Insular Southeast Asia." *Current Anthropology* 2 (4): 403–44.

Fisher, Helen. 1995. "The Nature and Evolution of Romantic Love." In Jankowiak, *Romantic Passion*, pp. 23–41.

Hill, Jacquetta. 1985. "The Household as the Center of Life among the Lahu Shehleh of Northern Thailand." In K. Aoi, K. Morioka, and J. Suginohara, eds., *Family and Community Changes in East Asia*, pp. 504–25. Tokyo: Japan Sociological Society.

——. 2004. "Women and Men in Local Leadership among the Lahu Na Shehleh in North Thailand." In Anthony Walker, ed., *Leadership, Justice and Politics at the Grassroots*, published in *Contributions to Southeast Asian Ethnography* 12:35–64.

Hsu, Francis. 1981. *Americans and Chinese: Passage to Difference*. Honolulu: University of Hawaii.

Jankowiak, William. 1993. Sex, Death, and Hierarchy in a Chinese City: An Anthropological Account. New York: Columbia University Press.

——, ed. 1995. *Romantic Passion: A Universal Experience?* New York: Columbia University Press.

Jankowiak, William and Edward Fischer. 1992. "A Cross-Cultural Perspective on Romantic Love." *Ethnology* 31 (2): 149–55.

Jankowiak, William, Monika Sudakov, and Benjamin Wilreker. 2005. "Co-wife Conflict and Cooperation." *Ethnology* 44 (1): 81–98.

Lei, Bo and Junyong Liu. 1999. *Lahu Wenhua Daguan* (Perspectives on Lahu Culture). Kunming, China: Yunnan Nationalities Publishing House.

Lindholm, Charles. 1995. "Love as an Experience of Transcendence." In Jankowiak, *Romantic Passion*, pp. 57–71.

——. 1998. "Love and Structure." *Theory, Culture, and Society* 15 (3–4): 243–63.

——. 2001. *Culture and Identity: The History, Theory, and Practice of Psychological Anthropology*. Boston: McGraw Hill.

Matisoff, James A. 1988. *The Dictionary of Lahu*. Berkeley: University of California Press.

Milani, Farzaneh. 1999. "Mediatory Guile of the Nanny in Persian Romance." *Iranian Studies: Bulletin of the Society for Iranian Cultural and Social Studies* 32 (2): 181–201.

Moore, Robert L. 1998. "Love and Limerence with Chinese Characteristics: Student Romance in the PRC." In V. De Munck, ed., *Romantic Love and Sexual Behavior: Perspectives from the Social Sciences*, pp. 251–83. Westport, Conn.: Praeger.

Rebhun, L. A. 1999. "For Love and for Money: Romance in Urbanizing Northeastern Brazil." *City and Society* 11 (1–2): 145–64.

Smith, Daniel J. 2001. "Romance, Parenthood and Gender in a Modern African Society." *Ethnology* 40 (2): 129–51.

Walker, Anthony. 1974. "The Division of the Lahu People." *Journal of the Siam Society* 62 (1): 1–26.

———. 1995. *Mvuh Hpa Mi Hpa: Creating Heaven, Creating Earth.* Chiang Mai, Thailand: Silkworm Books.

Wang, Zhenghua and Shaoying He. 1999. *Lahuzu Wenhua Shi* (The History of Lahu Culture). Kunming, China: Yunnan Nationalities Publishing House.

Wang Zhengfang, ed. 1990. *Hanizu Shenhua Chuanshuo Jicheng* (A Collection of Hani Myths and Legends). Beijing: Chinese Folk Art Publishing House.

Wu Xiaodong. 1999. *Zhongguo Shaoshuminzhu Minjian Wenxue* (Folklore among Chinese Ethnic Minorities). Beijing: Central National University.

Yan Feng, Wang Song, and Dao Baoyao. 1995. *Daizu Wunxueshi* (The History of Dai Literature). Kunming, Conn.: Yunnan Nationalities Publishing House.

Zuo Yutang. 1999. *Lisuzu Wenxue Jianshi* (Concise History of Lisu Literature). Kunming, China: Yunnan Nationalities Publishing House.

5. Interplay of Love, Sex, and Marriage in a Polyandrous Society in the High Himalayas of India

Geetanjali Tiwari

Sur nar sab kaiy yaha reetee, swaarath lag karahi sab preetee *(Gods, humans, and sages all love to fulfill self-interests)* —*Tulsee Daas, Raamcharit Maanas*

This chapter explores love and marriage in the fraternally polyandrous society of Kinnaur. Using firsthand case studies, I demonstrate that marital satisfaction and stability can be achieved in fraternally polyandrous unions and that mature love relationships are not exclusive to dyads. The cases illustrate the diversity of marriages, the complex and sometimes fluid nature of plural relationships, and the open-mindedness of the people that practice them.

I begin by briefly introducing polyandry and the Kinnauri perspective on sex, love, and marriage. Next I present the study area and the methods used for this research. The bulk of the chapter is comprised of nine life history narratives. Last, I discuss some common themes involving love and marriage that emerge from the narratives.

POLYANDRY: A BRIEF OVERVIEW

Polyandry is a marriage in which one woman is married to more than one man at the same time.[1] Although polyandry has always been a rare phenomenon, its distribution before the European colonial expansion was more widespread globally (Asia, Africa, the Pacific islands, and the Americas). Today various forms of polyandry are practiced in isolated, small subsistence populations living in harsh and resource-limited regions in parts of Africa, South America, and Asia. The classic form of polyandry is fraternal polyandry, where one woman marries a set of brothers, moves into their house, and acquires their lineage (Crook and Crook 1988). The Himalayas are the home of the largest extant fraternally polyandrous societies in the world (Levine 1988; Haddix 2001; Tiwari 2001).

Bizarre as the institution of polyandry may seem, fraternal polyandry has been extremely valuable for the survival of families in high-altitude regions with scarce natural resources and unpredictable life-threatening conditions (Crook and Crook 1988). Fraternal polyandry limits population growth and prevents the fragmentation of agricultural lands, households, and other resources (Durham 1991; Goldstein 1987; Goody 1976). Polyandry also creates a high ratio of adults (including unmarried adult females) to children per household (Berreman 1975; Goody 1976). Unmarried females significantly raise the socioeconomic status of the households they live in by sacrificing reproduction and contributing valuable labor (Tiwari 2001). Polyandry minimizes financial risks by pooling benefits from diverse incomes. Polyandry also minimizes the chances of widowhood, and under life-threatening conditions this may be critical for survival and the success of the remaining family members, especially children. Thus polyandrous households are significantly wealthier and have higher socioeconomic status relative to monogamous ones (Tiwari 2001; see also Goldstein 1987). Such multiple benefits may have been instrumental, in the evolution of fraternal polyandry, when tough conditions made independent nuclear family life unaffordable.

Whereas fraternal polyandry pools resources and enhances cooperation between cohusbands, by maximizing inclusive fitness, nonfraternal polyandry, where cohusbands are not brothers, does the opposite. Nonfraternal polyandry tends to create competition between cohusbands because they do not share common economic and reproductive goals (Hartung 1985; Gaulin and Schlegel 1980; Kurland 1979; Alexander 1974). In this sense nonfraternal polyandry is similar to polygyny, where multiple wives compete for their common husband and resources.

Dyadic Love and Plural Love

A dyadic relationship is the simplest and smallest stable sexual reproductive unit and thus is preferred by most. Perhaps that is why a dyad is considered, by the majority of people, as the ideal form of a relationship. A plural relationship, in contrast, is larger, socially complex, and thus more challenging. In polyandry a wife forms multiple dyads with her cohusbands, whereas in a dyadic union, love, sex, and intimacy are coterminous and mutually exclusive.

Love that involves sex can be broadly divided into two categories, comfort love and excited love. Excited love (also called "romantic love" [Fisher 2004]) is characterized by an erotic component, an idealization of the other, and a strong desire to be with the lover at most times (Jankowiak 1995; Hatfield 1988). These characteristics make excited love highly time and energy consuming for its participants. Issues of jealousy often become exaggerated in an excited love relationship. For these reasons excited love tends to be dyadic, short lived, and usually absent in plural relationships (see introduction). In contrast, comfort love (also called "attachment" [Fisher 2004]) is defined as a fulfilling kind of sexual and emotional love that is mature, peaceful, enduring, and built upon a long-term association of the partners (Jankowiak 1995; Hatfield 1988; Liebowitz 1983). Humans have the capacity to develop comfort love that is intimate, settled, and deep in both dyadic and plural relationships.

Marriage and Love

Marriage is not always expected to be about love. In fact, many cultures regard marriage as a respectable practical relationship that provides essential mutual assistance for the purposes of reproduction, child rearing, and help during old age. Of course, if the spouses can develop love for each other within such a setting, it is considered a bonus. India is a prime example of a society in which arranged marriages are the norm. Arranged marriages aim to minimize unwise choice of partners and are based on the idea that falling in love is not a rational decision. Spouses have the opportunity to inculcate love for each other but are not expected to do so, as long as they can work out a practical caring relationship. Once the expectation of being in love or having a lover is removed from the equation of marriage, marriage becomes a much easier proposition.

Fraternal polyandry ideally has the following characteristics: (1) an impartial wife, (2) cohusbands who are kind and generous toward each other, (3) tolerant dyadic unions that may even be compassionate toward each other within the polyandry, and (4) a culture, such as that in Kinnaur, that discourages paternity allocation. A combination of these characteristics can and often does create conditions in which love matures over time into a plural comfort love.

THE KINNAUR COMMUNITY

Kinnaur encompasses a wide range of cultural values regarding intimacy and permitted marriage types. Kinnauris understand and respect arranged marriages but are also extremely open to behaviors that result from love, both excited love and comfort love. It is common for men and women to marry their lover and choose the type of marriage that they desire. Within fraternally polyandrous societies other marriage types are also found, and the various marital types found in Kinnaur include fraternal polyandry (27 percent), polygyny (0.8 percent), polygynandry (only two cases; polygynandry is marital union involving multiple males and multiple females), and monogamy (47 percent) ($n = 1,243$; 620 males, 623 females) (Tiwari 2001). In addition I found that 28 percent of adult females (and 21 percent of adult males) were unmarried (Tiwari 2001). Individuals also experience different forms of marriage as part of their life cycle. Most marriages commence in the teens or early twenties. Marriages are accomplished by bride capture, elopement, cohabitation, or parental arrangement. Court intervention is rare, and local, religious, or legal ceremonies are not mandatory. If people start to live as spouses, the villagers consider them married, and if they later separate they are then considered divorced. Divorce and remarriage are common. Extramarital affairs are discouraged but not usually stigmatized. I knew men who were aware that they had been cuckolded but were still raising the children as if their own, along with their own biological children. Many homes were raising children that were born out of wedlock. I met Kinnauri women who were significantly more proactive than the typical Indian woman in getting the kind of romance and intimacy they desired. However, it appears that the younger generations are losing this openness and are becoming engulfed by the larger mainstream culture of India.

Within villages and sometimes in nearby villages, everybody knows each other. Kinnauri people are extremely pragmatic and value qualities such as honesty, hard work, and practical skills. Scarce resources through most of Kinnauri history have made them such, and these exigencies are evident in every facet of their lives, including romance, sex, and marriage. Perhaps Kinnauri openness, marriage permissiveness, and diversity are examples of their pragmatism.

LOVE AND INTIMACY—THE KINNAURI PERSPECTIVE

Polyandry is more complex than monogamy, because love and sex form an enormous component of marriage, and the physical expression of love and sex usually still demands privacy between two individuals in Kinnaur. Not all cohusbands traditionally live at home all year round, which greatly simplifies the matter.[2] Based on my observation it was clear that a visiting cohusband has preferential sexual rights to the wife. Resident cohusbands facilitate this by keeping themselves busy away from home. Many times they are happy to take this break. Another helpful custom is that one of the cohusbands becomes the household man, who typically assumes responsibility for household decisions and usually is a full-time resident. Wives discuss and consult with their household man on household decisions. This makes decision making simpler, and the other cohusbands are expected to not complain about not being consulted. Yet matters may not be that simple. There could be more than one full-time and part-time resident cohusbands at the same time. And, especially in the winters, not only multiple spouses but also preadolescent children often sleep in the central room. In many cases cohusbands work together as partners in the day and still manage to work out their sexual lives. The spouses seem attentive of one another's body language with regard to sexual interest toward the wife. Often sex occurs in the central family room while everyone else is asleep. Alternatively, a couple may find another room later in the night for sex. Sex also may occur in the daytime at home or in the fields when conditions permit.

Research Site

The research site is in the district of Kinnaur, which forms the southeast corner of the state of Himachal Pradesh in India and shares its eastern border with Tibet. The district of Kinnaur lies in the Great Himalayan Range where the altitude ranges from 3,300 to 6,000 meters. Much of Kinnaur (47.5 percent) is extremely rocky, rugged, and uninhabitable. The remaining land is comprised of alpine pastures (44 percent), forests (7 percent), and cultivated land (only 1.5 percent) (Sharma and Minhas 1993). Kinnaur has seventy-seven villages and a low average population density, eleven people per square kilometer.[3] Most villages have a population ranging in size from 150 to 900 people distributed among 25 to 170 households per village (see Tiwari 2001). Villages are tiny, isolated oases that are fed by one or two natural streams and surrounded by barren, rocky, and precipitous mountains. Terraces have to be constructed for housing and farming in most cases. Since arable land is exceedingly scarce, particularly near the villages, most villagers have high-altitude pasturelands (usually a two- to five-hour hike from the village) that they cultivate for one crop during the short summer months.

The main historical link that Kinnaur has had with the rest of the world is the traditional silk route that the transhumants used.[4] After the Chinese invasion of Tibet the government of India started to construct the first road to Kinnaur in 1962. Although this road is poorly maintained, dangerous, and often impassable, it has permitted an enormous influx of external economic and cultural, as well as political, influences. This influx has been accompanied by a transition from traditional subsistence to a market economy in Kinnaur.

The people of Kinnaur are a mixture of Tibetan and north Indian populations. They speak various dialects of Kinnauri, a Sino-Tibetan language, although Hindi has been gaining popularity since the mid-1980s. The Indian government classifies Kinnaur as a tribal district, which implies that the government honors local customs and governance and will override them only on demand from the locals.

Methods

I collected all the data in 1999 (five months), 2000 (three months), and 2006 (one month). I collected quantitative and qualitative data at the individual, household, and village levels for all individuals ($n = 3,697$) and all households ($n = 387$) in three villages in Kinnaur. I used semistructured interviews for collecting most data on demography, genealogy, life history, occupations, and livestock. For collecting data on personal experiences and thoughts about love, intimacy, and marriage, I used an open interview format. I did not ask who fathered which child, though occasionally women would volunteer the information in private.

In order to obtain greater reliability I lived in the three villages with various host families for the entire time. I socialized with the villagers, participated in their daily activities, and became friends with them. Villages are small and homes are clustered, and within a few days most villagers perceived me as a sort of a student or an author. Because of the steep terrain, the lack of trees inside villages, and the flat rooftops, which are a favorite spot in the summers, it was easy to observe several people and their activities from one spot. I always dressed like a local woman and tried to speak like a local; having Hindi as my native language was a great help. I usually helped with household chores and in the fields. On festive occasions I dressed in traditional costumes and participated in communal singing, dancing, cooking, and feasting. I developed close ties with numerous individuals, and these friends helped me enormously in understanding the local points of view and practices. I created a reputation for confidentiality and trustworthiness. I cross-checked all data, and I am confident of the reliability of the data I have collected.

What follows are nine narratives that illustrate different aspects of love life in this fraternally polyandrous society. Some cases are complicated because they involve multiple people and their situations evolve. The names of individuals and certain details have been changed to protect privacy.

Case 1: Equality and Fairness

The life of a polyandrous wife is emotionally challenging. "To be a polyandrous wife is to be mute," said a woman in her seventies, referring to how a wife has to be careful, as anything she says might be construed as partiality. Not only that, the wives have to try to please each cohusband without creating a cause for jealousy. These tensions are evident in this case, in which Lal Devi explained to me the important role of a wife in the success of polyandry.

Lal Devi elaborated on how, in polyandrous marriages, the role of the wife is the most difficult, yet it was the husbands who complained and left. For no real reason they "feel bad, neglected, or jealous, and all of these feelings are really frequent . . . and then, in the end, it is the men that cheat on their wife and get another woman." Like many other women I spoke with, Lal Devi referred to husbands who are not faithful to their polyandrous wife as "cheaters," indicating that in Kinnaur polyandrous males are expected to be faithful to their wife. Lal Devi constantly churned yogurt in a large earthen pot as she spoke with me. She mentioned how her cohusbands develop jealousy by comparing the food she cooks when a certain cohusband is home or by comparing the quality of cloth or clothing she makes for each of them. Lal Devi said she always tries to be impartial and never speaks when her cohusbands disagree, lest her thoughts be misunderstood as favoritism.

Lal Devi was the wife in a respected polyandrous household in her village. Her three husbands were half of the six sons born to their polyandrous mother and two fathers. All six brothers had once been married polyandrously to another woman. Together they had two boys and three girls. When the youngest child was about ten years old, the oldest cohusband died, and soon after the youngest two cohusbands left the polyandry to make separate monogamous unions with other women. Six years after the death of the oldest cohusband, the polyandrous wife also died. Then the three remaining cohusbands jointly decided to take Lal Devi as their wife, using the custom of bride capture. Lal Devi was then asked to be the polyandrous wife of the three brothers and she agreed. They now have three more children and still care for the children born to the first wife.

All three husbands of Lal Devi were pastoralists, in charge of separate herds located in different regions. Consequently, they were all part-time residents. The oldest brother became the de facto head of household. All three brothers were highly respected in the village and were known for their kindness, hard work, and forgiving nature. The oldest brother elaborated on the hardships that pastoralism entails. He did not, however, talk about the challenges his wife skillfully overcomes in managing emotions within the polyandrous marriage.

Lal Devi was extremely mature. She recognized the importance of being generous, patient, and impartial in her dealings with her cohusbands. She also understood the practical and emotional aspects of managing three cohusbands. She did not expect praise, or even acknowledgment, for her generous and impartial behavior from any husband. She knew that village gossip was trouble and distanced herself from it. She worked hard at home and in the fields. She cared for and loved all the children equally. On many occasions her stepdaughter would invite me "to meet 'my mother,'" whom she was sure I would like.

Lal Devi's case illustrates a successful polyandrous marriage in which three brothers have managed the pragmatic and emotional challenges typical of plural relationships. They have proved their ability to share their wife and avoid domestic disputes. For twenty-six years the brothers have shared two wives in succession and taken the responsibility of caring for all the children produced by their two wives. It is possible that Lal Devi may be more intimate with one cohusband, but there was no indication of that within this polyandrous family. In fact, the family success arose precisely because of her impartiality and the generosity of all the spouses.

Case 2: Passionate Dyads Become Polyandrous

Many polyandrous relationships begin with a dyadic love affair. For example, Namgyal Dorje explained that "I fell in love with Shyam Moni and wanted to marry her. She too wanted the same. As per custom my second younger brother, Bhisham Singh, and Shyam Moni were asked during the wedding if they would both agree to be polyandrous; both agreed. My two youngest brothers were too young then, but later, as they grew, they too joined in the polyandry, and nobody minds." The age difference between the four brothers ranges from two to ten years. Two brothers have local jobs and live at home. The youngest brother has a job in another village, and the second oldest is a pastoralist, which makes two part-time resident cohusbands. The household also includes the parents of the four brothers. Shyam Moni's father-in-law's first marriage was polyandrous, but he broke away and remarried monogamously to father the four sons whom Shyam Moni married.

Namgyal Dorje observed that "we all have respect for elders, understand each other's habits, and know that we all have equal rights at home." It is clear that the brothers consult each other and care for each other. The brothers respect Namgyal Dorje not only because the culture values respect for elders but also because of his wisdom, fairness, and consideration. Namgyal Dorje noted, "For polyandry to work there must be understanding between brothers on all topics, and all cohusbands should not stay at home all the time." The second-oldest brother added, "Polyandry is good because cohusbands can choose a profession that permits them to travel all the time, as I do, without worrying about the wife or children. Similarly a cohusband can choose to stay at home and take care of household matters and the wife, with whom he can be sexually active regularly." He said he wanted to continue his pastoral lifestyle for a few more years, noting, "It is true I do not get the luxuries of staying home in comfort, but being mostly alone and traveling is good for my brain."

This case illustrates how passionate dyadic love can mature into a settled plural comfort love. The family's successful marriage stems, in large part, from the wife's consistent impartiality in her love for her cohusbands. This was probably hard, because at first she may have been passionately in love with Namgyal Dorje, but as their love matured they learned to integrate the other cohusbands into the plural relationship by behaving impartially toward one another. Indeed, it appeared to me that Shyam Moni was almost more considerate of the younger husbands and that Namgyal Dorje was extremely generous with his brothers. It was as if Shyam Moni and Namgyal Dorje had an implicit understanding, that their love for each other would not waver and that extra kindness and generosity would only benefit them and the family. I did not find such an understanding among spouses to be common in Kinnaur. Indeed, such deep, steady, and generous love is hard to find anywhere.

Case 3: Cohusband Jealousy

"Jealousy is really common regarding food, clothing, and sex," said a wife with three husbands. Cohusbands must experience jealousy at some point, even under the best circumstances. A polyandrous wife in her thirties once told me, "The role of a polyandrous wife is the most crucial and the most difficult, yet it is the cohusbands that fight and leave." My data support this view (see also Levine and Silk 1997). It is less common for a wife to break away from her polyandrous union because of her emotionally challenging role than it is for cohusbands to fight and break away. Cohusbands express jealousy and competition in various ways, including earning capacity, working capacity, physique, and status. The example that follows illustrates how Kinnauri men and women deal with jealousy.

Thirty-seven-year-old Krishn Lal is the oldest of five brothers. Their parents arranged a polyandrous marriage of all five sons with Ringchin Dolma thirteen years ago. Ringchin Dolma is a year older than Krishn Lal. Both Krishn Lal and Bagh Sen, his next younger brother, started off as wage pastoralists but later managed to own enough animals to become small-time owner pastoralists. A few years ago the parents of Krishn Lal started to encourage their sons to get another wife because Ringchin Dolma had not had any children. Krishn Lal and his brothers resisted breaking from polyandry at first, but then the third and the youngest brother got another wife jointly, and the fourth married monogamously. Krishn Lal and Bagh Sen had to move out of the parental house in order to keep Ringchin Dolma as their polyandrous wife. Krishn Lal said, "It was not right that my parents wanted us to leave Ringchin Dolma; it is not her fault and maybe we will have children later. I did not want to separate from her." Krishn Lal loved his wife and was happy that at least two brothers were loyal to her, although at times jealousy issues arose.

When Bagh Sen joined the army, he sold his herd so he could spend more time with Ringchin Dolma. He invested the profit in building a new house for them. Ringchin Dolma readily acknowledged being completely impartial. What she found difficult, however, was convincing her two husbands of this impartiality. She offered this example: "I got some *patti* [locally woven woolen material] and got a local tailor to make two traditional vests for my husbands. Then I gave both my husbands the vests on the same day. But over time Bagh Sen's vest looked better than Krishn Lal's. So Krishn Lal complained that I gave a better vest to Bagh Sen." Krishn Lal looked away and smiled. "I explained to him that Bagh Sen has access to the army dry-cleaning facility, whereas he has never dry-cleaned his vest, and that is why it looks dirtier," she said, looking at Krishn Lal, who was still smiling. Ringchin Dolma touched Krishn Lal lightly and smiled, then went on: "I always try to cook their favorite foods, too. So I cook Bagh Sen's favorite food when he comes home, but Krishn Lal lives with me, and so of course I cannot cook his favorite food every day, yet sometimes Krishn Lal says that I cook more for Bagh Sen."

Case 4: Heartfelt Feelings and Sex

A woman in her fifties told me how, in her experience, "honesty is hard, too hard sometimes to keep in polyandrous marriages." Palmo was the polyandrous wife of three husbands. Now in her early fifties and the mother of six children, Palmo was captured for marriage by her husbands when she was in her early twenties. "I had no idea about it and did not want to be married then, but my parents had secretly consented to this capture," she said. "At first I hated being married, and so after a few months I sneaked away, to my aunt's village." But soon her husbands found out, and the entire family pressured her to return to her husbands. When she returned, she realized that her middle husband had disappeared, and no one has heard of him since.

I got to know Palmo very well. She was smart and strong and could read slowly but not write. She was also verbal, open-minded, generous, and resourceful. She would not hesitate to talk with me about anything and always wanted to learn more. Palmo was now happy and proud of her well-respected home and of her younger husband, who was a part-time teacher and farmer and a full-time resident. He was respected and liked in the village for his kindness and impartiality. Palmo's older husband worked in a city and visited the village only a few times a year. "In the beginning," Palmo said, "I tried to love both the husbands equally, but it got harder. My older husband even fathered five of my children, but the two men are so different. My older husband has lived away from home since the age of twelve or thirteen and has become habituated to his independence, I guess. Really, the younger husband is a gem." She continued, "My younger husband is so gentle, he listens to me and does what he says, and I know I can trust him. I discuss everything with him, and I realize that by having him, I am the luckiest woman."

Over the years the distance between her and her older husband grew, and now she does not feel comfortable expressing herself to him. Palmo now even suspected that her older husband was cheating on her, because even on his short visits home he did not spend time with her. She mentioned how the younger husband would always sleep in a different room when the older husband visited, yet the older husband often would not care. "Last night my older husband came home after so many months, but he did not sleep with me," she said. She paused and looked away before continuing: "Perhaps he is having an affair with some woman. I know he buys lots of things that I never see. My children tell me that he gives them to her." Two of their children live with their older father in the city. I asked Palmo if she had ever asked him why he does not come into her room at night, and she said, "He always brings male friends from the city with him and says he needs to take care of them and make them feel welcome." Palmo also chose not to confront her older husband, because she felt it could make the situation worse since he lived so far away. At least because of him the children had access to better education in the city. Palmo was clearly intimate with her younger husband and loved him dearly, and their relationship had reached a deep, stable comfort love.

Although Palmo had begun to give up hope with her older husband, the younger husband was always generous toward his older brother. I had several conversations with the older cohusband and once asked him what he thought of his polyandrous situation. He said, "You do not enjoy the comfort and happiness of living at home, and your wife and children become strangers. Then, by the time you retire and return to the village, all the children are gone and your wife is old."

This case illustrates how, in a marriage in which the spouses started off as strangers, the wife attempted to be impartial in her love for both husbands but ended up with an intimate, peaceful, and fulfilling monogamous union and only namesake polyandry. She wanted intimacy with her older husband too, not just physically but emotionally. She wanted to be able to confide in him and trust him, but she would not approach him and talk about any of these issues. Perhaps she felt it was a losing battle and that by confronting him she risked losing even the financial and educational benefits that he provided for the children. The older husband was not interested in developing intimacy with his wife. It is possible that in the early stages of marriage he developed a romantic and excited love relationship with his wife, for he fathered most of her children, but this love did not mature and over the years withered away. We can only speculate that if he had lived in the village, his behavior may have been completely different. This couple may also develop love toward each other in old age. It is also possible that he may have wanted a monogamous relationship after he realized that he would reside in the city, but, either way, now he has enough respect for polyandry or Palmo, or both, to not break away from them.

Case 5: Does the Wife Have a Favorite Husband?

This case illustrates how men and women break arranged marriages, have extramarital affairs, and how polyandrous wives may have a favorite cohusband. Buddha Pati was a beautiful sixty-six-year-old woman who had told me many stories of her life while braiding my hair into hundreds of long thin braids called *kra*, the traditional hairstyle for women in Kinnaur. I had talked with Buddha Pati on a number of occasions and had also participated in the celebration of the birth of her grandson. Buddha Pati was passionate as she told me how she left her first monogamous marriage because she fell in love with the youngest of four brothers; he was polyandrously married in a neighboring village at the time. The man Buddha Pati loved also fell in love with her, and he left his polyandrous wife to form a monogamous union with her. Later, two of his brothers also broke away from the polyandry to form separate monogamous unions.

Buddha Pati's first two children died as infants; the third child, a son, survived. Later, Buddha Pati's husband had an affair with Buddha Pati's younger sister that resulted in the birth of a son.[5] Buddha Pati did not express any anger or regret while speaking of her sister's affair with her husband. I asked how she felt about it, and she said, "Sometimes it happens in the heat of the moment, and my sister is married now." Buddha Pati's sister left the child and moved to her husband's village. This affair appears to have not threatened the intimacy and love between Buddha Pati and her husband, even though they had an illegitimate child to care for. Buddha Pati then had four more children, including two more boys. When her four sons (including her sister's son) grew up, Buddha Pati chose a wife for them. "I chose a girl who did not even complete elementary school, because I think the educated ones take the husbands away," she said, meaning away from polyandry and extended households. "But you did the same," I said, and she replied, "I know, but none of the men were happy with her [the first wife of her current husband]. See, the others also left her; she was not good." I then asked if her *bahu* (daughter-in-law) loved all her sons equally or if she had favorites. "My *bahu* is a good wife to all my sons and sleeps with all of them. But I think she loves my sister's son the most—I've seen how she prefers to sleep with him and will sneak away from the others to be with him sometimes," she said with a smile and dancing eyes. Buddha Pati was not disappointed or embarrassed that one of her biological sons was not the favorite. She was simple and transparent. If the mother-in-law could see this preference, I am sure the cohusbands were aware of it, too.

This case illustrates how a favorite dyad can exist inside polyandry and how the other cohusbands may simply come to terms with the situation. Why some men reconcile while others do not may reflect personality differences. Once a carpenter told me in reference to his brother, "He is real good, not just to her [their wife] but in general. He never gets angry and always helps everybody, so it makes sense that even she might prefer him." He continued with a smile, "But she is a good woman and puts up with my idiosyncrasies." Some men told me that it is understandable that a polyandrous wife would prefer some characteristics of one cohusband and other characteristics of another cohusband, yet overall appreciate them all more or less equally.

Case 6: It All Depends on the Wife

This case describes how an older brother can dominate the spousal relationship to such a degree that his younger brother leaves the house. Tenzing Gyacho, a thirty-seven-year-old man, came up to me as I was walking in the village and started to talk. He lived alone and had only one brother, Ghava Chering, who was six years older. The two brothers had married polyandrously three times. The first marriage, to a woman who was twelve years older than Ghava Chering, was arranged. She bore two infants fathered by Ghava Chering. Both infants died. The wife then had an extramarital affair and left. Ghava Chering then chose a wife who was six years older than he, but she too left him after a year. Ghava Chering then got the third wife, who was only two years older than he.

"I did not choose any of the wives, although my brother did obtain my consent before getting them," Tenzing Gyacho told me. "I was too young to be a husband to the first two wives and tried to be polyandrous with the third wife, but she did not like me. She never respected me or let me get close to her. I tried talking with her, but it looked like she did not want me. Polyandry is too difficult for me now. I think the success of polyandry depends entirely on the wife, and I cannot do it anymore, so I live alone" (see Haddix 2001 for comparable cases). Ghava Chering never went to school, while Tenzing Gyacho completed middle school. Both brothers had government jobs.

It is hard to know exactly why the younger brother was not liked by the third wife, who clearly expressed her preference for Ghava Chering. Perhaps she did so because she assumed that she could have the economic benefits of polyandry without being polyandrous; she was sure that Tenzing Gyacho would not find another woman and thus saw little risk that the household property would be divided. Maybe she did not care if he got a wife. Ghava Chering, unlike other men I knew in Kinnaur, did nothing to encourage the polyandrous union. He was no longer close to his brother; both he and his wife wanted a monogamous relationship, and they were very clear in expressing it.

Case 7: Commitment to Polyandry

This case is an example of the loyalty of a polyandrous wife to her unfaithful husband. Sharan Devi became the second wife of her five husbands, after the first wife left them within a few months of their polyandrous marriage. Sharan Devi's oldest husband was ten years her senior, while her youngest husband was seven years her junior. Twelve years into her marriage, an unmarried village girl accused Sharan Devi's middle cohusband of rape. The girl's parents, who were extremely well respected, would have helped the daughter abort had they known early enough. At first the accused man agreed to provide child support. But later Sharan Devi convinced her husband to deny the rape accusation. Sharan Devi did not want to believe the accusation. The girl's family took the case to the district court, which decided in favor of the girl. Sharan Devi had a reputation for keeping "all her husbands satisfied" and of being immensely loyal. However, Sharan Devi looked sad and angry when she acknowledged that "they wrongly accused my husband of a rape, when actually the girl is of loose character. Now my family has to provide child support every month."

While talking with Sharan Devi, it was clear that she was strong and influential in her family. Only her second-oldest cohusband was a home farmer; all the others were part-time residents who worked outside the village. She maintained a good, healthy relationship with each of her husbands and visited them regularly out of town. She said that when they visited her or she visited them, she would cook their favorite meals and treat them well. "After all," she said, "they only get the comfort of a home for a few days." Sharan Devi had six children, and her family was one of the wealthier families in the village, with large farmlands and a big house. She could easily have survived without the earnings from the accused husband and without his share of inheritance, but she maintained that "it is important to not cause a rift in the family as one crack leads to more cracks in a wall."

Case 8: Excited Love versus Arranged Marriage

This case is complex and illustrates tensions between excited love and arranged marriages. "Heartfelt feelings toward a particular individual are sometimes independent of wealth or marital status," a middle-aged polyandrous woman acknowledged when referring to the story of Urgyn Pati. Urgyn Pati was taken for marriage (bride capture with parental consent) by a man from a neighboring village. At the time Urgyn Pati was having an affair with an unmarried man named Gyan Vir in her natal village. Urgyn Pati could have opposed the marriage but instead accepted it. However, even after her marriage Urgyn Pati continued her affair with Gyan Vir, although more secretly than before.

Gyan Vir was the oldest of five brothers, and soon after Urgyn Pati's marriage all these brothers consented to an arranged polyandrous marriage with Leela Rani. Like Urgyn Pati, Gyan Vir also did not protest or opt out of this polyandrous marriage at the time. A few years later, however, Gyan Vir told the second-oldest brother, who was the household man, that he wanted to marry Urgyn Pati.[6] The latter agreed not only to let Gyan Vir marry his lover but also to care for the remaining polyandrous family. Gyan Vir, however, did not ask Leela Rani. Then Gyan Vir and Urgyn Pati both broke their marriages and started living together. Later the second-youngest brother also left Leela Rani to become polyandrous with Urgyn Pati. They have been married for more than a decade now and have children.

Some years later the third brother and the youngest brother also left Leela Rani and married different women monogamously. Thus

Leela Rani's first pentapolyandrous marriage became monogamous. The second-oldest brother remained loyal to Leela Rani and took care of all the children, even those born when they were polyandrous. But she was not a happy woman. Polyandrous wives profusely resent such breeches of trust by cohusbands. Leela Rani has very bitter feelings because none of her ex-husbands kept the promise he had made, to pay her a fixed amount of cash or land if he left her. They did not contribute financially or otherwise to the care of the children whom she claims they fathered with her. Ironically, she was also angry with her only loyal husband because he permitted his brothers to break away and did not demand financial compensation from them. She and her husband did not appear to have an intimate relationship, but neither wanted to dissolve their monogamy, either. "Monogamy from the start is better than polyandry, when husbands do not remain faithful," she said bitterly.

Case 9: Preferential Intimacy

This case illustrates the complexity and fluidity of marriage types within a household: from polyandry to monogamy to polygyny. As I was walking one day along the *khool* (irrigation canal) in a village, I was greeted by a happy young woman who invited me to her house. The house was large and even had a ceramic toilet with a septic tank. Gyan Pati, a short thirty-year-old, offered me tea. Within minutes she showed me around the house and invited me to stay with her family. We were soon joined by her oldest sister, Suraj Moni, and their husband, Deva Singh. Deva Singh was the second son of seven brothers. He had a local part-time job, and he had a small-scale cash crop business in the summers.

Initially, all seven brothers were polyandrously married to a woman for some years, when Deva Singh, who was the second oldest, had an extramarital affair with Suraj Moni. Deva Singh then decided to break away from the first wife and marry Suraj Moni; at the time Deva Singh's oldest brother, Padam Singh, joined to make the union polyandrous. Within a year Deva Singh had captured Amir Dasi, the younger sister of Suraj Moni, thus creating a polygynandrous union. Padam Singh was a pastoralist, and when it was time for him to go to the winter pastures, Suraj Moni agreed to accompany him, thus creating a temporary monogamy with him and leaving Deva Singh and Amir Dasi monogamous. After a year the sisters decided to switch their "monogamous husbands" because of their personal preferences. Thus Suraj Moni became monogamous with Deva Singh, and Amir Dasi became monogamous with Padam Singh. Amir Dasi said that she wanted to be with Padam Singh because he was a very calm and quiet man with hardly any demands. It was clear that Suraj Moni has much higher energy and in this way is more similar to Deva Singh.

A few years later Deva Singh started to have an extramarital affair with Gyan Pati, the younger sister of Suraj Moni and Amir Dasi. Soon Gyan Pati joined Deva Singh and Suraj Moni to form a polygynous union. The household became a joint family household with one polygynous and one monogamous unit. Each year the monogamous unit went away for the winter with the livestock, while the polygynous unit resided full time in the village. All three sisters got along well and always helped each other with household chores, farming, and parenting. The two older sisters had two sons each, and Gyan Pati told me, "I have a daughter and that is enough because my daughter already has many siblings." While I helped cook in the evenings, sometimes Suraj Moni would go to the next room to talk with Padam Singh. On one such evening Gyan Pati laughed as she told me how Suraj Moni still likes to tell Padam Singh about her day's experiences because she had spent time with him in the past. Clearly, Suraj Moni and Padam Singh have maintained a kind of comfort, albeit sexless, intimacy.

Usually Suraj Moni and Gyan Pati slept with Deva Singh and their children in one room while Amir Dasi and Padam Singh slept in the neighboring room with their children. Not once in the numerous months I spent there did I observe any form of jealousy or any other form of marital tension. Sometimes the sisters would laugh about Deva Singh and his lust for all of them.

SELF-DECEPTION OR IMPARTIALITY

These case histories provide a sense of the complexity, open-mindedness, and pragmatism of Kinnauri love lives. Some common themes emerge from these narratives. At a personal level impartiality is probably the single most important characteristic in a situation of plural love; in all probability self-deception (Trivers 1985) plays a critical role in achieving impartiality. A parallel situation that helps us understand multiple spouses is that of parenting multiple children. Ideally, parents never express partiality toward any child. Similarly, if a polyandrous wife feels a special intimacy for one of her cohusbands but refuses to acknowledge and express this partiality, even to herself, she will be considered impartial. By never allowing any expression of partiality, even to herself, the risk of dealing with the consequences of partiality is minimized. Thus self-deception can be extremely beneficial in promoting impartiality, especially for parents and polyandrous wives. It is possible that the polyandrous wives in cases 1, 2, 3, 7, and 8 used denial to a lesser or a greater degree in order to uphold their marriage as one grounded in impartiality.

Men Breaking Away from Polyandrous Unions

More men than women defected from their polyandrous marriages to marry monogamously (24 percent males, 3 percent females) (Tiwari 2001). This trend is increasing rapidly as men choose alternative options that are becoming affordable with the introduction of the market economy. "When I was a child there were only sixty-seven households in this village, and all of them were polyandrous," said Shyam Lal, who was born in 1929 and had seen enormous changes in people's lifestyles during his lifetime. Now the total number of households has more than doubled ($n = 143$), and fewer than a third remain polyandrous. Kinnauris are embarrassed by polyandry when living or traveling outside Kinnaur because outsiders often ridicule polyandry. Most households are monogamous.

The market economy has introduced wage jobs and thus made monogamy affordable for most (Tiwari 2001), or as a thirty-nine-year-old Kinnauri woman put it, "In olden days people were simple and stupid, now each is smarter than the other, and also the economic standards and options have risen and so people are not obliged to comply with polyandry." Or as a middle-aged Kinnauri man said, "Lack of wage jobs in the past forced men to be polyandrous."

Many Kinnauris agreed that polyandry was good in the past but that it is impractical in today's world. Another man aptly noted that "traditional values discourage independence, but today independence is considered superior." Many women thought that in the past polyandry was the best option but now the fear of having a cohusband leave the family to get another wife has caused a change of preference. A woman whose cohusband had left her acknowledged that there is "no peace of mind in polyandry, so who cares for wealth [that polyandry brings]?" Polyandrous women who have had a cohusband defect tend to be the most resentful. These women felt that they had been used, ill treated, and then abandoned by their ex-husbands. Most Kinnauris agreed that polyandrous marriages are extremely prone to breaking now and that if men are to break away to remarry monogamously, they should decide before children are born. This would avoid unfair treatment toward the polyandrous wife, and it would also avoid the unfair economic burden of supporting children fathered by defectors.

EXTRAMARITAL AFFAIRS

In Kinnaur men who break away from polyandry usually do so after having an extramarital affair. The married men who have an extramarital affair usually do so with single women (see case 3, the three husbands of Ringchin Dolma; case 4, Palmo's suspicions about her older husband; case 5,-Buddha Pati's second husband; case 7, Sharan Devi's middle husband; and case 9, Deva Singh's affairs with three sisters). Occasionally, both partners in an extramarital affair are married to other people (case 8). I also learned of two cases (not discussed in this chapter) in which wives (both monogamous) had extramarital affairs with and became pregnant by married men (one monogamous and one polyandrous). The husbands of both women had had vasectomies performed years before their wives conceived these children. Both children looked like their biological fathers, and everyone in the village knew of the affairs, yet the cuckolded husbands continued to care for their wives and accepted the illegitimate children as their own. My informants said that neither husband demonstrated any enmity toward his wife or the man with whom she had had an affair.

In some cases women tend also to accept their husband's extramarital affairs. For example, Buddha Pati (case 5) was not truly bothered when her husband had an extramarital affair with her sister. In addition, Buddha Pati did not mind taking care of the child that resulted from this affair. Similarly, the wives of Deva Singh (case 9) did not object to his extramarital affairs and the polygyny that resulted from it. Nevertheless, many wives do experience deep pain when their husbands cheat on them. The injured woman's response, however, is not to leave or initiate divorce. For example, both Palmo (case 4) and Sharan Devi (case 7) would not consider divorcing or even confronting their husbands. It is not that women fear dishonor, because divorce is not stigmatized in Kinnaur. I suspect the primary reason is economic. As Sharan Devi noted, "One crack leads to more cracks in the wall." These women tend to feel that an extramarital affair will be short lived, as will its related costs, compared with the costs of terminating their marriage. In this way the material benefits obtained from a husband far outweigh the emotional costs of infidelity. This is especially so if children are involved. They also know that children fathered out of wedlock (particularly children from unmarried women) do not inherit family property automatically. Kinnauri wives also know that the guilt of having been unfaithful may change a husband for the better. If a wife insists that a cohusband leave the family, she may harm herself financially, by losing his share of family inheritance. Most women feel that it is in their long-term interest to swallow the emotional pain in order to carve a richer future. Of course, no wife wants to see any signs of defection, but if that cannot be helped, tolerance or pretending to ignore the issue may save the family from dissolving.

Professions that earn money and keep men away from home are most closely associated with extramarital affairs, because men flirt and show off the money they earn. Migratory pastoralists are also prone to extramarital affairs. Of course, distance and money are known to increase the risks of breakups in modern societies, too. "Money was rare throughout my childhood," explained an elderly man, "then, in the sixties, for the first time money came in after people started to plant cash crops of apples and peas." Money brought with it an enormous transformation, including alternative economic options and access to the outside world. The market economy buffered the dependence of the Kinnauri people on their tough and unpredictable environment by offering them alternative reliable and relatively risk-free economic alternatives. The Kinnauri people thus are no longer required to depend on polyandry for economic backup and diversification. Introduction of the market economy is the most important factor in the increase in extramarital affairs and the push toward monogamy.

FRATERNAL POLYANDRY: REDUCTION IN
COHUSBAND CONFLICT

Polyandry, like most polygamous marriages, can be challenging, but fraternal polyandry is probably the least challenging of all polygamous marriages, especially when resources are extremely limited. Scholars have found that nonfraternal polyandry (especially when coresidence is involved) has a higher probability of breaking up than fraternal polyandry (Crook and Crook 1988; Levine 1988; Tambiah 1966). Locals in Kinnaur say that full brothers are now breaking from polyandry, so what chances are there for unrelated or less related males (such as half siblings) to be polyandrous? A young man in his late thirties commented, "It is easier for cohusbands to understand their differences than for a common wife to understand each husband." In polygynous marriages, even sororally polygynous ones, co-wives compete for resources for themselves and their children.[7] In fraternally polyandrous marriages, on the other hand, cohusbands have been important allies for the survival and success of their children.

Having grown up in the same house, brothers are more likely to share common styles of working, values, customs, daily rituals, and habits than are nonbrothers. Brothers also share larger economic and reproductive goals and thus make better team partners. More important, because cohusbands share a wife, the children are either biologically their own or they are nieces or nephews. Additionally, in Kinnaur cultural values strongly discourage differentiating the biological fathers from the nonbiological ones, thereby culturally minimizing competition between cohusbands and partiality toward one's biological children. The children differentiate their fathers as "oldest, middle, second youngest, youngest father," and so on. The avoidance of identifying the biological father also avoids the issue of fertility, and dominance with respect to fatherhood and sexual access to the wife, at home as well as socially. In contrast Levine and Silk (1997) found that one factor contributing to marital instability among the Nyinba people of Tibet was that the cohusbands tracked and competed for allocation of paternity. In addition, since Kinnaur is traditionally a fraternally polyandrous society, the Kinnauris (especially the sons of polyandrous parents, and even, as case 2 illustrates, sons of monogamous parents) are more likely to understand and respect the daily mechanisms of polyandry.

Twenty-four of thirty-seven women interviewed (65 percent) preferred polyandry to monogamy, with eight women preferring more than two cohusbands. The majority ($n = 16$), however, prefer only two cohusbands as the best way to compromise the desire to maximize income while minimizing conflicts as well as age differences between the spouses (Tiwari 2001).

That 36 percent of married individuals chose to be fraternally polyandrous, in a society where monogamy is becoming affordable, demonstrates that Kinnauris continue to believe that fraternal polyandry is worth the effort. Fraternal polyandry certainly has economic benefits, and among all polygamous systems, fraternal polyandry provides maximum inclusive fitness and minimum competition. This chapter suggests that marital satisfaction can be found in fraternally polyandrous plural relationships.

***

I am indebted to the people of Kinnaur for accepting me so open-heartedly. Without their friendship, confidence, and kindness, none of this would have been possible. I would also like to express my gratitude to Alan J. Redd, William Jankowiak, Stephen Beckerman, Gregory Hart, and my father for their encouragement and valuable suggestions.

NOTES

1. Polyandry is prevalent in the animal kingdom, including some species of birds (Lack 1968; Clutton-Brock 1991), tamarins (Goldizen 1987), amphibians, and other animals.

2. Transhumant cohusbands manage to visit home only twice a year. Other cohusbands may be part-time residents who have private, government, or wage labor jobs away from their village.

3. The average population density for Himachal Pradesh is 92.9 people per square kilometer (*District Census Handbook* 1991) and that of India is 312 people per square kilometer.

4. Traditionally, pastoralists were also long-distance traders along the silk route, bartering items such as salt, metal utensils, wool, dried fruits, and nuts.

5. Such affairs between men and their wife's sister are not unheard of, and in many cases sororal polygyny or sororal polygynandry result. Locals believe that plural sororal marriages are more stable than those in which unrelated women are married to the same spouse(s).

6. In this case Gyan Vir was respectful enough to ask his then-cohusband permission to marry Urgyn Pati. In many cases men who break away from polyandry do so without asking anybody for permission. Perhaps that is why it is common in polyandrous weddings for the bride's family to ask each groom to promise to pay

an agreed amount, either in cash or in kind, in case he breaks away to form another marital union.

7. Jankowiak, Sudakov, and Wilreker's 2005 cross-cultural study of cowife conflict also found competition markedly reduced among sisters, as case 9 demonstrates.

REFERENCES

Alexander, Richard. 1974. "The Evolution of Social Behavior." *Annual Review of Ecology and Systematics* 5:325–83.

Berreman, Gerald D. 1975. "Himalayan Polyandry and the Domestic Cycle." *American Ethnologist* 2 (1): 127–39.

Clutton-Brock, T. H. 1991. *The Evolution of Parental Care*. Princeton, N.J.: Princeton University Press.

Crook, John H. and S. J. Crook. 1988. "Tibetan Polyandry: Problems of Adaptations and Fitness." In L. Betzig, M. Borgerhoff Mulder, and P. Turke, eds., *Human Reproductive Behavior: A Darwinian Perspective*, pp. 97–114. Cambridge: Cambridge University Press.

Daas, Tulsi. "Kishkindhaakaand." *Shree Raam Charit Maanas*. Gorakhpur, Uttar Pradesh: Geeta Press, n.d.

District Census Handbook of Kinnaur. 1991. Series 9, part 12 (A&B). Himachal Pradesh, India: Director of Census Operations.

Durham, William. 1991. *Coevolution: Genes, Culture and Human Diversity*. Stanford, Calif.: Stanford University Press.

Fisher, Helen E. 2004. *Why We Love: The Nature and Chemistry of Romantic Love*. New York: Henry Holt.

Gaulin, Steven J.C. and A. Schlegel. 1980. "Paternal Confidence and Paternal Investment: A Cross Cultural Test of a Sociobiological Hypothesis." *Ethology and Sociobiology* 1:301–9.

Goldizen, Ann W. 1987. "Facultative Polyandry and the Role of Infant-Carrying in Wild Saddle-Back Tamarins (Saguinus-Fuscicollis)." *Behavioral Ecology and Sociobiology* 20 (2): 99–109.

Goldstein, Melvyn C. 1987. "Pahari and Tibetan Polyandry Revisited." In M. K. Raha, ed., *Polyandry in India*, pp. 198–219. Delhi: Gian Publishing.

Goody, Jack. 1976. *Production and Reproduction*. Cambridge: Cambridge University Press.

Haddix, Kimberly A. 2001. "Leaving Your Wife and Your Brothers: When Polyandrous Marriages Fall Apart." *Evolution and Human Behavior* 22:47–60.

Hartung, John. 1985. "Matrilineal Inheritance: New Theory and Analysis." *Behavioral and Brain Sciences* 8 (December): 661–70.

Hatfield, Elaine. 1988. "Passionate and Companionate Love." In R. J. Sternberg and M. L. Barnes, eds., *The Psychology of Love*, pp. 191–271. New Haven, Conn.: Yale University Press.

Jankowiak, William, ed. 1995. *Romantic Passion: A Universal Experience?* New York: Columbia University Press.

Jankowiak, William, M. Sudakov, and B. Wilreker. 2005. "Co-wife Conflict and Co-operation." *Ethnology* 44 (1): 81–98.

Kurland, Jeffrey A. 1979. "Paternity, Mother's Brother, and Human Sociality." In N.A. Chagnon and W. Irons, eds., *Evolutionary Biology and Human Social Behavior.* North Scituate, Mass.: Duxbury Press.

Lack, David Lambert. 1968. *Ecological Adaptations for Breeding in Birds.* London: Methuen.

Levine, Nancy E. 1988. *The Dynamics of Polyandry.* Chicago: University of Chicago Press.

Levine, Nancy E. and Joan B. Silk. 1997. "Why Polyandry Fails: Sources of Instability in Polyandrous Marriages." *Current Anthropology* 38 (3): 375–98.

Liebowitz, Michael R. 1983. *The Chemistry of Love.* Boston: Little, Brown.

Sharma, P.D. and R.S. Minhas. 1993. "Land Use and the Biophysical Environment of Kinnaur District, Himachal Pradesh, India." *Mountain Research and Development* 13 (1): 41–60.

Tambiah, Stanley J. 1966. "Polyandry in Ceylon—With Special Reference to Lagala Region." In C. von Furer-Haimendorf, ed., *Caste and Kin in Nepal, India and Ceylon,* pp. 264–358. London: Asia Publishing.

Tiwari, Geetanjali. 2001. "Polyandry versus Monogamy: Social and Economic Evidence from the Northwest Himalayan Region of Kinnaur, India." Ph.D. diss., Pennsylvania State University.

Trivers, Robert. 1985. *Social Evolution.* Menlo Park, Calif.: Benjamin/Cummings.

6. Voiced Intimacies
Verbalized Experiences of Love and Sexuality in an Indonesian Society

Birgitt Röttger-Rössler

ETHNOGRAPHIC BACKGROUND: SOCIAL ORGANIZATION AND GENDER RELATIONS OF THE MAKASSAR

The Makassar live in the south of the Indonesian island of Sulawesi. They number about two million and are spread along the coast or in the mountainous regions of the interior.[1] Whereas the economy of the interior is based on wet rice cultivation, fishing and seaborne trade play a central role on the coast. Although the coastal regions were Islamized relatively early and the majority of the Makassar practice Islam, this religion has managed to establish itself only weakly in the highlands.[2] Makassar society is characterized by a strict hierarchic organization. The apex of the social pyramid is formed by the high nobility of the former Kingdom of Gowa, headed by the maternal and paternal descendants of the kingdom's mythical founder and first queen.[3] The lowest level is formed by descendants of former serfs, or slaves. Although this latter class no longer exists officially, it continues to be anchored in people's minds. Between these two poles society is divided into various strata and substrata. Membership in a particular social stratum is based on individual descent and the rank assigned to an individual on the basis of the bilateral kinship system determined by both matrilineal and patrilineal origins.

The individual social strata and substrata are—at least ideally—demarcated according to endogamous principles: a woman should never marry below her descent rank, which significantly links together the aspects of hierarchy and gender. This cultural norm is backed up by being linked directly to the indigenous conception of honor: through a "false marriage," that is, by marrying a man of lower rank, a woman and her family will show themselves to be people without honor (*siri'a*). The logical consequence of this doctrine is that marriages are arranged by families and not by the partners themselves on the basis of their mutual attraction. This is one reason for the strict separation of young men and women of marriageable age: to minimize the risk of the development between young people of liaisons that run counter to marriage policy and might lead to elopement and secret marriages. However, only interaction between young men and women of marriageable age is strictly taboo. Boys and girls can play together relatively freely as children but are strictly separated by puberty at the latest. As they grow older, in contrast, men and women can interact increasingly more freely. Nonetheless, the last two to three decades have seen a clear relaxation of the separation between boys and girls after sexual maturity because of mixed school classes. They are now able to converse in public places without causing offense, whereas previously even eye contact was forbidden. Gender separation was predominantly achieved by drastically limiting the freedom of young girls, who could move freely only within the house and backyard. Public places were accessible to them only under the supervision of older women.

However, in daily life men and women hardly interact. Their walks of life are generally clearly separated and characterized by different conditions and responsibilities. Men and women do not possess higher or lower social standing through their gender; they adopt different but equally valued roles within society. The genders also have equal rights in the economic sphere. There is even a kind of separation of property in marriage, with marriage partners retaining the rights of ownership and access to the personal property and real estate each brings into the marriage. In the case of divorce each retains her or his own property, and property acquired during the marriage is either divided or passed on to the children of the marriage.[4] Houses are assigned in principle to the woman. Traditional local inheritance laws also do not favor either gender. Islamic law, with its bias toward sons, remains irrelevant in the highlands. In the contemporary education and job sectors, boys and girls generally have equal opportunities, and married couples in which the woman is more highly qualified and has a better job are quite common in Makassar society. There is no ideology that casts the man as the "family provider" and limits the role of women to reproductive tasks. Instead, earning a living both within and beyond the agrarian context is taken as a joint task for both genders. Another decisive aspect in this context is that child care and child rearing are not the primary responsibility of parents or even mothers but are understood as a common task of the extended family, with great importance assigned to a division of labor between the generations.

All other domains of social life reveal a complementary distribution between the genders as well. This applies not only to the division of labor in agriculture but also to the distribution of sociopolitical and religious positions. For example, although men generally hold the traditional political offices, women hold the decisive ritual positions in the local shrines (*kalompoang*), which represent incarnations of political power, according to indigenous belief. In general, women function as "protectors" of the shrines. This means that they are responsible for maintaining them and performing the rituals pertaining to them that play a central role in socioreligious life.[5]

CULTURAL PATHS TO CONJUGAL LOVE AND INTIMACY

Within Makassar society two different forms of marriage coexist, namely, arranged versus self-made marriages. These correspond to two competing models of conjugal love and intimacy. The normatively "correct" path to conjugal intimacy is that of the arranged marriage. Self-made marriages in the form of elopement are considered to be a deviant behavior that threatens the honor of the family. Nonetheless, such elopements form the basis of about 35 percent of all marriages.

ARRANGED MARRIAGES

Marriages are of central importance in Makassar society because they not only forge or consolidate decisive bonds in terms of sociopolitical and economic status but also maintain the rank endogamy. As a result an individual's marriage (particularly the first one) should not be left to "chance" individual attraction but is arranged by families. (Once a socially acceptable marriage has produced children and descent is ensured, individuals have much more freedom of choice regarding further polygamous or later monogamous marriages.) Nonetheless, family marriage policy does not focus only on the economic and social status of the potential partner but is, to a large extent, aimed at matching the future couple in terms of character, attitude toward life, and values, thus ensuring that positive and close emotional bonds will emerge and lead to a long-lasting and harmonious marriage. This ideal of a gradual development of love can be traced clearly in the different everyday terms in the Makassar language for describing different forms of affective bonds between woman and man.[6] These terms can be understood only against the background of arranged marriages between partners who did not know, or hardly knew, each other before. At the beginning of a marriage, the Makassar believe, there are either no feelings at all or *cinna-cini'a*. *Cinna-cini'a* is a feeling of affection, of being attracted by the external appearance and behavior of a potential marriage partner—by their physical attractiveness, demeanor, voice, and expression. However, this is not taken in any sexual sense; the expression *ero'* (wanting, strong desire) is reserved for this form of desire. Ideally, *cinna-cini'* and *ero'* should merge at the beginning of a marriage, and partners should like the "taste" of each other (*a'kanjame*) in a physical, sexual way as well. Over the course of a marriage this should lead first to the emergence of *singai* (liking each other), thus bringing together personality characteristics that neither partner had been aware of in the other before. For this reason older informants (born before 1960), who experienced a far stronger norm of strict gender separation, believe that *singai* can emerge only at the beginning of a marriage, whereas the younger generations (born around 1970 and later) consider that *singai* may also develop before marriage (when the man and woman know each other before getting married).

During the course of a marriage *singai* often turns into *sikarimangi*, that is, a mutually caring, understanding, and respectful love. The prerequisite for this feeling is for partners to already be familiar with each other's personal idiosyncrasies and feel attracted to each other. *Sikarimangi* implies the emergence of a completely specific, loving, and trusting form of interaction. The liberal younger generations also believe that *sikarimangi* becomes possible only within marriage. An intensification of this bond is *ammaling-maling*, a form of intimacy, of love, in which the other is always present in one's thoughts and actions. *Ammaling-maling*, like *sikarimangi*, is not restricted exclusively to the marital context but may also develop between other people who have a close relationship. Another form of emotional bond between marriage partners is *sikatutui* (mutual respect). *Sikatutui* is independent of mutual attraction (*cinna-cini'*) and deeper mutual care and understanding (*sikarimangi*). However, *sikatutui* implies a respectful interaction within a couple that aims to always avoid offending and hurting each other, and it is valued highly in Makassar society. *Sikatutui* seems to imply a conjugal relationship based on less intimacy between partners. They do not have such close emotional bonds as those who feel *sikarimangi* for each other. Nonetheless, many successful and long-lasting marriages characterized by little strife and tension are based, according to my informants, on *sikatutui*, which is also held to be an emotional ideal in the context of polygynous marriages.

The basic precondition for the formation of a positive emotional bond between marriage partners is, as I mentioned earlier, having the most in common, not only in social and economic terms but also in terms of such mental aspects as temperament and personality. This is why the reciprocal "observation of the behavior" (*accini' angka*) of potential marriage candidates by each party's relatives is such a major activity long before any official marriage negotiations commence. In an endless chain of visits and return visits, the different parties try to gain an insight into family relations as well as an idea of the character of the marriage candidate. Close and trusted friends of the potential bride and groom also attend these visits and then give personal reports on the future marriage partner. Only just before the official start of marriage negotiations—given that the *accini' angka* process has a positive outcome—is the future couple given an opportunity to see each other. If one or the other is then opposed to the planned marriage, in most cases marriage negotiations will not commence.[7]

Marriage is the most elaborate rite of passage in Makassar society. It is made up of a host of discrete rituals that extend over weeks and represent a gradual bringing together of a bride and groom who are generally more or less strangers to each other. A marriage does not just take a lot of time but is also enormously costly in economic terms, particularly for the family of the groom. The financial costs to the groom's family are linked directly to the rank (in terms of descent) of the bride. They break down into two parts: the bridewealth (*sunrang*) and the spending money (*balanja*). The latter consists of rice, cattle, and cash for the wedding feast, whereas the former serves as a social insurance for the bride in the case of divorce or the death of her husband.

Two dozen marriage rites successively annul all the regulations limiting contact between the genders before marriage. I have room to sketch here only the most important. The formal start to the marriage process is the announcement of the official proposal by members of the man's family and its acceptance by the representatives of the bride. This has been preceded by successful negotiations about the amount of the spending money (*balanja*). Some time later—between one week and one year—the agreed-upon *balanja* is handed over in the house of the bride's parents. The date of the marriage is set on this day and will generally be one to two weeks hence. The actual marriage ceremony consists of two central acts: the handing over of the bridewealth (*sunrang*) by members of the groom's family to representatives of the bride and the subsequent Islamic *nikka* (marriage ceremony) performed by the imam and the bridegroom in the presence of a male representative of the bride's family. These two key actions are embedded in a host of ritual sequences that stretch out over several days and gradually bring bride and groom, along with their families, closer together. I will analyze only two of these sequences in more detail here: the "making into speaking partners" (*appasiurang akkana*) and the "reconciliation" (*pappasiama*'), because their symbolic meaning casts light on the indigenous conception of conjugal relations.

Bride and groom first meet after the completion of the *nikka*. However, they are not allowed to talk to each other or to look at each other directly before completing the *appasiurang akkana* ritual. Until then they have to use intermediaries if they wish to communicate. In this rite the couple sit together on one sarong on the bed in the bride's chamber. The bride and groom are served with food containing specific symbolic ingredients that have been blessed by a specialist, the "marriage mother" (*anrongbunting*). They have to put this in each other's mouth. The groom then takes his bride's hand, saying: "Speak to me; I have been in your house for a long time." The bride answers with a plain yes. In earlier times this ritual was delayed until the tenth day after the marriage ceremony. Today it usually is completed on the second or third day after the *nikka*. Nowadays this is also the day of the ritual "reconciliation" (*pappasiama*') of the bride and groom that allows them to engage in sexual intercourse. Until the early 1970s this rite, which brings the marriage process to a close, did not take place until forty days after the marriage ceremony. Nonetheless, this "reconciliation," often also called *nipabajikang* (making mutually good or well disposed), is still of central importance. The bride and groom are bedded for their first night together in the bride's house by the "marriage mother" (*anrongbunting*), within the context of various ritual acts. According to local belief, the success of the marriage, particularly in terms of a mutually harmonious sexuality, depends on the effectiveness of the *pappasiamaʾ* and, hence, on the competence of the *anrongbunting*. If the marriage has still not been consummated sexually in the months after the "making mutually good or well disposed," the *anrongbunting* will repeat the ritual. If this too does not lead to success, the marriage will be annulled—as long as one or both partners wish it. Thus a mutually harmonious and satisfying sexuality is considered an important element in positive conjugal relations. Nonetheless, there is no "cultivation" of eroticism. Sexual desire is viewed as a basic human need, like the desire for food, water, sleep, and so forth. This is underlined by the lack of any special term for sexual lust. It is designated with the general term *eroʾ*, signifying strong wanting, wishing, and desiring. According to local belief, sexual lust is particularly strong in young people and is viewed as a natural urge that brings young couples together and may lead to a positive conjugal relationship—as long as the fundamental social, economic, and personality parameters match.

The multitude of sequences in the Makassar marriage rituals are designed to overcome the distance between unacquainted partners. It can be argued that the diverse taboos making it harder for the couple to interact freely and delaying sexual contact make things easier for bride and groom. Older couples report, for example, that the speech prohibition still lasted ten days when they got married and that this taboo frequently provided opportunities for comic situations and liberating laughter that helped break down the barriers between bride and groom. The lengthy taboo on sexual contact was also perceived as a relief, and couples frequently maintained it voluntarily beyond the *pappasiamaʾ* ritual. Even though the "reconciliation" is now performed at an early stage, the younger generation still finds it completely normal to wait several months after marrying before initiating sexual contact—particularly when couples are very young.

SELF-MADE MARRIAGES

In reality a large proportion of marriages are not the outcome of familial arrangements but of elopement (*silariang*). This provides a kind of institutionalized safety valve enabling young people to assert their own partnership wishes against the interests of the family. In such cases the couple flees to a distant village and asks to be taken in by one of its houses, usually that of the village headsman or the local imam. The elopers (*tau nyala* = people who have committed a mistake) now have to watch out for the woman's family, because a *silariang* violates the honor of all consanguinal kin of the woman, obliging them to compensate this loss of honor by killing the elopers. The elopers are married as quickly as possible by the local imam in the place to which they have fled. However, even after this marriage they both still have to fear the compensatory acts of the *tumasiri'* (people who have been dishonored), that is, the woman's kin. The couple is safe only within the house of the host, because custom forbids the killing of people in the house of another. In public places, in theory, the newlyweds must continuously fear for their lives. Nonetheless, the killing of elopers is rare, because the *tumasiri'* generally do not search for elopers systematically or for long. The community to which the elopers have fled also protects the bride and groom and warns them when a member of the woman's family is approaching. As a result direct encounters between *tau nyala* and *tumasiri'* are rare. In most cases after some time has elapsed, the elopers have the possibility of making a "good return" (*ammotere' baji'*), that is, a ritual taking-back of the bride by her family, and this dissolves her family members' *tumasiri'* status (i.e., the duty to kill the couple). In some cases only a few weeks pass before they are taken back, in other cases several years. This depends on how acceptable the bridegroom is to the bride's family. If, for example, he has the same rank as the bride, a good reputation, and an acceptable economic status, agreement is generally soon reached on an *ammotere' baji'*. Only when a couple's elopement violates central marriage taboos, for example, when a woman marries a man of much lower rank, no return is possible. In such cases the family of the woman who has eloped generally declares her to be dead, which means lifelong and irrevocable banishment.

But if the bride's side has agreed to n *ammotere' baji'*, the man's family has to pay the bride money, although the sum is always smaller than that for a normal marriage, because an *ammotere' baji'* costs less than a normal marriage ceremony. It should be noted that *silariang* is also often used as a deliberate policy-making strategy in marriage and status affairs. It serves as an important medium for manipulating the rigid social hierarchy. Marriages through elopement are frequently organized deliberately in order to forge ties that would otherwise be impossible because of differences in rank.

The marriage ceremony in an elopement is restricted to the *nikka* performed in a completely nonfestive, formal atmosphere by the local imam in the house that has taken in the eloping couple. All ritual acts characterizing a normal marriage are dropped. This includes the "reconciliation," even though this rite is in no way restricted to a first marriage but is also performed at further marriages of older widowed or divorced people, that is, people with previous sexual experience. This makes it clear that the *pappasiama'* ritual is a form of ritual legitimization and empowerment of a couple's sexuality. This legitimization and the positive "charging" of sexuality associated with it are not available to *silariang* couples. Because they lack the protection of ritual, marriages through elopement are believed to be generally unstable and at risk, as well as especially susceptible to negative magical powers. Marriage by elopement is seen as kind of dangerous "jump start" into marital life that hinders the "normal" step-by-step development of conjugal love and intimacy. According to dominant beliefs, elopements are not the outcome of intense feelings or deep affectional bonds between two people but of a mainly sexual attraction (*ero'*) or magical factors (love magic). Although mostly young men, with their strong libido, are believed to use magic (*pa'balle*) to make a particular woman want them, the use of magic by young women is in no way considered rare. In this context it is important to note that Makassar society does not possess any elaborate model of falling in love (Röttger-Rössler 2002). Emotional states, like those considered typical for falling in love in Western societies, such as continuously thinking about and idealizing the loved one, euphoria, restlessness, hyperactivity, sleeplessness, and the neglect of all other aspects of social life (Hatfield 1988; Hendrick and Hendrick 1992; Tennov 1979), are viewed as an illness. Young people of both genders are particularly susceptible to this illness, called *garring tau lolo,* and treatment is considered essential. Makassar society certainly recognizes the phenomenon of being so intensely drawn to one particular person that it takes over both body and mind, seeming to leave hardly any cognitive and emotional capacities for dealing with other concerns in daily social life. However, it is not viewed as a positive and desirable emotional state but as something pathological, a mental and physical illness that may be socially destructive and a threat to the structures and harmony of family life.[8]

PERSONAL NARRATIVES OF CONJUGAL LOVE AND INTIMACY

I will use five personal narratives to examine how individuals talk about their start into married life and their early experiences of sexual intimacy. The first three involve arranged marriages; the last two, marriages through elopement. All five are so-called conversational narratives (Quasthoff 1980a, b; Riessman 1993), that is, spontaneous accounts of personal experiences emerging within the context of everyday conversations rather than experience reports elicited in artificial interview situations. My main research aim here had been to investigate how emotional experiences of developing conjugal relations are communicated in everyday conversations and what these communicative acts reveal about the underlying cultural "feeling rules." Narratives do not reflect experience directly but continuously stage it anew (Boothe 1994:35). In the narrative act, which is always an interactive process, individuals interpret their experiences and feelings within the cultural schemes and models available to them; they consolidate, categorize, and reconstruct their complex emotional experience and translate this into a communicable code. For this reason I shall sketch the context in which each narrative emerged, which should also make more vivid the process of "communicative meaning making" (Riessman 1993:4) inherent to daily conversations. Primarily, these narratives provide information about the cultural "feeling rules," rather than about how people actually experienced the beginning of intimate conjugal life—without even considering the issue of whether emotions can in any way be verbalized in a direct form.

In this context it might be important to note that Makassar society, like other Southeast Asian societies, does not encourage self-centered and self-reflective autobiographical narrations. It is generally considered inappropriate to present oneself to others as the focus of a narrative, making it hard to carry out explicitly autobiographical interviews in this society (see Röttger-Rössler 1993 and 2004:284–90). Personal experiences and feelings are mostly communicated indirectly, either in the form of episodic descriptions or through brief asides during the course of biographical narratives concerning the community. My focus on "conversational narratives" also constitutes a methodological adaptation to these narrative traditions.

WEDDING NIGHT STORIES

Uma's Marriage

The conversational context. I heard this narrative in 1991 during an ethnographic conversation I was holding with three women, then aged forty-five
to fifty, about how marriage rites used to be.[9] Uma, one of the official
"marriage mothers" (*anrongbunting*) in the village, had just embarked on
a detailed description of a ritual sequence when she suddenly paused and
commented that earlier marriages were not only far more lavish but also
more exciting. Without being asked, she then began to describe her own
marriage:

> I only found out that I was going to be married three days before my
> *nikka;* I wasn't told to whom. I only found out that it was Bossong on
> the day of the marriage ceremony. Bossong was a very tall, strong, and
> very light-skinned man. He was handsome. He had Dutch blood. He
> was a brave man. . . .
>   I didn't even know when the spending money (*balanja*) was handed
> over. I was in my aunt's house at the time. She'd asked for my help.
> Later, I realized it was just an excuse so that I wouldn't find out about
> the *balanja* being handed over in my parents' house. I really didn't
> know what was going on. On the day my *balanja* was handed over, I
> was pounding rice in front of my aunt's house. Suddenly, my brother
> turned up. He took the rice pounder out of my hand and said: "Don't
> pound so much. Take a break!" He was crying. I thought he was all
> worked up because he was just about to get married himself. A little bit
> later my aunt brought me a silk sarong and told me I would be married
> off in three days. She didn't say to whom, just that it was somebody
> from our family who lived in the village of Tompokang. Then I knew
> that it could only be my second cousin from there. I should wear the
> sarong when the horse brought me from my aunt's house to the *a'ba'ra*
> (literally: the powdering) in my parents' house. From that time on all
> I did was cry. I must have been about fourteen years old. I had only
> just had my first period. My breasts were still really small; they were
> just beginning to grow and they were very sensitive. . . . The "making
> mutually well disposed" didn't work at all for Bossong and me. We
> were both frightened. We used to wrap ourselves up from head to toe
> in our sleep sarongs and lie down in bed as far away from each other as

possible. That went on for about half a year. Then the "making mutually well disposed" was repeated. That made us a little braver; we even
started to stretch our feet out of our sarongs and touch each other with
them. Later on we slept close together in each other's arms. But it took
roughly another half a year before we really "met up."

This was the end of Uma's narrative, and Naiba, one of the other two women
present, added a description of her own behavior after the *pappasiamaʾ*:

They had to repeat the "making mutually well disposed" with us, too.
I refused to lie in the same bed as Itung's father (*puanna* Itung) for
months.[10] I slept with my parents and he lay alone in our chamber.
Then my mother said enough was enough. We'll send for the *anrongbunting* again and repeat the *pappasiamaʾ*. Then you'll sleep with him.
You'll see; it'll be all right then. However, I was still scared (*mallaʾ*).
In the night following the second *pappasiamaʾ*, I lay down under the
bed. Then Itung's father laughed and said: "Come on, let's switch
places. You lie in the bed, and I'll lie underneath it." We kept that up
for a while. Then, finally, I invited him to lie down in bed with me.
I'm not frightened of him or "meeting each other" any more. The
second *pappasiamaʾ* was a strong one!

Lempang, the other neighbor who was also the same age as Uma and
Naiba, said nothing about her own marriage experiences during this conversation. However, when she and I were walking back alone through the
fields to the village from Uma's outlying house, Lempang explained to me
that most young girls were frightened of "meeting each other," and they
would threaten to scream when touched, which would frighten the young
men in turn. However, it had been different for her. She had been more curious than frightened after the *pappasiamaʾ*. For her the "making mutually
well disposed" had been powerful. There had been no need to repeat it.

Ratna's Marriage
The conversational context. I was sitting with Ratna (born in 1961) and her
mother on the veranda of their house. We were waiting for some neighboring women to join us so that we could go to the *aʿbaʿra* ritual of a young
woman from the village. The coming marriage ritual inspired Ratna to describe her own marriage.

Ratna: I didn't know *puanna* Hasan [Hasan's father] at all. I'd never seen him, except once as a child. But I couldn't remember that anymore. I was frightfully afraid of the marriage. All I did was cry.

Mother: Oh, yes, she cried all the time, didn't want to get married, wanted to drink poison instead. My brother eventually threatened to become frightfully angry if she didn't stop.

Ratna: Ugh, I was scared (*malla'*)! I kept on trying to find somebody who knew Hasan's father, but hardly anybody knew him. Eventually, a [female] cousin came to stay who had seen him occasionally. I made her tell me about him all through the night. Over and over again. Because she couldn't tell me much, either, only that he seemed quite nice and wasn't bad looking. In the time just after the marriage, I didn't talk to Hasan's father, not a word, even though we had already done the "making into speech partners." When he came in through the front of the house, I went out the back. However, most of the time Hasan's father hung about outside anyway; he didn't want to meet me, either. That went on for a long time. We did sleep in one bed; we had to. However, we lay down as far away from each other as possible. I always put pillows between us. Hasan's father didn't do anything to stop me. He was frightened, too. I was eighteen or seventeen years old when I got married. Hasan's father is about the same age as me.

Mother: But the *pappasiama'* didn't have to be repeated!

Ratna: No. Both my grandmother and my mother thought that the *pappasiama'* had been good. It would just take a while. That was true, too; eventually, we cleared away the pillows between us.

The Marriage Nights of Rani and Minne

The conversational context. As often happened late in the afternoon, some people living in the house next door gathered on their veranda with some other neighbors for a chat. When I went over and joined the group on the veranda, they immediately asked me what I'd been doing all day. I told them that I'd been sorting through and revising all my notes on marriage rites and that I had noticed that even at the beginning of the 1970s, the "reconciliation" (*pappasiama'*) of the bride and groom was not held until forty days after the marriage. In this context Rani (born in 1961) began to talk:

Rani: We already had our "making mutually well disposed" after ten days. I was frightfully scared (*malla'*). During the *pappasiama'* I lay in bed and shook. However, *puanna* Darmawati was just as frightened and didn't even try to touch me. We then simply fell asleep—a long way apart from each other. Later, we came closer, but it took months before we "met each other." During the daytime as well, we always avoided each other at first and we hardly talked to each other, either. I was *siri'-siri'*, and *puanna* Darmawati doesn't talk much anyway. We had only seen each other once before our marriage. When my parents asked whether I would be prepared to marry *puanna* Darmawati, I said: I want to see him first.

Ngalle (Rani's father): Why shouldn't she? Her aunt then went with her to visit his family in Matanna. So that the two of them could get an impression of each other. The grandparents were outraged. They thought this was a very improper thing to do. So she saw him and agreed to marry him.

Rani: Yes. I agreed, but of course I was scared (*malla'*). I got married about two years after Minne. I was about sixteen years old when I married; Minne was twelve or thirteen when she was married to Taba.[11] She was still a child, hadn't even menstruated. Minne was frightfully afraid before the night of the *pappasiama'*. She had asked me to stay with her; she didn't want to be alone whatever happened. So I hid under the bed in their chamber while the *anrongbunting* performed the *pappasiama'* ritual. I was curious as well; I wanted to see what happened during the ritual and what Taba would do with Minne afterward. Minne cried horribly the whole time. Taba tried to calm her and said: "Come on, we'll just go to sleep now, you don't need to be afraid. I can also lie down in front of the bed if you want." Then I came out from under the bed and said: "If that's all you're going to do, then I can go now." Taba couldn't stop himself from laughing, and then all three of us slept in the bed together and talked halfway through the night.

R.R.: Is it that easy to slip into the bridal bedchamber without anybody noticing?

Rani: Of course. There's always a lot going on at a wedding, and a lot of guests stay overnight, so nobody notices if somebody

suddenly disappears. The other girls I was with knew what I was
up to. They didn't tell on me. They wanted to know what goes on
themselves.

    Binto (Rani's mother): That happens more often than you think. The
bride and groom frequently don't spend their first night alone;
they don't want to, either.

Interpretation

The marriage stories presented here are selected from fifty such narratives
that I have documented over the years. They all discuss fear as the predominant emotion in the context of the marriage ceremony. In almost all
these narratives fear emerges within two central scenarios, first, within detailed accounts of their own reactions to being told that they are going to
be married. According to the narratives, each found out either just before
or after the spending money (*appanai' balanja*) was handed over. Second,
fear emerges within their reaction to the *pappasiama'* topos, that is, within
the narrative account of the fear they felt before their first sexual encounter.
In all these narratives the *appanai' balanja* and the *pappasiama'* are singled
out from the elaborate course of the marriage and tagged as special experiences. However, it is questionable whether these women experienced the
fear they describe most intensively in these contexts or in completely different ones. That nearly all narrators use these two stages within the marriage
ritual for the narrative modulation of their emotional climax suggests that
these are established narrative topoi for communicating their fear of the
arranged marriage.

    A completely different issue is whether each narrator really experienced
the fear she describes or whether all simply pretend to have done this in
their narratives because fear is the culturally prescribed emotion in the
context of arranged marriages.

    The cultural elaboration of the emotional dimension of fear can be in-
terpreted in terms of the prolonged incremental ritual of bringing together
bride and groom as a psychologically meaningful model within the arranged marriage context. It enables what are generally very young couples
to cope with what is, in many cases, an undeniable uncertainty and fear
about getting married to an unknown partner and to move gradually toward each other and their new status. On the other hand, the elaboration
of this emotional domain has also turned this fear into a rigid convention.
For a bride and groom to display fear in a marriage ceremony is good form.

It is related to a central behavioral norm and is in no way automatically an outcome of the direct emotional experience of the individual. For example, girls are expected to cry at their marriage ceremony or at least look very unhappy. Twenty years ago young brides were even pinched until the tears came so that they could deliver the necessary emotional display. This norm also applied, and still applies, to men although not so rigidly. They are allowed to wish for marriage to fulfill their sexual desires and therefore do not need to feel any overwhelming fear of this event. Nonetheless, men should also not show joy. In sum, within the context of marriage ceremonies the demonstration of fear—also in narrative form—becomes a matter of social etiquette, of cultural convention. It does not necessarily reflect the actual emotions of the individuals involved. I see further support for this interpretation in that I was unable to document any conversational narratives in which the speakers characterized their marriage as a positive emotional experience. Indications that individuals did not find their marriage or their first sexual contacts frightening were always communicated to me privately and without witnesses—and never during conversations involving several people. Just as, following Uma's narrative, Lempang waited until we were going home together before confiding in me that she had not experienced any problems with her *pappasiama'*, other individuals also made similar statements when nobody else was present. Another, related aspect is that individuals who had chosen their own partner never talked in the presence of other people about how they experienced their marriage ceremony and their *pappasiama'* night. Descriptions of first sexual contacts are also omitted in the various reports about marriages by elopement that form a further domain of egocentric conversational narrative.

Elopement Stories

Couples were happy to give detailed accounts of their marriages by elopement as long as these, along with the ritual reacceptance in the family, had occurred a long time ago and all associated resentments had faded away. In general, these narratives are very action oriented and more like adventure stories. Here I shall report two highly prototypical elopement stories. Both were recounted within the context of the afternoon chats among neighbors on the veranda mentioned earlier. These provide a typical framework for personal narratives in the village environment. Nonetheless, these narratives were directed primarily toward me as a person who was not yet familiar with these stories and journeys through life.

Nurwati and Cala's Elopement

The conversational context. This "chat on the veranda" occurred in 1985. In addition to the two protagonists of the narrative, one of Cala's brothers was present. The narrative had been triggered by my ethnographic questions about marriage taboos.

> NURWATI: We had known and liked each other ever since we were children. When the family of a man from Lappara' asked for my hand and offered a *balanja* payment way beyond what Cala's family could ever pay, it was clear that the only thing we could do was elope. Actually, my parents would have accepted Cala but not my uncle. We had an auspicious day identified and agreed that the best thing would be for me to elope while I was going to do the laundry. That way I would be able to hide a few things among the dirty washing. Most of the time the girls in our neighborhood went to the springs alone to bathe and do laundry, but now, all of a sudden, one of my aunts or my mother always came with me. Perhaps they suspected something. Twice Cala had to wait for me in vain.
>
> *Cala:* Yes, that was awful. I didn't know whether she had been caught or had suddenly changed her mind. Whether I should carry on waiting or go into hiding. If everything had been found out and Nurwati's family had caught me, I'm sure I would have been stabbed!
>
> *R.R.:* Even if the elopement hadn't taken place?
>
> *Cala:* Most likely. It would have been obvious what we had intended. At least I'd have been beaten until I was half dead.
>
> *Nurwati:* I was also very frightened that our plan would be discovered. It was very difficult for me to hide my things under the washing. But then it worked. However, we had to elope during the night. I crept out of the house and thought I could hear my own heart beating. If anybody had heard me, I was going to say that I had to go out, and then I would have gone back into the house. I had already hidden a bundle with some things in the garden.

Cala: On the third attempt, however, it worked. I was also completely nervous while I was waiting; I was shaking. I'd brought a horse with me so that we could get to a village on the other side of the river as quickly as possible. We fled to the house of the *imam kampong* there. The *nikka* was held on the next day.

Nurwati: But we were able to come back quickly. It took only two months for my parents to consent to the *ammotere' baji'*. They didn't actually have any objections to Cala.

I asked them whether any kind of *nipabajikang* had been held for them. They said no, something like that was not customary for *silariang* couples and also not necessary, because they already had the desire to meet each other (*ero' baratammu*).

Ratna and Ancar's Elopement

The conversational context. After returning from the market with them, I was sitting with Ratna, her neighbor Nuri, and two other women on Ratna's veranda. Nuri told us how the marriage negotiations were proceeding for one of her nieces whom the family wanted to marry to a second cousin. This triggered Ratna's narrative.

I was supposed to be married to a second cousin whom I didn't know and had never seen. At one of my cousins' weddings I got to know Ancar. I liked him straight away. He was very handsome, tall, and he was very good at telling funny stories. I could see him very well from the corner in which we girls were sitting. He had noticed me too and kept on looking over to me. I could tell that he liked me because he then kept on starting to turn up with some people or other at my parents' house. He tried to get to know people who came to see us, and then he joined them. He was well received, he often helped my father, and everybody liked him.

But my mother soon became suspicious about his frequent visits, and she warned me: "If his intention is to ask for your hand, it won't work. You're going to be married to your cousin from Sironjong." I then sent out tentative feelers to find out how serious these marriage negotiations were and found that everything was very advanced and that Ancar didn't stand a chance. I told him that in a letter. We never talked about it openly, only three or four times secretly. Mostly, we exchanged letters—hid them in a tree.

After Ancar got my news, in his next letter he asked me if I was willing to elope with him. I was. Then Ancar organized everything. He let two of his cousins into the secret so that they would help and got a *dukun* [seer] to predict the best days to elope. A cousin of mine was having his marriage festival on one of these days. That was a great opportunity. There's always a lot going on at a wedding; loads of people get together, and nobody notices straight away when someone disappears. We had agreed on a time and a place for Ancar to be waiting with his cousins. When the time came, I said to my companion: "I'm just going to go back into the house and take another look at the bride and groom and see what's happening inside." I then secretly disappeared around the side of the house. I didn't have anything with me, just the clothes on my back. Anything else might have aroused suspicion. Ancar and his cousins were waiting for me. We then went to B. as quickly as possible, where we were expected in the house of Ancar's relatives. We left there very early on the next morning and came here [Ancar's home village].

I lived in his aunt's house until our *nikka,* and Ancar stayed with his parents. Then the *imam kampung* started negotiating with my parents, but they refused to send a representative (*wakil*) for me, and they let me know that there was no question of an *ammotere baji'* as long as my father was still alive. My father was a hard man and frightfully angry that his daughter had been seduced by a boy whom he had welcomed into his house. After the *nikka* we moved to Ujung Pandang. It was too dangerous to stay here in the villages. My *ammotere baji'* did not occur until nine years later and after my father had died. He had stuck to his word, and he did not allow me to return for the rest of his life.

Ratna ended her narrative here, and I asked whether she had found it hard not to be able to return to her family and whether she had ever regretted eloping. Of course, it had been difficult, she answered, and she had often felt homesick for her family, but Ancar had been worth paying the price. "When I had to cry, and then looked at him, I knew that it is good the way it is. It's still the same today. It's very hard for me now that Ancar is so far away for such a long time. Sleeping alone is terrible."[12] At this point Nuri asked mockingly: "Is Ratna still that hungry (*nafsu makan*)?" "That's still there, but that's not what I mean. It's simply better when you are always together and you can go to sleep together and wake up together. But perhaps that's something that only people who have 'chosen' their marriages 'for themselves' (*kemauan sendiri*) can understand." When I subsequently asked her what her first sexual contact with Ancar had been like, and whether she had also been frightened like most girls say they were on their marriage night, she replied with a laugh, "Frightened? No! Why then? It was self-chosen (*kemauan sendiri*). I wanted him (*ero'*)! I was nervous but in a happy way and not a fearful one."

Interpretation

Each of the thirty-five elopement stories that I have documented over the years reveals the same construction as those reported here. They always begin with an explanation of the motive for elopement, and mostly—as here—point to existing marriage arrangements elsewhere, and they do this regardless of the real reasons. In addition to the named motive, these are generally that the partnership violates endogamy, one partner comes from a family with a bad reputation, the man's side is unable to raise the necessary bride money, or the woman is already pregnant. Because each of these reasons is shameful for one side or the other, any public conversations generally fall back on the topos of formal marriage negotiations' having been commenced already, even when everybody present knows the real reasons for elopement. This is always followed later in the narrative by a description of the actual elopement, its organization, implementation, and special risks. These narratives close with reports on the length of time and circumstances surrounding the reacceptance (*ammotere' baji'*). In contrast, the first nights together, the first sexual encounters, are never depicted narratively in elopement stories. I was only ever told about such matters when I asked directly, as the conversation protocols here show. These statements seem to indicate that, in contrast to arranged marriages, sexual intimacy does not form a problem, a tense scenario, in the context of elopement. The amazed and amused replies I always received to such questions were similar in content to those reported here: A ritual "reconciliation," a "making mutually well disposed," is not considered necessary for eloping couples because mutual attraction—including its sexual elements—is already present.

However, the dominant moral discourse evaluates this attraction as a purely sexual "appetite" that leads people to enter into ill-considered, economically and mentally unsuitable, partnerships that are, accordingly, doomed to failure. Once again it is important to emphasize here that sexuality is not regarded negatively and devalued in itself but that it is viewed as a force that needs to be channeled and exploited positively—that is, in the interests of the family. The dominant Makassar "theory of love" is simple: If the preconditions are auspicious, if a couple is matched in terms of social, familial, religious, economic, character, and physical aspects, a mutual attraction and a positive emotional relationship will form almost automatically with the help of basic sexual desire. Over the course of time spent together, this may consolidate into an intimate bond in the sense of the greatest possible mental and physical harmony. The indigenous conception of "love" seems to be less a mystery that befalls people and far more an emotional consequence in a developmental psychological sense, a feeling that can be planned and evoked deliberately. Self-made marriages, according to the dominant ideology, are determined primarily by sexual elements. They lack the necessary "ingredients" for a positive marriage relationship. This is why—according to the dominant discourse—they will rarely lead to higher forms of intimacy in the sense of always being together in thought and deed and caring for each other (*sikarimangi, ammaling-maling*).

However, Ratna counters this dominant concept in her answer to Nuri's mocking interjection. She formulates the belief, held by most couples who have eloped, that only self-made marriages can generate a high degree of emotional closeness and that couples whose marriages—like that of Nuri—have been arranged are simply incapable of building up comparably close and intimate bonds. We can see how two, so to speak, competing cultural models of love and intimacy are embedded in this short and half-joking dialogue between Ratna and Nuri.

CONCLUSION: IT'S ONLY MAGIC—OR IS IT?

A closer inspection reveals that what seemed to be two competing models of love are really just different ideas about which is the best path to conjugal love, harmony, and intimacy. When it comes to what constitutes a loving marriage and what characterizes deep and close bonds (*sikarimangi, amaling-maling*) between partners, in contrast, there is scarcely any divergence of opinion. These common criteria emerge clearly in the discussions and narratives about the end of a marriage, be it through divorce or the death of a partner. These conversations provide a context for the emergence of collectively fabricated marriage biographies that reflect the values that the community attributes to each specific type of marriage. In a case of divorce the love components are depicted negatively. Accounts of the reasons for the failure of a relationship clearly reveal what are held to be the significant elements of a good marriage.

However, an even more subtle access to local conceptions of love and intimacy is found in the marriage descriptions that emerge when what has been held to be a good, long-lasting marriage ends through the death of a partner. I shall close this chapter with two narratives that provide a good illustration of local concepts of intimacy.

The first involves Nuri, the approximately fifty-year-old woman mentioned earlier who lost her husband after a stable and harmonious arranged marriage that lasted more than thirty years. Two years after the death of her husband, I met Nuri again. Our first conversation took place in the presence of some of her female neighbors. One neighbor was commenting on Nuri's loss: "Nuri, poor thing! She had a really good man. Bossong looked after his family well; he was capable, reliable, good humored. They never argued, those two. They were very fond of each other; they always cared for each other (*sikarimangi*). It was a good marriage. It's not easy for Nuri to manage on her own now, particularly as she's still got two sons to marry off."

Nuri herself, who, at least superficially, continued to radiate the same relaxed contentment so typical of her all the years before, then turned to me and said: "I really miss Bossong! I know, we were often apart, when he was off traveling for weeks on end. But that's something else, something completely different. It's not just that I have to make all the decisions about our sons by myself; no, it's that nothing feels good anymore. I've become restless, I feel lonely, even when everybody else is around me."

The second narrative concerns Tokeng, who was about seventy years old. She had lost her husband, Tobo, after an arranged marriage that lasted more than fifty years. The first time I met Tokeng again was three years after her husband had died. The very lively, agile, and always cheerful woman I had known before had changed completely. She had become listless, introverted, remarkably still, and had lost a lot of weight. During a visit to Tokeng's house we were discussing all sorts of different things together with her daughter-in-law Pia as well as her neighbor Nuraeni, when Pia suddenly grasped Tokeng's hand and turned toward me:

> *Pia: Tokengku kuringi* (my Tokeng is consumed with grief)! Since Tobo died, she's like a different person. They were always in each other's thoughts (*ammaling-maling*). They were right for each other. They never spent a night apart.
>
> *Nuraeni:* Tobo was a handsome man! Tall and light skinned! And he was a very good flute player. Fine! All the women would have liked to marry a man like that. But Tokeng and Tobo had a strong *baca,* so that Tobo never yearned for other women.
>
> *Pia:* Oh, yes! Tokeng also knows a lot of *bunga-ria-ria.* She learned all that from her mother. She had told her: "Take care! It's up to you whether your man only looks at you or at other women as well!" My husband's parents really suited each other. They also never argued; they crossed words sometimes but never "deep in-side" (*pa'mai'*).
>
> *Nuraeni:* Yes, that's really true. Only a few people have marriages like that.
>
> *Tokeng* (*turning to me*): Nothing feels (*kasia'*) good anymore. Not eating, not drinking, not sleeping, not talking. Nothing is good anymore.

According to their families and neighbors, both women had had good marriages characterized by mutual care, consideration, respect, and close emotional ties. Each woman said that she still felt very alone and alienated from life even years after the death of her husband: "Nothing feels good anymore." In their arranged marriages both had attained forms of intimacy and emotional closeness that turned the loss of their partner into a heavy emotional burden.

However, what is interesting here is that their contemporaries attribute different degrees of emotional bonding to the two couples. Nuri and Bossong's marriage is never characterized as an *amaling-maling* relationship but always as *sikarimangi,* whereas Tokeng and Tobo's relationship was mostly classified as *ammaling-maling,* that is, as the most intimate form of love, as "always in each other's thoughts" and never apart. This classification is justified by describing Tokeng's emotional state after the death of her husband, which is interpreted as *kuring,* that is, an all-consuming form of sorrow accompanied by marked physical symptoms (loss of weight and appetite, listlessness) and a risk of serious illness. This most intensive form of sorrow is interpreted as an indicator for the exceptionally close emotional bond in this couple.

Furthermore, the decisively magical, supernatural components (*baca; bunga-ria-ria*) in these marriage narratives are also important. Intimacy is presented as the outcome of supernatural interventions. The phrase "had a strong *baca*" refers primarily to the *pappasiama'* ritual designed to exert a positive influence not just on the first sexual encounter but also on the entire course of the marriage. The emotional quality of a marriage is always correlated with the quality of the *baca* performed by the marriage mother (*anrongbunting*) during the *pappasiama'*. The term *baca*, which, translated literally, means "to read, to recite," describes the casting of magical spells (and also religious blessings) designed to influence an event or an intention in a positive way that will lead to success. Mostly, *baca-baca* (the plural form) are combined with specific ritual acts (*sara'*) that are attributed with the power of also bringing about that which they symbolize. The comment that Tokeng knows many *bunga-ria-ria* indicates that Tokeng, who is generally considered to have not been particularly pretty, must have used various "love charms" to keep her good-looking man from straying.

Public discourses always fall back on magical components when events or social relationships are considered to be outside the norm—in either a positive or negative sense. The close and exclusive bond between Tokeng and Tobo does not fit the typical expectations for a marriage; it is an exception that has to be explained. At this point Ratna's comment, that a high degree of intimacy can be attained only in self-made marriages, once again appears as a clear counterproposal. She expressed the belief that intimacy and bonding develop of their own accord in self-made marriages without any need for external powers or the ritual empowerment of a *pappasiama'*. In this—in no way new—discourse, love and intimacy are removed from the domain of the family and become the responsibility of the autonomous individual. The coexistence of two antagonistic conceptions in Makassar society may well be due to the simple knowledge, based on experience, that intimacy, closeness, and familiarity can be attained by taking either an externally arranged or a personally chosen path.

Notes

1. The data in this article come from several longer field studies in Sulawesi in the years 1984–85, 1989, 1990–91, 1993, and 1997.
2. For further information on Islamization, see Rössler (1990) and (1997).

3. At the peak of its power during the seventeenth century, the Kingdom of Gowa controlled an area extending from the Philippines to northern Australia. This powerful, highly organized kingdom successfully withstood the encroachments of the Dutch colonial power, which gained a foothold in Makassar only at the beginning of the twentieth century.

4. Divorce is unproblematic and a relatively frequent occurrence. Current divorce law is based on a mixture of Islamic and traditional common law that is interpreted very flexibly. In former times it was enough for both marriage partners to utter a ritualized formula to end a marriage. Nowadays, the imam desa performs divorces in an official process. To reduce the costs of an official act, all divorces carried out by mutual consent are only de facto but not de jure. As a result no reliable divorce statistics are available (see Röttger-Rössler 2004:127).

5. For more detail see Röttger-Rössler (2001).

6. Only the most important terms can be described here. For a more detailed discussion see Röttger-Rössler (2004).

7. Although now taken for granted, this was in no way the rule for the marriages of those now aged forty to fifty.

8. This is not peculiar to the Makassar. Numerous societies view the emotional phenomenon of falling in love as a "madness" or mental disease. Examples can be found in Sri Lanka (De Munck 1998:294), the Taita in Kenya (Bell 1995), and Japan (Simmons, Vom Kolke, and Shimizu 1986).

9. All narratives reported here are based on protocols that I wrote down from memory immediately after hearing the narratives in a mixture of the Indonesian and Makassar languages. Even though I always took great pains to recapture the wording of these narratives as exactly as possible, they are, nonetheless, inevitably texts that I have constructed. Tape-recorded interviews would not have been possible in the informal conversation situations in which these narratives occurred, never mind that the Makassar fundamentally reject all recorded narratives and interviews.

10. Naiba talks about her husband only by using the locally practiced teknonym: father of [name of firstborn child]. Uma, in contrast, talked about her man without using a teknonym. This may well be because he had been dead for a long time.

11. Rani married in 1977; Minne (born in 1963), in 1975. Individuals are rarely aware of their concrete biographical data. However, this can generally be reconstructed with the help of other dated events.

12. When this conversation occurred, Ancar had been working for several months on a plantation in a distant region of Sulawesi Tengah.

REFERENCES

Bell, Jim. 1995. "Notions of Love and Romance among the Taita of Kenya." In William Jankowiak, ed., *Romantic Passion: A Universal Experience?* pp. 152–65. New York: Columbia University Press.

Boothe, Brigitte. 1994. *Der Patient als Erzähler in der Psychotherapie*. Göttingen, Germany: Vandenhoeck and Ruprecht.

De Munck, Victor C. 1998. "Lust, Love and Arranged Marriages in Sri Lanka." In Victor C. De Munck, ed., *Romantic Love and Sexual Behavior: Perspectives from the Social Sciences*, pp. 285–300. Westport, Conn.: Praeger.

Hatfield, Elaine. 1988. "Passionate and Companionate Love." In Robert Sternberg and M. Barnes, eds., *The Psychology of Love*, pp. 191–217. New Haven, Conn.: Yale University Press.

Hendrick, S. and C. Hendrick. 1992. *Romantic Love*. Newbury Park, Calif.: Sage.

Quasthoff, Uta. 1980. *Erzählen in Gesprächen: Linguistische Untersuchungen zu Strukturen und Funktionen am Beispiel einer Kommunikationsform des Alltags*. Tübingen, Germany: Narr.

Riessman, Catherine Kohler. 1993. *Narrative Analysis*. Qualitative Research Methods Series, no. 30. Newbury Park, Calif.: Sage.

Rössler, Martin. 1990. "Striving for Modesty: Fundamentals of Religion and Social Organization of the Makassarese Patuntung." *Bijdragen tot de Taal-, Land-en Volkenkunde* 146 (2–3): 289–324.

——. 1997. "Facets of Islamization and the Reshaping of Identities in Rural South Sulawesi." In Robert W. Hefner and Patricia Horvatich, eds., *Islam in an Era of Nation-States: Politics and Religious Renewal in Muslim Southeast Asia*, pp. 275–308. Honolulu: University of Hawaii Press.

Röttger-Rössler, Birgitt. 1993. "Autobiography in Question: On Self-presentation and Life Description in an Indonesian Society." *Anthropos* 88:365–73.

——. 2001. "Shared Responsibility: Some Aspects of Gender and Authority in Makasar Society." In R. Tol, C. van Dijk, and G. Acciaioli, eds., Authority and Enterprise: Transactions, Traditions, and Texts among the Bugis, Makarese, and Selayarese, pp. 143–60. Leiden, Netherlands: KITLV Press.

——. 2002. "Aspekte ethnologischer Emotionsforschung." *Zeitschrift für Ethnologie* 127:147–62.

——. 2004. "Die kulturelle Modellierung des Gefühls. Ein Beitrag zur Theorie und Methodik ethnologischer Emotionsforschung anhand indonesischer Fallstudien." *Göttinger Studien zur Ethnologie*. Vol. 12. Münster, Germany: LiT.

Simmons, C. H., A. Vom Kolke, and H. Shimizu. 1986. "Attitudes toward Romantic Love among American, German, Japanese Students." *Journal of Social Psychology* 126 (3): 327–36.

Tennov, Dorothy. 1979. *Love and Limerence: The Experience of Being in Love*. New York: Stein and Day.

7. Love Work in Sex Work (and After)
Performing at Love

Denise Brennan

This chapter explores the shifting meanings and practices of sex, marriage, and romantic love in a sex-tourist destination in the Dominican Republic.[1] I argue that in a place where sex and tourism are the main industries, what I call a sexscape, sex and love between foreigners and Dominicans take on new meanings and purposes. Of course "love" cannot be measured or proved in any setting. But what is of interest for this book is that practices that are assumed to indicate romantic love in many cross-cultural settings are suspected of having other purposes in this tourist setting. No relationship between foreigners and Dominicans escapes scrutiny. After all, successful performance of love can lead to marriage, which can lead to legal migration off the island. In this context of transnational desires and economic ambitions, these relationships become fodder for the gossip mill. "So are they really in love?" is a common response by both Dominicans and foreign residents living in Sosúa, a tourist town on the north coast, when they hear about a relationship between a Dominican and a foreigner. The possibility of love for migration is mentioned almost immediately and then either waved away or confirmed.

In Sosúa we see how Dominicans may try to maximize sexual opportunities and use marriage as a migration strategy. Marriage in a tourist economy—especially in an internationally known sex-tourist destination—often has nothing to do with emotion-driven love or romance. In fact, in

Sosúa, Sosúans talk about two kinds of marriage that grow out of different understandings and uses of love. There is marriage *por amor* and marriage *por residencia*. Marriage *por amor*, the "real thing," is understood by Sosúans in the context of Sosúa as sexscape, as driven by romance and emotional needs rather than strategy and financial needs (*marriage por residencia*, or for a visa). At the discos, bars, and beaches any Dominican can meet—and perhaps marry—a foreigner. Love takes on multiple meanings when resort workers (men and women), female sex workers, and the men known as "sanky-pankies" try to parlay their access to foreign tourists into marriage proposals and visa sponsorships.[2]

This chapter recounts how sex workers—and former sex workers—marry individuals as a strategy to get ahead. They use the discourse and practices of romantic love to secure marriage proposals for a visa. Why waste a marriage certificate on romantic love when it can be transformed into a visa? In Sosúa there is a kind of sexual labor continuum onto which we can map times in poor women's lives when they might work in the formal sex trade, as well as other times when former sex workers might build transactional sexual relationships outside the formal sex trade.[3] This continuum of women's strategic use of sexual labor—and of "love work"—underscores how difficult it is for poor women to get themselves and their families out of poverty.

MANIPULATION AND LOVE

Rebhun aptly expresses just how difficult it is to do research on love because of the "slippery nature" of emotions: "Now conscious, now unconscious, now openly expressed, now indirectly expressed, and always manipulated" (1999:11).[4] Even though sex workers in Sosúa talk about the possibility of marriage *por amor*, I only rarely heard sex workers describe having experienced this kind of emotion-driven love as opposed to strategy-driven love. Rather, sex workers' descriptions of what they want in relationships—in marriage or in consensual unions with either foreign or Dominican men—center not on emotions but on financial security. For Sosúa's sex workers choosing to "fall in love" with one man over another is a rational process with serious material consequences. Contrary to the notion of "falling in love" as a kind of elation that comes with losing control of one's senses or wits, for these women being in love—or pretending to be in love—requires alertness, savvy, and determination. Rebhun comments on this idea that in the United States "we tend to believe that sentiment is genuine only if it is spontaneous; conventional, required, manipulated sentiment seems false . . . and its falseness morally reprehensible." But, continues Rebhun, "deliberation and requirement are as much a part of emotion as spontaneity" (Rebhun 1999:29–30).

Some relationships are not easily described, however. Many relationships that start out as transactional (by one or both parties) can transform into something else entirely. In the sex trade, in particular, the line between love and money can become "very fuzzy," as Yos Santasombat has observed in relationships between Thai sex workers and farang men (white-skinned Westerners) (1992:15–17, cited in Hamilton 1997). In fact, many sex workers and resort workers in Sosúa hope for romantic love even while they doubt the "authenticity" of the relationships around them. Sosúans understand— indeed, expect—that many relationships beginning in their town are strategic performances on the part of Dominicans. Their skepticism about love emerges from Sosúans' knowledge that, in Arlie Hochschild's language, "active emotional labor" (1983:ix) is involved—indeed, demanded—in jobs at hotels, bars, and nightclubs. If we focus simply on the exchange of sex for money (or goods) in Sosúa, we will miss "a sense of the active emotional labor involved in the selling" (1983:ix). Sosúans know that many sex workers— and former sex workers now working at restaurants and hotels—are hard at work selling romance and love along with the other services they deliver.

MARRIAGE AS TRANSACTION

Sosúa's sex workers' transactional use of marriage is an age-old story. What is new is how marriage-as-transaction operates in a globalized world where legal crossing of national borders requires passports and visas. In Sosúa's sexscape marriage between Dominicans and Europeans (usually Germans) emerges as an economic strategy as well as a legal route to securing the papers necessary to migrate off the island. Within what Constance Clark calls the "the politics of border crossing," research on so-called mail-order brides vividly underscores how marriage to foreigners is often the only viable option for legal migration for citizens of certain countries (Clark 2001). For example, young Chinese women are able to gain the exit visas and passports that most Chinese spend years waiting for—or never get—by marrying men from Japan or Singapore through marriage introduction agencies (Clark 2001:105).[5] Research on marriage-as-transaction, such as Nicole Constable's work on marriage introduction agencies, throws into relief Western "culture-bound assumptions about what constitutes a 'good' marriage." It also demonstrates that the Western, white, and middle-class feminist critique of marriage based on traditional division of labor does not consider the calculus of women who have "worked in fields or a factory for subsistence since childhood" (Constable 2003:65). For them, marriage, even marriages that take the most traditional forms—and are not based on "love"—can be a vacation from back-breaking work and daily financial crises. With their own workload lightened (Constable describes how, for example, working-class or rural Filipinas' workdays may involve "a combination of hard work in shops, factories, or rice fields combined with domestic chores and responsibilities for an extended household" [2003:66]), their material comfort improved, and the possibilities to remit money to their families expanded, marriage for migration and economic security can be good enough. Love may not be missed.

Although some Dominican sex workers ideally might hope for love and greater gender equality in the household (as an alternative to Dominican machismo) within marriage to foreign men, most regard these marriages strictly as a business transaction.[6] I cannot attempt to determine which relationships were rooted in emotion or which grew out of strategy; however, when sex workers told me that their own relationships were based on strategy and not on emotion, the guessing was removed. Elena, a former sex worker, laughed when I asked if she was in love with the German man she married in the spring of 2001: "You know how it is. It's not love. My children and I will have more opportunities in Germany." However, it is important to keep in mind the various motivations that could shape self-reporting on love. Positing love could make Sosúan sex workers appear foolish. No matter what they feel for their foreign boyfriends, these women have an incentive to portray themselves as not naive enough to actually fall in love. Elena, for example, had earlier been abandoned by another German man, Jürgen, with whom she had set up a household in Sosúa and had a son. Elsewhere I write about this relationship as defying easy categorization, but at times it seemed to be based on emotion and at other times on strategy (Brennan 2004). And, later in this chapter, I examine a more recent turn of events in Elena's romantic and economic life.

Since Sosúan sex workers (and former sex workers) do not see marriage to foreign men as ending other romantic and sexual relationships, they know they still can share love and engage in sex they enjoy with other partners. Sex workers maintain relationships—with Dominican and foreign men—while they are married to foreign husbands. Lauren Derby's description of the "complex and contradictory structure of the Dominican family" as "characterized by concubinage, serial unions, female-headed households, de facto polygyny" helps explain why Sosúan sex workers do not conceive of marriage as either restricting their sexual life or as permanent (Derby 2000:217). Nor do they necessarily imagine living their life out in Europe but rather know they can always return to the Dominican Republic, especially after accumulating some savings.

SEXSCAPES

With its constant influx of Dominican and Haitian migrants for work in the sex and tourist trades and of European tourists for play, as well as a large foreign-resident community living there year-round, Sosúa has become a transnational sexual meeting ground. Since Sosúa has become known as a place where tourists can buy sex, Sosúa and Sosúans have experienced monumental changes. Because sex tourism has played a critical role in the town's transformation, I see it as a space inextricably tied up with transactional sex—it has become a "sexscape" of sorts. I use the term *sexscape* to refer to both a new kind of global sexual landscape and the sites within it. The word *sexscape* builds on the five terms Arjun Appadurai has coined to describe landscapes that are the "building blocks" of "imagined worlds": "The multiple worlds which are constituted by the historically situated imaginations of persons and groups spread around the globe" (1990:4). He uses the suffix -*scape* to allow "us to point to the fluid, irregular shapes of these landscapes" (with such terms as *ethnoscape, mediascape, technoscape, finanscape,* and *ideoscape*) as he considers the relationship among these five dimensions of global cultural flows (1990:6–7). Sex for sale is one more dimension of global cultural flows, and Sosúa is one site within a global economy of commercialized sexual transactions.

Sexscapes link the practices of sex work to the forces of a globalized economy. Their defining characteristics are (1) international travel from the developed to the developing world, (2) consumption of paid sex, and (3) inequality. In a sexscape such as Sosúa there are differences in power between the buyers (sex tourists) and the sellers (sex workers) that can be based on race, gender, class, and nationality. These differences become eroticized and commodified inequalities. The exotic is manufactured into the erotic—both privately in consumers' imaginations and quite publicly by entire industries that make money off this desire for difference.[7] Let me be clear: these differences, between sex workers in the developing world and sex tourists traveling from the developed world, are essential in distinguishing sexscapes in the developing world from red-light districts (or other sites where paid sex is available) in the developed world. So too are the radiating effects of consuming practices—of paid sex—that undergird social and economic life in sexscapes. Within sexscapes the sex trade becomes a focal point of a place, and the social and economic relations of that place are filtered through the nightly (and daily) selling of sex to foreigners. In contrast, the sex trade in red-light districts in the developed world—such as in Frankfurt, Rome, Brussels, or New York—by no means defines social and economic life outside these districts. Nor do the female citizens of these places necessarily become associated with sexual availability or proficiency. As Altman notes in his book *Global Sex*, although sex is "a central part of the political economy of all large cities," few cities can base their economies on sex (2001:11).[8]

When sexscapes emerge within a globalized economy, globalized hierarchies of race, class, gender, citizenship, and mobility create undeniable power differentials between the actors in these geographic spaces, which, in turn, give them unequal opportunities.[9] Sosúa offers different and often uneven opportunities for foreigners and locals, and men and women, while race and age also are factors in the differentiation of power.[10] The asymmetries and inequalities that result from the mix of differences in Sosúa reveal the "unevenness" that Appadurai describes in his discussion of modernity as "decisively at large, irregularly self-conscious, and unevenly experienced" (1996:3). In this sexscape the buyers eroticize these differences—particularly gendered and racialized differences—as part of their paid-sex experiences. Meanwhile, the sellers often struggle to capitalize on these differences. One way is through their "performance of love."

PERFORMING LOVE

Beyond the assumed transaction of sex for money, complex politics of relationships are at work in the encounters between Sosúa's sex workers and sex tourists. While sex workers represent themselves as sexually desirable and available to both attract and to anchor sex tourists to their own life and future, they also deploy love strategically. This role playing is not without costs, however, as sex workers find themselves both exploited and exploiter in a cascade of customers, suitors, boyfriends, and partners. Dominican sex workers' strategies to get ahead (*progresar*) through Sosúa's sex trade with foreign tourists—successful or not—can be viewed as an example of what Michael Smith and Luis Guarnizo (1998) label transnationalism "from below."[11] Their strategies often hinge on their performance of love. Of course, the sex trade in any locale relies on the charade that sex workers desire their clients and enjoy the sex.[12] Yet in Sosúa's sexscape some sex workers also pretend to be *in love*. Sex workers candidly admit that their relationships with foreign clients are *por residencia,* not *por amor*. In this distinction Sosúan sex workers' use of sex and marriage has a highly strategic element. With so many financial demands on them as single mothers (nearly every sex worker I met was a mother), and so few well-paying jobs available to them, Dominican sex workers in Sosúa who perform well at being in love have much at stake. Keeping transnational ties open is a daily task for some sex workers. Many send faxes simultaneously to four or five foreign clients with whom they have ongoing relationships (it costs less than US$1 to send or receive a fax at Codetel, the national phone company). For some, dropping by the Codetel office to check for incoming faxes is a daily ritual. They are considered lucky if they receive a fax instructing them to pick up money at the Western Union office in downtown Sosúa. Others receive word that their European or Canadian client/boyfriend is planning a return visit. The most envied women receive a "letter of invitation," essential to obtaining a tourist visa to visit the man in his home country.

Sex workers' active emotional labor is clear in their performance of "love" in their faxes. Sex workers less experienced at building transnational relationships come to their colleagues, such as Elena who has a proven track record of receiving money wires and return visits from clients. Elena has helped compose letters and faxes for women who were uncertain about what to do with the addresses, fax numbers, and telephone numbers clients gave them. She helped a sex worker, Carmen, for example, write a letter to a Belgian client who had sent her a money wire and then abruptly stopped corresponding with her. Carmen came to Elena because, at the time, Elena was living with Jürgen and was experienced—indeed, successful—at transnational courting. Elena's advice was simple and centered on Carmen's "performance of love": "You have to write that you *love* him and that you miss him. Write that you cannot wait to see him again. Tell him you think about him every day." Following Elena's guidelines, Carmen composed the following letter, which I helped her translate into English (his English was better than his Spanish):

> *Dear _____,*
> *I have been thinking of you every day and have been waiting for a fax to hear how you are. I got your money wire, thanks. But I still want to see you.*
> *Please send me a fax at the following number, _____, and, if possible, a fax number where I can reach you.*
> *I miss you very much and think of you all the time. I love you very much. I wait to hear from you. I hope you come to visit again very soon.*
>
> *Many kisses,*

Carmen never heard from this client again. Sensing which men are not already married, and are likely to continue corresponding and to return for future vacations (the most certain first step to receiving an invitation to visit Europe or Canada), often proves an elusive skill. While sorting through all the pictures and letters from her European clients, Nanci, for example, commented on which ones seemed the most serious about keeping in touch. She pronounced several too young and thus not likely to follow through on the relationship. During her four years in Sosúa Nanci had honed her ability to detect which transnational suitors were worth pursuing. She had been receiving money wires on and off from five or six European men at the same time. Her many and varied transnational ties were envied and difficult to replicate, yet many tried. Nanci kept a bundle of letters and faxes stashed in a spare pocketbook. She also had photos— photos of the men back home and photos of her with the men during their vacation in Sosúa. Taped to her wall were photos of at least fifteen different foreign men. Several had returned to Sosúa to see Nanci and expressed interest in bringing her to Europe and marrying her. Expressing her love for them, and how much she missed them, were central themes in Nanci's performance of love with her suitors.

SEX TRADE AS MIGRATION STRATEGY

Poor women use the sex trade as a first step to marriage and greater financial security in other sex-tourist destinations. Kamala Kempadoo, for example, writes about migrant Colombian and Dominican women who work in the sex trade in Curaçao's Campo Alegre Mirage and whose work with a client might develop into a "close and intimate" relationship that leads to marriage (Kempadoo 1998). Sylvia Chant and Cathy McIlwaine (1995) also write about the sex trade as a route to marriage—and sometimes to migration—between Europeans and Filipinas. Much like their Dominican counterparts, Filipina sex workers perceive a better life for themselves and their children in Europe. And like their Dominican counterparts, these Filipina women are locked out of opportunities for legal migration (1995:248).

Edward Bruner's (1996) description of "touristic borderzones" as "performative space[s]" calls attention to the performative aspects of tourist encounters. He writes, "The touristic borderzone is like empty space, an empty stage waiting for performance time, for the audience of tourists and for the native performers" (1996:158). Tourists on vacation often engage in behavior and activities they would never engage in at home, such as paying for sex or, as Deborah Pruitt and Suzanne LaFont observed in Jamaica, having cross-racial relationships (1995). When I interviewed male tourists in Sosúa, they often told me that they never had paid for sex at home, but since they were on vacation they thought, "Why not?" Chant and McIlwaine also found that some foreign men—who had not intended at the outset to pay for sex—buy sex in Cebu's bars in the Philippines because of "peer pressure." One man boasted to his friends, for example, that he had bought five women in one night (1995: 225). In encounters between locals and foreign tourists, locals often have more practical goals—such as laying the groundwork to receive money wires from tourists once they return to Europe—and might need to "perform" for tourists to achieve these goals, whereas foreign tourists primarily seek fun and pleasure.

Relationships in Sosúa *por residencia* also can be a kind of stage upon which Dominicans can resist racial hierarchies as well as inequalities based on gender, class, and citizenship. For example, the strategizing of Dominican women within Sosúa's sex trade sometimes has economically advantageous results. Some clients have paid for the education of the children of their "girlfriend" or have helped a sex worker get a fledgling business off the ground (such as a clothing store or hair salon). In these cases sex in a postcolonial context, much like in a colonial context, can be used as a "vehicle to master a practical world" (to achieve privileged schooling, a well-paying job in the civil service, or access to certain residential quarters) (Stoler 1997: 44). Because any use of sex between black local women and white foreign men in a postcolonial context is a "crucial transfer point of power, tangled with racial exclusions in complicated ways" (Stoler 1997:44 on Fanon 1967:63), today's sex trade is inextricably linked with the violent colonial history for Hispaniola's women. In the relationships between sex tourists and sex workers, there are similarities to the relationships between the colonizer and the colonized. I do not mean to suggest, however, that Dominican sex workers (or resort workers) are "enslaved" but want to underscore that they stand to lose more—materially—than love gone awry.[13]

Of course, not every Dominican worker in Sosúa's tourist economy tries to parlay access to foreign tourists into a marriage proposal and visa sponsorship, yet many are perceived as doing so. Sosúans (Dominicans and foreign residents) and Dominicans who live outside Sosúa brand as "sankies" a wide range of men who do not trade their bodies for money. For example, young good-looking Dominican men who have migrated to work in Sosúa's hotels, bars, and beaches often are glibly referred to or derided as sankies. Male resort workers, particularly "activity directors," often are talked about as sankies. By referring to male resort workers as "sanky-pankies," Sosúans see these men as prostituting themselves as well as sacrificing love for migration. The term is now loosely used throughout the Dominican Republic to refer to Dominican men who hit on tourist women—especially women older than they.

Female resort workers too undergo public scrutiny and risk being stereotyped as a *puta* but usually from Dominicans outside Sosúa, as Sosúans know that most women who clean, serve food, and cook in the hotels and other tourist businesses are from Sosúa, Puerto Plata, and other nearby towns. Sosúans also know that women who enter the sex trade are not from Sosúa but migrate from towns throughout the island (to protect their families left behind). However, to Dominicans outside Sosúa, women's claims that they work in Sosúa's hotels and restaurants can appear to be a cover story for working in the sex trade. Indeed, most sex workers I interviewed concealed their participation in the sex trade from their family and neighbors by claiming instead to work in Sosúa's tourist hotels and restaurants.

Without the transnational connections that can grow out of relationships with foreigners—faxes, money wires, clients' return visits, and the possibility of traveling to or moving to a client's home country—Sosúa's sex trade would be no different from sex work in any other Dominican town. Sosúa's sex trade also stands apart from many other sex-tourist destinations in the developing world because it does not involve pimps or the coercion of women into selling sex, and therefore it allows sex workers a good deal of control over their working conditions. I do not suggest that these women do not risk rape, beatings, arrest, and HIV infection; the sex trade can be dangerous, and Sosúa's trade is no exception. However, Dominican women are not trafficked into Sosúa's trade but usually are drawn to it through female social networks of family and friends who work or have worked in it. The absence of pimps in Sosúa is critical to sex workers' lives. Without them Sosúan sex workers keep all their earnings, essentially working freelance. They decide how many hours they will work, with whom, and for what price. Sosúa's sex trade allows women more choices than they would have in other sites.[14]

SEX WORKERS' ROLLER-COASTER LIVES

Despite sex workers' strategizing, however, a recurring story seems to unfold: most sex workers in Sosúa end up just getting by, rather than improving their own or their children's lives. Dominican women's migration strategies cannot work, for example, unless the European or Canadian client follows through on his promises of visa sponsorships and marriage. At any time these foreign men could stop sending money wires or decide to withhold help in the visa process.[15] Since the late 1980s, when Europeans began vacationing in Sosúa in significant numbers, only a modest number of European men have married Dominican women, let alone sponsored their migration to Europe. And while stories circulate in sex workers' circles about women living in Europe with former clients-turned-husbands, nearly every sex worker also recounts stories in which foreign men break their promises to Dominican women. Particularly striking about women's participation in Sosúa's sex trade is the impermanence of their "successes" and "failures." Foreign men are as unpredictable about stopping the transmission of money wires as they are about sending them. Promises to sponsor a woman's visa can go unfulfilled. And, of course, marriages can come to an end. Moreover, the women themselves move in and out of sex work. Kamala Kempadoo also has observed that commercial sex work is not always a "steady activity" but might occur in conjunction with other income-generating activities. It can be an activity that women (and men) take up for short periods or as part of an "annual cycle of work" (1998:3–4). In Sosúa's sex-tourist trade women engaging in paid commercial sex with foreign tourists do not simultaneously work in other income-generating activities. However, former sex workers may combine paid work (outside the sex trade) with "love work": a transactional approach to romantic and sexual relationships with foreign men as boyfriends. And, of course, since sex work and the relationships that grow out of it—both long-term relationships and marriage—are business transactions, sex workers and former sex workers do not see these relationships with clients as restricting their sexual or romantic lives. Rather, sex workers maintain sexual—and possibly romantic—relationships with Dominican men while they simultaneously build and maintain a roster of transnational suitors.

Only a few women I met during my first trip to Sosúa in 1993 were still working in Sosúa's sex trade in 2003. Most had long since returned to their families in towns and cities throughout the island. Those who stayed in Sosúa had moved on from sex work. Some married Dominican men—usually a man who was their boyfriend while they were in sex work. These marriages, sex workers explain, are for "love." Others still look to foreign men for resources and visas. I never could have predicted back in 1993 that some of them—who had no ties to men overseas and who were not actively seeking to establish them—would eventually marry foreign men and move to Europe. And of course, the reverse has happened: women who moved with foreign men to their home countries in Europe have seen the dissolution of their relationship, usually resulting in the woman's return migration from Europe to the Dominican Republic and downward mobility.

LIFE AFTER SEX WORK

Former sex workers who stay on in Sosúa (rather than return to their home villages and cities), may continue to look for foreign men, but this time as boyfriends, not as clients. Like the liaisons that grew out of the women's participation in the "formal" sex trade, these relationships, they candidly explain, also are for practical reasons. We cannot call postformal sex-work relationships *sex work* in a strict sense of the term since their boyfriend/husband does not hand them money after each sexual act. But a transaction transpires nonetheless. Years after Elena and Mari left the sex trade, foreign men still figured in their income strategies.

ELENA AND MARI

Elena's life, like that of so many poor women, has been full of changes—some as a result of her decisions and actions, others as a result of forces out of her control. After working as a server in several of Sosúa's restaurants, dancing in bachata contests, and "investing in" successfully—various illegal pyramid schemes and lotteries, Elena married a German man (not Jürgen) she met while she was a server. She calculated that this marriage *por residencia* was the only way that she could establish an economically secure life for her family. In her nearly ten years of living in Sosúa's sexscape, Elena had seen thousands of foreign men hanging out in Sosúa's bars and nightclubs looking to have sex—and in some cases for romance—with Dominican women. She watched countless Dominican women (and men) migrate to town from throughout the island to find work and/or to meet foreign lovers. And she had said goodbye to friends as they moved to Europe with foreign men. In short, Elena knew as well as any veteran of Sosúa's sex trade that unless she married a foreign man who could sponsor her overseas migration, she would continue to live hand to mouth. She busied herself that spring with the details of getting a visa to visit her husband, who lived permanently in Germany, as the first step to moving there with her family.

Yet more changes were to come for Elena. Elena's new German husband is no longer in her life. He never returned to Sosúa, nor did he make arrangements to secure a visa for her to travel to Germany. They speak on the phone occasionally, but Elena is sensible enough to recognize that it is foolish to wait for him to send money, let alone for his help with a visa. In fact, she waits for nobody and instead solves problems on her own when they arise. After working for a few months at a bar in downtown Sosúa, she quit because the German bar owner paid poorly and was verbally abusive to her and to the other Dominican employees (calling them stupid and incompetent). Since then she has been working at a bar on the beach, with her friend Mari. Elena selected this job because the owner, a Dutch citizen, works most of the year in Santo Domingo. In his absence she manages the bar and answers to no one. She continues to be the sole breadwinner, taking care of her two children, and she has been helping one of her older sisters who lives with her and has work, cleaning hotel rooms, only occasionally.

Both Elena and Mari have been out of the formal sex trade for years. They do not go to bars to find clients who are looking to pay money in exchange for sex. Yet sex and romance—or the performance of romance and love—with foreign men is still an earning strategy for them. Mari had lived in Germany with a German man she married, left him, and then moved back to Sosúa, where she took up with a Dutch man, Edgar. Quite unexpectedly, Mari's German husband followed her to Sosúa. A quiet man in his early to midsixties, Claus decided to live half the year in Sosúa because, he explained, referring to Mari and her daughter, "his wife and daughter were here." Although he is not the biological father of his stepdaughter, Claus is a caring and generous father, Elena and others report. Mari is unimpressed, however, and is bored with Claus. She had initially left him in Germany because she "did not love him." But his move to Sosúa has translated into greater material comfort for Mari and her daughter. The three of them live together, renting the second floor of a cement house in Sosúa that has the nicest kitchen I have seen in Los Charamicos (the "Dominican side" of Sosúa), with a refrigerator, stove, sink with running water, Formica countertops, and wooden cabinets. Mari explains that she continues to work at the bar on the beach with Elena as a way to "get out of the house," but most afternoons Claus is there anyway. He watches her flirt with male customers, usually younger than he. He sits quietly while Mari bounces from one customer's lap to another, boisterously teasing them, as they lavish attention on her.

Mari has sex with Claus, and in exchange he pays the bills for her and her daughter to live well. Her countertops and matching cabinetry—which none of her friends' homes has—are symbols of their arrangement. Mari, however, risks having no long-term benefit from this relationship. If she and Claus split up, she is likely to end up empty-handed, just like Elena when Jürgen kicked her out and eventually sold off the furniture he had purchased. Mari would have to leave behind the living-room furniture set, television, and, of course, the kitchen. Claus has given Mari jewelry, including a sizable gold heart necklace with four small rubies, that she could always pawn. Moreover, since Claus pays all household expenses, Mari could save the money she earns at the bar. But, unlike her girlfriends, nearly everyday Mari has on a new outfit, which provokes criticism from Elena and her sister: "Mari loves money. It is all she cares about. She spends any money she gets." And, they emphasized, she spends it only on herself. Whereas Elena had negotiated with Jürgen for him to pay for her daughter to attend private school, Mari has not tried to work out the same arrangements. In fact, Elena and her sister are worried about Mari's daughter, since Mari often has left her in the care of others—a long and rotating list of female family members scattered throughout the island, and friends, including Elena and her sister. Elena took care of Mari's daughter while Mari lived in Germany, and not once, Elena explained, did Mari send money to help with the girl's care.

Mari's obvious impatience with Claus, indicated by the rolling of her eyes when he is around, and the silent treatment she gives him, along with her flagrant flirting with other foreign men, does not bode well for their relationship. Claus is also well aware that Mari is still involved with her Dutch boyfriend, Edgar, also in his early sixties, with whom she had been living in Sosúa after she left Claus in Germany.

***

Since her relationships with both Claus and Edgar have collapsed, Mari lives in a smaller apartment with her daughter. And Elena married a Dominican man (in a consensual union) and had a baby girl. But Elena faces ongoing challenges in this relationship; her "husband" has another family—and financial obligations—in a nearby town. Both women still work on the beach where they meet foreign men every day. This access to foreigners provides them with opportunities to feign love and use sex as short-term survival earning and long-term advancement strategies. In this sexscape this kind of "love work"—and the sex that is a part of it—will continue to forge new meanings and uses for marriage, sex, and romantic love.

NOTES

1. I have changed all the names of Sosúans, including sex workers, their boyfriends, husbands, and clients. This chapter draws from field research that I conducted in Sosúa in the summer of 1993, 1994–95, the summer of 1999, and January and July 2003. I owe a great debt to the Dominican HIV outreach and education nongovernmental organization CEPROSH, especially to its peer educators (known as *mensajeras de salud*).

2. Men who are gossiped about as sankies do not use this term to describe themselves. Mark Padilla's findings in a research project with two hundred male sex workers in Santo Domingo and Boca Chica suggest that only a small minority of those interviewed use this term to describe themselves. Rather, more commonly, the men pejoratively apply the term to others and sometimes use it when ribbing one another. Padilla finds that the term carries less stigma than the terms *puta* or *prostituta* for female sex workers, because male sex work (with female clients) seems less transgressive than female work and more in line with norms of male gender and sexuality (Padilla 2003).

3. Mark Hunter (2002) writes about schoolgirls and older women as engaging in "transactional sex" with men, either to help with subsistence or to increase their consumption possibilities.

4. Linda-Anne Rebhun was also interested in how people "describe sentiment" but moved past "vocabulary to discourse: what people talk about in relation to sentiment, how they communicate, what they say, as well as what they leave unsaid and they act out in wordless practice" (1999:11).

5. These Chinese women's transnational use of marriage, Constance Clark writes, has earned them a reputation similar to that of Sosúan sex workers', as "gold diggers" searching for foreign "airplane tickets" (2001:105).

6. Eva Illouz explores the connections between romantic love and the marketplace (1997). Marriage has long served, in many cultures, as a site for the exchange of wealth. She comments that until the beginning of the twentieth century marriage was considered to be, by all classes except for those that could not afford a ceremony, "one of the most, if not the most, important financial operations of their lives" (1997:9). Of course, reality television shows—such as *For Love or Money*, in which participants have to perform love convincingly enough to win money—have certainly served as crass pop cultural reminders that all marriages potentially contain transactional elements. In contrast, Laura Ahearn (2001) charts how Nepalese women's increased literacy has allowed them to seek love marriages—facilitated through love-letter writing—rather than "capture" or arranged marriages.

7. Analyzing exotic and erotic representations of the Pacific—such as in the movie *South Pacific*—Margaret Jolly examines how difference "stimulate(s) desire" (1997:100). Writing about Brazilian women, Angela Gilliam finds that part of the appeal of women characterized as exotic "rests within the unequal economic and social exchange between visitors and the places to which they travel as tourists" (2001:174).

8. Cities with foreign military bases are an exception. For example, see Kathy Moon's book on the sex trade that grew up around the U.S. military bases in South Korea (1997), Cynthia Enloe's analysis of the links between militarization and women's exploitation (1989), and essays in Saundra Sturdevant and Brenda Stoltzfus's edited volume (1992).

9. Although this chapter focuses on women sex workers' experiences, see Mark Padilla's 2003 research on Dominican male sex workers.

Mahler and Pessar discuss globalized hierarchies as operating "at various levels that affect an individual or group's social location" such that they "shape, discipline, and position people and the ways they think and act" (2001:446).

10. Within Sosúa's sex-tourist trade I never met women older than forty who went to the tourist bars to find foreign clients.

11. Dominican Sosúans—both sex and other workers—often use the verb *progresar* to refer to improving one's economic status.

12. See sex workers' accounts of their experiences with clients in Delacoste and Alexander (1987), McClintock (1993), Bell (1987), and Nagle (1997).

13. Angela Gilliam (2001) and Susanne Thorbek (2002a, 2002b) examine the relationship between the colonial eroticization of non-European women and the contemporary exoticization of sex workers in underdeveloped countries. In particular, both essays consider the role that the brutal display in Paris's Musée de l'Homme until the 1970s of Saartje Baartman (a young woman taken from what is now South Africa to be exhibited like an animal in Europe) has played in shaping colonial and contemporary views of black women's sexuality. The display of her body "was placed at the unsavory intersection of slavery, an Enlightenment classificatory system, and quasi-pornographic notions of medicine" (Gilliam 2001:179).

14. The debate about how scholars, activists, and sex workers understand women's sexual labor centers on issues of agency and victimization, as well as economic empowerment and powerlessness. Some assert that women are forced to choose sex work because of their race, class, nationality, colonial status, and gender and do not have a "choice." To these critics all forms of sex work are exploitative and oppressive, which is why they usually use the terms *prostitute* and *prostitution* rather than *sex worker* and *sex work*. The latter terminology recognizes that selling one's body is a form of labor that—under certain contexts—women can *choose*. While grappling with the thorny issue of whether sex work is inherently oppressive, Anne McClintock issued a warning against conflating agency with context in discussions about sex work that is helpful: "Depicting all sex workers as slaves only travesties the myriad, different experiences of sex workers around the world. At the same time, it theoretically confuses social *agency* and identity with social *context*" (1993:2–3). Rather than lumping all sex workers in all places together as victims with no control over their lives, I suggest a nuanced understanding of women's room for maneuvering within the sex trade. Sosúa's sex trade is not a story of women who use sex work simply as a survival strategy but also of women who try to use sex work as an *advancement* strategy. Marriage and migration off the island are the key goals of this strategy.

15. Constance Clark describes a similar dependency on foreign Asian men's whims as Chinese women wait for these men to pick one of them from the video collections of marriage introduction agencies. She draws on Doreen Massey's idea

of "power geometry" that "some are more in charge of [mobility] than others," with Clark's potential brides, much like Sosúa's sex workers, on the "receiving end of mobility" (Clark 2001:104; Massey 1993:61).

REFERENCES

Ahearn, Laura M. 2001. *Invitations to Love: Literacy, Love Letters, and Social Change in Nepal.* Ann Arbor: University of Michigan Press.

Altman, Dennis. 2001. *Global Sex.* Chicago: University of Chicago Press.

Appadurai, Arjun. 1990. "Disjuncture and Difference in the Global Cultural Economy." *Public Culture* 2 (2): 1–24.

——. 1996. *Modernity at Large: Cultural Dimensions of Globalization.* Vol. 1. Minneapolis: University of Minnesota Press.

Bell, Laurie, ed. 1987. Good Girls, Bad Girls: Feminists and Sex Trade Workers Face to Face. Toronto: Seal Press.

Brennan, Denise. 2004. *What's Love Got to Do with It? Transnational Desires and Sex Tourism in the Dominican Republic.* Durham, N.C.: Duke University Press.

Bruner, Edward M. 1996 "Tourism in the Balinese Borderzone." In Smadar Lavie and Ted Swedenburg, eds., *Displacement, Diaspora and Geographies of Identity,* pp. 157–79. Durham, N.C.: Duke University Press.

Chant, Sylvia and Cathy McIlwaine. 1995. *Women of a Lesser Cost: Female Labour, Foreign Exchange and Philippine Development.* London: Pluto Press.

Clark, Constance D. 2001. "Foreign Marriage, 'Tradition,' and the Politics of Border Crossings." In Nancy N. Chen, Constance D. Clark, Suzanne Z. Gottschang, and Lyn Jeffry, eds., *China Urban: Ethnographies of Contemporary Culture,* pp. 104–22. Durham, N.C.: Duke University Press.

Constable, Nicole. 2003. *Romance on a Global Stage: Pen Pals, Virtual Ethnography, and "Mail-Order" Marriages.* Berkeley: University of California Press.

Delacoste, Frederique and Priscilla Alexander, eds. 1987. *Sex Work: Writings by Women in the Sex Industry.* Pittsburgh: Cleis Press.

Derby, Lauren. 2000. "The Dictator's Seduction: Gender and State Spectacle during the Trujillo Regime." In William H. Beezley and Linda A. Curcio-Nagy, eds., *Latin American Popular Culture: An Introduction,* pp. 213–39. Wilmington, Del.: Scholarly Resources.

Enloe, Cynthia. 1989. *Bananas, Beaches and Bases: Making Feminist Sense of International Politics.* Berkeley: University of California Press.

Fanon, Frantz. 1967. *Black Skin, White Masks.* New York: Grove.

Gilliam, Angela M. 2001. "A Black Feminist Perspective on the Sexual Commodification of Women in the New Global Culture." In I. McClaurin, ed., *Black Feminist Anthropology: Theory, Politics, Praxis, and Poetics,* pp. 150–86. New Brunswick, N.J.: Rutgers University Press.

Hamilton, Annette. 1997. "Primal Dream: Maculinism, Sin and Salvation in Thailand's Sex Trade." In Manderson and Jolly, *Sites of Desire, Economies of Pleasure,* pp. 145–65.

Hochschild, Arlie Russell. 1983. *The Managed Heart.* Berkeley: University of California Press.

Hunter, Mark. 2002. "The Materiality of Everyday Sex: Thinking beyond 'Prostitution.'" *African Studies* 61 (1): 99–120.

Illouz, Eva. 1997. *Consuming the Romantic Utopia: Love and the Cultural Contradictions of Capitalism.* Berkeley: University of California Press.

Jolly, Margaret. 1997. "From Point Venus to Bali Ha'i: Eroticism and Exoticism in Representations of the Pacific." In Manderson and Jolly, *Sites of Desire, Economies of Pleasure,* pp. 99–122.

Kempadoo, Kamala. 1998. "The Migrant Tightrope: Experiences from the Caribbean." In Kamala Kempadoo and Jo Doezema, eds., *Global Sex Workers: Rights, Resistance and Redefinition,* pp. 124–38. New York: Routledge.

McClintock, Anne. 1993. "Sex Workers and Sex Work: An Introduction." *Social Text* 11 (4): 1–10.

Mahler, Sarah J. and Patricia R. Pessar. 2001. "Gendered Geographies of Power: Analyzing Gender across Transnational Spaces." *Identities* 7 (4): 441–59.

Manderson, Lenore and Margaret Jolly, eds. 1997. *Sites of Desire, Economies of Pleasure: Sexualities in Asia and the Pacific,* pp. 145–65. Chicago: University of Chicago Press.

Massey, Doreen. 1993. "Power Geometry and a Progressive Sense of Place." In John Bird, Barry Curtis, Tim Putnam, G. Robertson, and Lisa Tickner, eds., *Mapping the Future: Local Culture, Global Change,* pp. 59–69. New York: Routledge.

Moon, Katherine. 1997. *Sex among Allies: Military Prostitution in U.S.-Korea Relations.* New York: Columbia University Press.

Nagle, Jill, ed. 1997. *Whores and Other Feminists.* London: Routledge.

Padilla, Mark B. 2003. "'Me la busco': Male Sex Work, Political Economy, and Sexual Identity in the Dominican Republic." Ph.D. diss., Emory University, Department of Anthropology.

Pruitt, Deborah and Suzanne LaFont. 1995. "For Love and Money: Romance Tourism in Jamaica." *Annals of Tourism Research* 21 (2): 422–40.

Rebhun, Linda-Anne. 1999. *The Heart Is Unknown Country: Love in the Changing Economy of Northeast Brazil.* Stanford, Calif.: Stanford University Press.

Smith, Michael Peter and Luis Eduardo Guarnizo. 1998. *Transnationalism from Below.* New Brunswick, N.J.: Transaction.

Stoler, Ann. 1997. "Educating Desire in Colonial Southeast Asia: Foucault, Freud and Imperial Sexualities." In Manderson and Jolly, *Sites of Desire, Economies of Pleasure,* pp. 27–47.

Sturdevant, Saundra Pollock and Brenda Stoltzfus, eds. 1992. *Let the Good Times Roll.* New York: New Press.

Thorbek, Susanne. 2002a. Introduction to Susanne Thorbek and Bandana Pattanaik, eds., *Transnational Prostitution: Changing Global Patterns*, pp. 1–9. New
York: Zed.

——. 2002b. "The European Inheritance: Male Perspectives." In Susanne Thorbek
and Bandana Pattanaik, eds., *Transnational Prostitution: Changing Global Patterns*, pp. 24–41. New York: Zed.

8. "She Liked It Best When She Was on Top"

Intimacies and Estrangements in Huli Men's Marital and Extramarital Relationships

Holly Wardlow

*A*nthropologists and other scholars often invoke New Guinea to provide evidence of the myriad social, ethno-ontogenetic, and cosmological meanings that humans can confer on sexual practices, substances, parts, and relationships. Lest students assume that genital interactions are always about pleasure, pair bonding, or reproduction, ethnographic cases from New Guinea show that "sexual" practice can also be about ensuring proper masculine growth and development, revitalizing the body politic, or replenishing the fecundity of the earth (Herdt 1993; Knauft 1986, 1993; Kelly 1976). Indeed, the purposes of precolonial ritualized sexual practice in some New Guinea societies departed so markedly from naturalized Western assumptions about sex that scholars have questioned whether they should be considered "sexual" at all, raising the question of what exactly is meant and demarcated by the term *sex* (Elliston 1995; Clark 1997; Jolly and Manderson 1997; Pigg and Adams 2005).

Perhaps because of the engrossing metaphysical nature of such questions, somewhat less ethnographic and theoretical attention has been paid to love, romantic attachment, and the intricate emotional intimacies of marital sexuality or, in the era of HIV/AIDS, of extramarital sexual liaisons (but see Leavitt 1991; Wardlow 2006a). This scholarly neglect of love probably also stems from ethnographers' observations of pronounced male dominance, gender avoidance, and even "sexual antagonism" in many traditional Papua New Guinea societies (Herdt and Poole 1982; Meggitt 1964; Langess 1967, 1974; Glasse 1974). As Carol Jenkins describes a recurrent theme in contemporary male discourse about women, "the female is objectified as the seductive, dangerous other. . . . Intimate relations of long duration with females should be avoided . . .[and] it is considered a sign of weakness and threatening of future sickness and misfortune should a man spend time with a woman for anything more than the pursuit of reproduction" (1996:198; see also NSRRT and Jenkins 1994). Jenkins's recent research, as well as that of other scholars (Borrey 2000; Hammar 1999; Knauft 1997; Wardlow 2006b; Zimmer-Tamakoshi 1997), indicates that male misgivings about female personhood—and about the threats that women are perceived as posing to male dominance—persist in the contemporary context and are often intensified by increasing class distinctions, declining economic opportunity, increased female mobility and autonomy, and the emergence of criminal gangs and other masculinist subcultures.

And yet it is also important to bear in mind that Papua New Guinea has experienced a long history of Christian missionization—which tends to emphasize the sanctity of marriage and the importance of mutual respect between spouses (if not necessarily gender equality)—as well as exposure to globalized popular media (Wardlow 1996), such as Hollywood films and, more recently, bootleg Nigerian video compact disks (which almost invariably concern love, marriage, and infidelity). Thus contemporary gender relations are shaped by myriad influences and, of course, are not characterized only by new forms of "sexual antagonism." In this chapter I discuss Huli men's attitudes toward, and experiences of, marriage, marital sexuality, and extramarital sexual liaisons. What is revealed is a complex sexual and emotional landscape in which precolonial ideologies and practices remain compelling for many men, although they may now confine these ideologies to certain kinds of marriages or certain stages of the life cycle. Moreover, there does seem to be a significant pattern in which men abide by traditional sexual taboos in the context of their marital life but seek out "modern" sexualities in their extramarital life.

CONTEXT AND METHODS

I draw on data from two research periods for this chapter. From 1995 to 1997 I conducted doctoral fieldwork about Huli women's experiences of marriage and about *pasinja meri* (literally, passenger women; women who exchange sex for money; see Wardlow 2004, 2006b). In 2004 I returned for six months of research on married women's risk for HIV. Much of the latter research entailed interviews with married men of different generations about their marriage and their extramarital relationships.[1] The 2004 research was part of a larger comparative project in which four other researchers and I used the same methods and asked the same interview questions in our respective field sites (Papua New Guinea, Nigeria, Uganda, Mexico, and Vietnam) with the goal of identifying the social and economic structures that put married women at risk for HIV.[2] In the seven years between these two research periods, my field site, Tari, Southern Highlands Province, had declined dramatically.

Tari is a small town built around an airstrip. On one side of the airstrip is the hospital and a primary school, and on the other is the market, some small retail stores, the courthouse and police station, and housing for civil servants. Outside town are three large mission stations (Catholic, United, and Evangelical Church of Papua) and a large boarding high school run by Catholic nuns. Even in the mid-1990s Tari was not considered a safe or pleasant place. The one large store and the small bank had been held up by armed criminal gangs, and vehicles were also often held up on the roads around Tari and on the main road between Tari and Mendi, the provincial capital. In 2004, however, the situation seemed much worse. The kina, Papua New Guinea's currency, was worth approximately one-third of its value ten years earlier, and the costs of basic goods had risen accordingly, but people's wages and the prices they could demand for their goods at market had not. Increasing crime and election-related violence in 2002 had resulted in the closure of many stores, the post office, and the bank; the phones and electrical power were also not in service. This situation had precipitated the exodus of many government employees, which resulted in the closure of some primary schools and health centers in the area. The services that remained open were often understaffed and had ongoing problems obtaining essential supplies.

The principle effects of this situation on marriage and sexual practice were twofold. First, it was increasingly difficult for young people to get married. Bridewealth remains a robust institution among the Huli, and, in fact, the amount demanded by women's families had increased from an average of twenty-four pigs in the mid-1990s to thirty pigs in 2004. Moreover, although people typically speak of bridewealth in terms of pigs, most families demand that some of the amount be given in cash, and because economic opportunities have declined, young men and their families find it difficult to obtain the money. Young men with whom I spoke talked of having to leave the community to find work elsewhere, and one popular strategy was to go to Porgera, site of the Porgera Joint Venture gold mine, in order to search (illegally) through the mine's scrap heaps for whatever gold they could find. The danger of this strategy, and the perpetual postponement of marriage, was distressing to the women waiting at home, and it often put them in conflict with their natal family when they tried to persuade the family to lessen the amount of bridewealth required. A second consequence of the economic deterioration was the increasing numbers and visibility of women who exchanged sex for money. One theme that emerged in almost all the men's interviews was just how easy it was to saunter through the marketplace and find women who were willing to meet up later for a brief, paid sexual rendezvous. Indeed, many men articulated this as a reason for their extramarital relationships: the availability of women who wanted to exchange sex for money was too great a temptation for the men to decline. As one man said, "We would have to blindfold ourselves not to see all the willing women here now."

MARITAL INTIMACIES AND ESTRANGEMENTS

Health surveys, such as the widely used Demographic and Health Survey (DHS), often ask questions about "marital coital frequency"—that is, how often a person has sex with his or her spouse—typically in order to assess a couple's potential need for contraception.[3] In this study we also asked about "coital frequency," both in order to get a sense of typical marital practice in each of our research sites (or at least a sense of whether there was such a thing), and—in combination with a number of other questions—as a potential index of emotional closeness between spouses. However, many Huli men, particularly of the older generation but also in the middle-aged group, forthrightly asserted that the question made no sense and that they couldn't answer it. "That's not how we do it. It's not a matter of number of times per week or per month. We do it during the times that we are supposed to do it" was a typical response.

What these men were referring to was the traditional Huli practice in which spouses had sex only on days 11–14 of the wife's menstrual cycle

(Frankel 1980, 1986). This sexual regimen was one among a range of practices intended to protect the male body and ensure a married couple's fertility. More than the female body, the male body is conceptualized as naturally beautiful, pure, and socially compelling but also highly vulnerable to the powerful and potentially deleterious effects of female reproductive substances. Having sex at any other time than these four days was considered—and still is by some men—dangerous to a man's health, leading to premature aging, bodily decline, the loss of one's social appeal, and worsening economic fortunes. In the past, when husbands and wives lived in separate residences, a woman would hang red leaves outside her house to indicate to her husband that her period had begun. Her husband would then stay away for ten days but during this time would—in concert with his wife—engage in cleansing rituals, with the understanding that married bodies are permeable to each other's states and thus that a husband is weakened by his wife's condition, even in the absence of actual physical contact.

Even now, when most married couples live together in one house (though they usually do not sleep in the same room and often keep themselves and their belongings on their respective sides of the house), a husband will decamp to the local clan's men's house (still a highly robust social space) when his wife is menstruating. Alternatively, a wife will make a point of circumscribing her body's powers by not touching, cooking for, speaking to, or handing objects to her husband for the duration of her menses. In the 2004 interviews the men who followed such practices expressed a variety of emotional investments in them: a few were anxiously focused on their own bodily health, some asserted that the practices were as much for family well-being as their own, and some, with lots of chuckles, made a point of informing the interviewer that they enjoyed themselves sexually as much as possible during the four "safe" days and that abstinence during the rest of the month was merely a prudent and ingrained healthy habit.

Many also said that they had been taught that not only was a wife's body least dangerous and most fertile on days 11–14 of her menstrual cycle but also that she was most concupiscent during that window of time. As one older man said, "Nowadays men don't know when a wife is eager for it or not. Before, when we followed the ancestral ways, there was a date—meaning we knew how to count from when her period began, count one day, then another, then another, then you reach day nine, then day ten, and then the woman is eager for it, and you can go have sex with her." Men repeatedly used the Huli word *pobo,* which literally means heat, to refer both to a woman's reproductive energies, which were said to be at their most powerfully fertile on days 11–14, and to refer to a woman's sexual desire, which was also said to be at its peak during this time. Indeed, for some men these were not two different things: reproductive "heat" and desire were synonymous, or at least always concurrent, and thus one benefit of the traditional sexual regimen was that a husband never had to worry—as more modern men do nowadays, older men said—about whether a wife was in the mood and what to do about it if she wasn't.

Most men in the older generation and many in the middle-aged generation had, upon marriage, also received official instructions from a *gamuyi* (literally, holder of spells) or *manayi* (literally, holder of wisdom or cultural knowledge), men known to be well versed in traditional gender-avoidance taboos and ritual healing. These instructions consisted primarily of rules, taboos, and spells, about how to have marital sex safely and how to ensure fertility and success in reproduction. For example, two old men spoke of learning to apply sticky red tree oils to both their own and their wives' genitals before sex in order to enhance fertility and to avoid unprotected contact between powerful reproductive parts. Many more men spoke of learning to carry out postcoital ablutions that involved drinking bespelled springwater (see also Frankel 1986:104–8 for a similar description of these instructions). In general, these teachings emphasized that marital sex was strictly for reproduction and should be scrupulously managed in terms of timing, venue, and bodily technique. One should not "*guap guap nating,*" which literally means "go up, go up nothing"—that is, have sex with no purpose or just for pleasure.

Fertility, health, and proper conjugal interpersonal relations were also articulated by most older and many middle-aged male interviewees as the reasons why spouses should have sex only in the "traditional" position with the man on top. The linguistic anthropologist Laurence Goldman pointed out long ago a gendered pattern that reverberates throughout Huli language and practice in which "women should be underneath men" (1983). This commonplace aphorism refers broadly to the cultural imperative of male dominance in politics, religion, and the domestic sphere, but it is also instantiated in more literal ways, both spatially and corporeally: men's houses are always located higher up on a hillside than women's houses, women should never stand while men are still sitting, men often stand upright during public forums while women sit on the ground, and, in the past, when there were separate walking paths for men and women in some areas, men always took the higher path. Not surprisingly, this spatiomoral rule is also meant to be followed in sexual practice. Thus, as one old man said about the sexual education he had received upon marriage, "The *manayi* did not teach me about different sexual styles or positions—he said that the woman should be underneath and that the man should lift himself up on his hands or elbows in order to minimize contact with his wife's body. And with all my wives I have followed these teachings and only done this style. . . . And what the traditional healer said has come true. I still have lots of strength to do agricultural work, and I attribute my strength, my good fortune, my renown in the community, and my longevity to the fact that I always followed the rules taught to me." Further, some older men and middle-aged men said that they had been taught that spouses should remain partially clothed during sex and that a man should not gaze at or touch his wife's genitals, again in order to minimize any contact that might be deleterious to a man's beauty, health, and economic fortunes.

It is important not to assume that such practices automatically enforce emotional distance between spouses or diminish the erotic dimensions of marital sexuality. While these are, in fact, two of the overt purposes of these practices, it is possible, of course, for individuals to invest them with their own meanings. Thus, for example, two male interviewees hinted that such practices could be titillating. Moreover, many middle-aged and even some older men broke with these rules altogether. One old man, who was arguably the most "traditional" of the interview sample—as a young man he had participated in a "bachelor cult," he had married a woman chosen by his parents as soon as he left the bachelor cult, and throughout his married life he had had sex only with his two wives on days 11–14 of their menstrual cycles—had this to say about sex with his first wife: "My wife and I talked about the traditional customs regarding sexual technique and whether to follow them, and we eventually decided to abandon them. I know all the ancestral rules very well, but we really like to—. I mean she really liked me, and I liked her, and we really liked to have sex together, and we developed our own styles of doing it. She pulls on my beard, and I run my fingers through her pubic hair and throw her arms over her head, and we—. Well, we have discovered our own ways of doing it. So we just decided to forget about the old rules." Nevertheless, most men who followed these sexual guidelines spoke of them as reinforcing what they considered not only a proper physical, but also a proper emotional, distance between husband and their wife.

Indeed, a few men in the study had deliberately adopted these practices in order to lend legitimacy to their already emotionally distant behavior with their wife. Specifically, there were a few cases of well-educated, middle-aged men who had chosen their first wife—often a schoolmate or coworker—and who said that since they and their wife were educated and loved each other, practicing the customary sexual taboos would have felt "strange" and "*bush kanaka tumas*" (too unsophisticated and backward). After the fractious dissolution of their intimate and companionate first marriage, these men eventually submitted to an arranged marriage, primarily because their kin were urging them to "behave like adult men" by settling down and having children. With the second wife, who typically was not well educated and did not have a job, these men often followed the "traditional" sexual practices—including living in separate houses, eating separately, and having marital sex principally for the purpose of reproduction. They even paid *manayi* to teach them the traditional rules of marital conduct since most had expressly rejected learning them for their first marriage. However, becoming rigid "neotraditionalists" appeared to be less about rediscovering and espousing custom and more about using customary practice to publicly defend an emotional distance from a wife they weren't in love with. In other words, these men didn't feel emotionally close to the wife of their second, arranged marriage, and they embraced traditional gender-avoidance practices in order to justify to this wife and her family not spending much time in the domestic sphere. As one forty-three-year-old man said,

> I just do it the traditional way with my second wife. My first wife and I tried some of the things that knowledgeable people do, some ways that are in books. We read a book and tried what we read. That was with my first wife. We met and were married outside of Tari, and we were in love. And so I would be completely naked, and she would be completely naked, and we would lie next to each other that way, in a bed, and I would hug her and we would kiss. I had seen this in movies where they showed people hugging and kissing. But the woman I am married to now, we don't do any of that. No styles. We just have sex the traditional way.

In this passage innovative sexual practice is associated with literacy, education, foreign films, urban life, modern housing, emotional intimacy, and, especially, progress. Indeed, when asked to discuss what in particular he liked about his first wife and some particular instances when she had made him happy, he talked about her having more education than he did, the classes she had taken in home economics, and how she was therefore able to take proper care of the urban house in which they were living and to teach him about nutrition, food groups, and how to cook modern store-bought foods. Novel sexual practices were similarly associated with being a modern person. In contrast, he practiced "traditional" sex with his second wife, not because he was worried about "sexual pollution" but because he didn't associate her, or this marriage, with modernity. Thus the performance of "tradition" should not necessarily be seen as the enduring, seamless, internalized continuation of earlier generations' practices. Instead, for some men it is a cultural resource expediently taken up in the context of a relationship that is less than emotionally satisfying or that doesn't match up to the "modern" marriage that they had envisioned for themselves. Also important to note is how the ideologies of progress so central to being "modern" seep into even the seemingly most private sphere of marital sexual practice.

Regardless of what these "traditional" practices meant to individual men, most of the study participants of all ages expressed far more anxiety about the potential emotional and interpersonal repercussions of departing from traditional bodily technique—in particular, the erosion of male dominance in marriage—than about physical consequences. They expressed particular concern about the likelihood of losing authority if they experienced too much sexual pleasure with a wife, who might then take the upper hand upon realizing that her husband didn't have complete mastery over his bodily desires and that she herself was the source of this chink in the masculine armor. For example, one fifty-four-year-old man who had had four wives said,

> Although I've seen blue movies, I haven't tried to do any of these things with my wives. I think the purpose of marital sex is to have children. This is our custom, and so I have sex the traditional way with my wife on her back underneath me. Actually, my second wife liked to try different kinds of styles; when I asked her to try things I'd seen in blue movies or magazines, she agreed and she enjoyed it a lot. But I think this is why she became so rebellious and defiant. She liked it best when she was on top. . . . But then I noticed that my body was getting weaker and weaker. Also I noticed that she was becoming more demanding in everyday life, and more likely to get angry with me, and that she no

longer showed me respect. So now I think all these different styles are bad. They are bad for marriage. I was really interested in trying all these different things with her, but my desire for this made me confused, and she took advantage of me. So I divorced her.

Much of the ethnographic literature about gender in Melanesia has focused on the power of reproductive substances, the vulnerabilities of the male body, and men's perceived need to protect themselves from the powerful and dangerous bodies of women. But in the 2004 interviews, as the experience of this veteran husband indicates, Huli men had more to say about the *emotional* dangers of marriage than the *corporeal* ones. In particular they feared being manipulated by a wife as a consequence of either becoming too emotionally or sexually attached to her, or being too open and allowing their wife to know them too well. Thus, as one man in his early forties said in response to a question about the nature of the conversations he typically had with his wife,

If I shared my thoughts with her—well, some women are very clever. They will study a husband, listen to him, and come to really understand his thoughts and his ways. And then they can take advantage of him and manipulate him. They have studied their husbands, and so they know them and they are better able to cheat on them or disobey them. So I follow the wisdom of the older generation. If I have instructions to give her, then I stand in the doorway or outside the house and give her the instructions while she's sitting inside the house. I am standing outside and she is sitting inside the house, and she cannot see my face or guess how I am feeling, what I am thinking, or what my plans are. There are lots of old, wise men who know our customs, and I paid one of them to teach me this kind of traditional knowledge about how husbands should interact with wives. You can have fun, relaxed conversations with a girlfriend or a sex worker but not with your wife; if you do, she'll use that information to dominate you.

Similarly, a fifty-year-old man, who asserted that he considered his wife a friend and that he would take her advice over his own natal family's, said, "My wife is not like my heart. I married her to have my children and take care of my pigs. My secrets are my secrets. That's my law for myself. I don't tell her my secrets. If I told her everything, she would use this knowledge to dominate me. That's the way women are. So I don't give or reveal all my thoughts to my wife. I think maybe coastal men do this, but we highlands men do not." Two of my four male field assistants were also adamant that a primary cause of marital strife in the contemporary context was excessive emotional intimacy between spouses. As one said, "You get to know her too well, and she gets to know you too well, and you stop respecting each other, and it's too easy to end up fighting, because you know what to say to hurt her feelings and make her angry and she knows the same about you." In fact, a few men told me that they were considering reverting to the custom of living apart from their wives in order to regain the distance that enabled smoothly functioning marital relations and the male dominance that made for a productive household. They were somewhat concerned about contravening what was seen as proper Christian practice (that is, living together in one house) but also were willing to entertain the possibility that the missionaries had simply gotten this one particular lesson wrong.

Because the 2004 research was part of a multisited comparative project, the interview protocol included questions that I might not have thought to ask. For example, one researcher had found during her earlier research in Mexico that marital sexuality was considered a kind of "emotional glue" by the younger generation and that one practice that distinguished the marriages of the younger generation from those of the older was candid discussion between spouses about sexual pleasure, what each spouse enjoyed doing during sex, and so on (Hirsch et al. 2002; Hirsch 2003). Thus, in order to get a sense of the meanings and purposes of marital sexuality, the interview questionnaire used by all the researchers in the project included a question about whether the interviewee made a point of communicating sexual pleasure to his or her spouse and whether he or she could request certain sexual acts or positions. Most Huli men of all generations were quick to say that men definitely should *not* do this—not because of embarrassment or modesty but because candid expressions of pleasure or forthright requests for certain practices would (1) express an inordinate preoccupation with sex, which showed lack of self-discipline about one's bodily desires, which might make a wife think you were weak and unworthy of respect, and (2) suggest an inordinate attachment to or desire for your wife, which she might use to her advantage in some way. As one old man said, "In the men's house they say that men should not fervently express their desire for sex or their pleasure during sex. If they do, their wives will easily dominate and control them."

Being able to count on regularly experiencing sexual pleasure, though asserted by men as one of the benefits of being married, was also described by them as a potential site of manipulation. As one man, a virgin at marriage, said of marital sexuality,

> I hadn't known that kind of pleasure before. . . . I came to think that everything begins and ends with a woman's vagina. All corners of the earth, everywhere you go, everything you do—it all ends with a woman's vagina. I realized that the most intense pleasure was hidden in a woman's vagina, and I hadn't known this before. When God created man and woman he hid pleasure inside a woman's vagina. . . . Women's talk and their behavior can be like a spear or a knife that causes the worst kind of pain and anger, but their vaginas are the source of the best pleasure. So it seems like there are these two opposite things inside women. But, in fact, they are not opposites. They are both resources that women have for subordinating and manipulating men—one through the pain of their talk and the other through the intensity of the pleasure you get from them.

Marital sex, he suggested, could be used against a man precisely because the means for securing its intense pleasure was located inside another person to whom he was bound, a person who not only might have other unknown aims and intentions but who also was his wife—in other words, a person who was motivated to resist a man's will and to attempt to impose her own will upon him.

Most older and middle-aged men were sure that their wives had been taught the same guardedness about marital sexuality by their mothers or other female kin. Although no female interview subjects mentioned this, most of the middle-aged and older men were convinced that women received instructions analogous to their own about the importance of marital emotional opacity, especially in sexual matters. Thus, as one man said, "Women's mothers tell them, 'When you are experiencing tremendous pleasure, you must not reveal this. You must say that it hurts. If you express your pleasure, your husband will not respect you, he will criticize you behind your back, and he will dominate you.'" In other words, mirroring what men were taught, women (men believed) also learned that for a wife to express too much pleasure or emotional attachment might make her appear weak in her husband's eyes. Inevitably, he would be tempted to take advantage of this power imbalance, knowing that her feelings for him would make her more willing to accept poor treatment at his hands.

Some men also said that they had been taught that women were taught to resist sex, particularly early in marriage, and thus that at least until the first child was born, marital sex was a ritual in which wives should *pindi pendi* (twist and turn in an attempt to get away), and husbands should respond with ritual displays of force in which, as a few men said, "I pull her legs out from under her, topple her over, and then she lets me." In sum, many men middle aged and older described marital sex, particularly early in a marriage, as a ritual in which neither partner should openly express desire or pleasure, and in which men played the part of aggressive initiator and women performed the role of reluctant participant whose opposition is overcome through a show of force. As one fifty-year-old man described it, "According to Huli tradition, it is forbidden for wives to ask their husbands for sex. Women may not do this. So a man must touch his wife or give her some signs, and then she'll know what he wants. And then she'll say she doesn't want to, but she's lying and making excuses. So then you push her down and she'll let you have sex with her. If she's your wife and you lie her down and put her in the right position for sex, your wife can't refuse. If a wife says no, a husband shouldn't listen to this kind of talk. He shouldn't walk away angry—he should just lie her down and have sex with her."

And, although men were clear that women should play the sexually reluctant wife for their own good—as a means of maintaining a husband's respect and thus some degree of power in the marriage—it was also clear that an erotic thrill—sometimes for both partners, though the interviews with women suggest that this is certainly not always the case—was derived from this ritual dance of conquered resistance.

Certainly not all—or even most—men in the study described what could be interpreted as marital rape. While most men expressed frustration about the times when a wife refused them sexually, and while most felt entitled to have sex with their wives when they wanted to because of the bridewealth they had given for them, many also said that if a wife refused, they would assume that she had a good reason and that, even if they were irritated, they would simply leave and try again at a later time. It is also important to bear in mind that there was variability in the extent to which men took cautionary warnings about marital intimacy to heart. As one man with three wives said,

Traditionally, the custom is that wives do not express sexual desire or sexual pleasure. If they do, they will be dominated by their husbands. . . . Their mothers teach them that if they express desire, their husbands will easily rule them. But my first wife really loved me, and so she broke this traditional custom. She would tell me when she was experiencing pleasure. She said, "My mother told me that I shouldn't express my pleasure to you, but I want you to know that I am enjoying this." And so I said, "You feel that this is sweet? I'm glad, because I feel the same way." So we both broke tradition in this way. But my first wife was the only one of my wives who ever said anything like this to me.

Other interviews showed that even if husbands did not explicitly verbalize their desire, pleasure, or attachment, they sometimes showed it in other ways—through unexpected gifts, gentle teasing, praising the wife to kin (both the husband's and the wife's), or offering to do a wife's chores. Nevertheless, most men interviewed expressed varying degrees of caginess about the candid expression of emotional closeness between spouses.

At same time, and often within the same interview, many men said that they enjoyed their wife's company, trusted their wife with the money to manage the household finances, would confide in their wife over other people when faced with health or interpersonal problems, and liked sharing jokes or gossip with their wife. Almost all the men in the interview groups that were middle aged and younger spoke explicitly of having learned in church that spouses should respect each other, listen to each other, and openly share concerns and grievances rather than let them fester silently. Moreover, almost all the men who were middle aged and younger considered themselves better husbands and fathers than their own fathers had been because they spent more time interacting with their wives and children and were more attentive to their desires and needs. Thus, according to the man who said he wouldn't tell all his secrets to his wife, "My mother's house was in one area, and my father's house was in a different area. They only came together to make children. They didn't sit down and talk. My wife and I also live in separate houses, but our houses are on the same area of land, and I come to see her, and we go to the market together, and we work in our fields together. We sit down and talk to each other everyday." Many men implied that with the arrival of the missions and the conversion of most Huli to Christianity, the masculine self of the past—and especially the emphasis on maintaining spatial and emotional distance from women—had become morally problematic (see also Tuzin 1997). God wanted people to live in nuclear family households and wanted men to listen to their wife over natal kin or male peers.

Moreover, many middle-aged and younger men saw traditional gender avoidance practices as backward and unmodern. As one man in his midthirties tellingly said in response to the question of whether he and his wife followed the traditional customs, "No, we have abandoned the ancestral ways. Now we use white people's ways. Actually, these ways of doing things don't just belong to white people. What I mean is that we do things the normal way now. We do what is normal." Thus "traditional" spousal relations were often described by men as too estranged, too male dominant, and too regimented—too "according to the law," as some men said, by which they meant too controlled by what are now seen as highly restrictive taboos and rituals. And although many of the men quoted in this chapter may strike the reader as having a high level of mistrust and emotional distance, in fact, almost all the men in the study saw themselves as having—and when compared with past ethnographic descriptions of the Huli (Glasse 1968; Goldman 1983; Frankel 1986), in fact, *were* having—far more intimate and companionate marriages than their forefathers.

Significantly, none of the younger men in the study had been taught explicitly the emotionally complex marital relationality discussed earlier. In fact, the study included few newly married young men, primarily because my field assistants, all middle aged or older, were far more comfortable discussing such issues with their peers and were reluctant to ask intimate questions of young men. However, of the few young men interviewed, most had learned a stripped-down version of traditional custom that focused principally on restricting sex to days 11–14 of their wife's menstrual cycle and on having sex with their wife in a supine position. They said they were following these practices, seeing them as the best means they knew for ensuring the reproductive success of their marriage, which they saw as the most important aim for newly married couples. As one thirty-year-old man said, "I've told my wife, 'This is the way the ancestors say we should do it. If we do it this way, we will have children. And so we must do it this way.'" Most young men also seemed to see the traditional regimen as important only during the early years of a marriage (something that many middle-aged men also expressed). In other words, for younger men these practices were less about safeguarding the health of a man's body or maintaining male dominance and more about using the technique that was said to ensure that a marriage would produce children (which is not to say that male dominance wasn't important to them; in most cases it was). None of the young men had seen a *manayi* upon getting married, either because they had learned about sex already in high school or because they had engaged in premarital sex and their families thus considered the teachings a waste of time and resources (one must pay *manayi* to pass on their customary knowledge).

EXTRAMARITAL INTIMACIES AND ESTRANGEMENTS

Almost all the men interviewed expressed unease about the ability of women to exploit male sexual desire; the erosion of male dominance; the fraught question of whether the "traditional" sexual regimen was backward, unmodern, and not "normal" or whether it was uniquely valuable knowledge that a man renounced at his own peril; and how best to create a conjugal bricolage from the expansive repertoire of relational practices available today. Given these anxieties—and men's concerns about health, fertility, and social efficacy—one might assume that Huli men would not be quick to engage in extramarital sex. Indeed, ethnographic research from the 1960s through the early 1980s (Glasse 1968; Goldman 1983; Frankel 1986) suggests that a number of factors worked effectively to deter male infidelity: pronounced gender separation, which meant that men were rarely in the company of women who weren't related to them; anxieties about female sexual fluids, menstrual pollution, and the vulnerability of the male body; and the married state of almost all nubile women, which therefore usually meant that extramarital sexuality constituted the appropriation of another man's wife, a situation that could lead to violent retaliation and tribal fighting. Further, Huli custom also emphasized the danger of a man's infidelity to his wife's and children's health and well-being. According to Frankel: "[T]he child would become weakly if exposed to a father who has been adulterous. In such circumstances they would say that the child was ill as *angua haya,* which means literally that '(the father) stepped over (the child).' *Angua* is used in a number of other contexts, including the problems that follow from a woman's 'stepping over' food and so contaminating it. But here it refers to the man having 'stepped over' his wife" (1986:102).

As both men and women explained to me, spouses' bodies become bound to each other through marriage and the exchange of bridewealth, and they are consequently more permeable or vulnerable to each other's behavior—especially transgressive sexual behavior—even with no physical transmission of dangerous substances. Therefore a man's extramarital sexuality puts his body into a state of pollution—somewhat like women's bodies during menstruation, at least in terms of the danger they pose to others—that can make his wife and young children sickly and feeble. This conceptualization of the body is still taught to men, and it was one of the reasons given by young men in the study for why they did not engage in extramarital sex: since they were only beginning their reproductive lives, they had to take every precaution to protect the health and fertility of their new family. *Angua,* and its harmful effects, was also the reason given by middle-aged and older men for why they typically stayed away from the domestic sphere for a few days after engaging in extramarital sex. Not exposing one's family to one's smell, touch, or talk was thought to minimize one's polluting effects.

And yet, despite all these concerns, most middle-aged and older men in the study did regularly have sex with women other than their wives, primarily with women who sold sex, called *pasinja meri* (passenger women) by the Huli (Wardlow 2006b; see also Clark 1997; Clark and Hughes 1995; Hughes 1995). This seemingly counterintuitive behavior is not as paradoxical as it might appear. Participant observation and interviews with men revealed a number of factors contributing to high levels of extramarital sex, the most important of which is probably male labor migration and the consequent separation from wives, children, and community. Rates of male outmigration among the Huli have been high at least since the mid 1970s, in part because of colonial period economic policies that were designed to shape Southern Highlands Province into a labor reserve for coffee, tea, and copra plantations located in other provinces (Harris 1972; Vail 2002). Migration data for 1982, for example, shows that in some areas of the Tari Basin, particularly those areas with the least fertile land, approximately 45 percent of men aged twenty to thirty-nine were absent (Lehman 2002; Lehman et al. 1997).[4] Lack of economic opportunity, the extension of a paved road to Tari in the 1980s, and daily plane service have contributed to continuing high rates of male outmigration, these days to mining sites more than to plantations.

For many men labor migration is associated with what I came to think of as men's "extramarital sexual debut"—that is, their first experience of extramarital sex.[5] The quotes that follow reflect the centrality of absence from home to many men's extramarital liaisons:

> After I was married, I left my wife and children and went to Goroka for work, and it was there that I had sex with another woman. That was the first time. I went with another man. It was his idea—he was my boss, and I was the driver. He said, "Let's go around and find some women. I'll pay for some food, and I'll pay for the guest house room." So I did this the first time because I was with him. We took a car and we went together. We impressed the women by riding around in a car. Lots of working men do this—they pressure each other to go drink and have sex with prostitutes.

> I started when I was far from home, and my wife wasn't with me. The time I was away from home went on and on and on, and I felt full of desire, and I wanted to—. Well, I noticed that there were women around who wanted money, and they didn't want anything else from men—just the money. And they didn't want very much—just five kina or six or eight. And so I would give them this and have sex with them. I had been married a while, and I knew that these women were "secondhand." But they looked fresh and new. So I had sex with them. It was just for a moment of happiness—it wasn't as if I was going to go around with them or marry them. That's the way it is when we men are living far from home. Our lust builds up, and it's hard to ignore it and hard to just give up having sex for such a long time. And all it takes is money—it's like buying sugarcane or fruit at the market. The women want to sell their bodies, we want to buy sex, so we have sex.

That labor migration was the context for many men's first forays into extramarital sex enabled them to conceptualize and experience extramarital sex in a particular way—that is, as something men do together for entertainment and relaxation; as a kind of consumption activity, like drinking (which was usually a precursor to buying sex); as a kind of harmless and inconsequential escape from the emotional hardships of family separation; and as an expression of modern, autonomous, worldly masculinity.

Perhaps not surprisingly, then, while many men's initial experiences of buying sex were tied to their experience of labor migration, their extramarital sexuality did not necessarily stop upon returning home. Although a few men in the study said that they confined their extramarital liaisons to the occasional trip away from Tari, most said they bought sex from passenger women in Tari at least a couple times a month, an activity that was greatly facilitated by the severe economic decline in Tari, which had, according to almost all the men interviewed, dramatically increased the number of women selling sex. Interview after interview contains something similar to the descriptions provided by these men:

> Sometimes these women know a little about your background—like if you own lots of pigs. Other times they just notice if you have a lot of money on you. They watch you in the marketplace, and they see that you have money, and so they are willing to do it. You can have an ugly face or crippled hands or a bum leg—it doesn't matter. They don't look at that—they just look at how much you have in your pocket. Even young women. They will hang around you at the market for no reason. They will do it with any man who has money.

> First I take a good look at them and try to catch their eye. If they look back at me in the same way, then I'll edge a bit closer to them. And then I'll give her some small thing like a Coke or some betel nut. And then just from the way we look at each other, I know that she's willing, and we'll agree to meet somewhere later. We talk about which road to take, and who will go to the agreed-upon location first and who will come later, and where exactly we will meet in the bush off the road. When a woman agrees to meet a man like that, it only means sex—that's the only reason for it, even if it's never actually said. So if a woman agrees to follow me to a certain place or to meet me there later, then I know she's willing to have sex with me.

Extramarital liaisons with passenger women seemed to appeal to men in two particular ways (besides the appeal of sexual variety—which men often described as being able to eat plantain after endless meals of sweet potato—they definitely wanted their regular diet of sweet potato, but a different taste was nice now and then). First was the possibility that men could experiment with innovative sexual practices with passenger women—something most men (though certainly not all) said they could not do with their wives:

> I do style-style sex with passenger women. Wives are not for doing this kind of thing. Wives are for making children with. So we just do it the traditional way. But I've seen blue movies, and so I've tried different styles with passenger women. Some passenger women don't know about these styles, and they just lie there. But some passenger women have seen these styles and are willing to try them. When I want real pleasure, I try these things with passenger women.

> Sex with passenger women is very different! When I'm at home with my wife, we just have sex the traditional way, but when I lived in Madang, those passenger women in Madang knew all kind of styles: backfire and all kinds of ways. They taught me all kinds of styles, and I really enjoyed sex with them.

> I try all kinds of styles with passenger women, but our Huli *mana* [traditional lore] says that you shouldn't do this with your wife. So with my wife I pretend I don't know about these different ways of doing sex, and we just do it the traditional way.

> I know there are different styles—like the woman on top and backfire. But our law is that a wife must be underneath the husband in all things, including sex. Wives may not be on top of husbands—this has been our law since forever. Before the first time I had sex with my wife, we spoke with a *manayi* to receive instruction in the traditional way of doing sex. But later I got ahold of some pornographic magazines, and I tried some of the things I saw in them with other women, passenger women. So first I learned the traditional laws, and then I learned new ways to have sex. These are white people's ways—our traditions are not this way. We can't violate tradition with our wives.

Men articulated a number of reasons why "untraditional" sex was inappropriate to the marital relationship. A few worried that "style-style sex," as many Huli refer to it, might damage a wife's fertility. Others worried that their wives would be so affronted by a request for specific sexual positions or acts that they might gossip to friends and kin, which would humiliate a man and "make people think he was a sex maniac," as one man said. Many men asserted that women were naturally more lustful and less self-disciplined than men, and thus if a husband introduced his wife to novel ways of experiencing sexual pleasure, she would be unable to control her desire for such pleasure and would inevitably seek out other men. Teaching her new styles was thus "setting a bad example," as a few men said, as well as asking to be made a cuckold. Many also asserted that requesting untraditional sexual practices would lessen a man in his wife's eyes: she would think that he had lost control of his bodily hungers, and she would stop respecting and obeying him. Finally, many simply said that a man should maintain traditional practice with his wife and, if he wanted, live a more modern kind of masculine sexual identity with passenger women.

In contrast, men articulated a number of reasons for why they felt comfortable asking passenger women to try novel sexual activities. Many men assumed, for example, that women who sold sex were already familiar with a variety of outré sexual styles—either because other male customers must have requested them in the past or because they were "the kind of woman" who engaged in all kinds of *pasin nogut* (no good ways; immoral activities)—such as drinking, smoking, petty theft, and watching pornographic videos. Other men assumed that since passenger women were primarily motivated by money, they would be willing to try a variety of styles as long as enough money was offered. Perhaps most important, men felt that the stakes were very low when it came to passenger women: a man didn't have a real relationship with a passenger woman; therefore, he didn't have to worry about how she would perceive him or whether sexual innovation might make her more wayward or disobedient.

In other words, men's comfort with asking for and trying "style-style sex" with passenger women was indicative of a more general kind of emotional ease that men felt with them, which is the second reason many men found them appealing. While it would be incorrect to describe these extramarital liaisons as emotionally intimate—most men said they typically had sex with the same woman not more than three times, and many could not remember or never knew the names of passenger women with whom they had had sex—men nevertheless characterized them as transactionally straightforward, inconsequential, and thus anxiety free in a way that marriage rarely was. Men suggested that while wives might have hidden motives and surreptitious schemes, passenger women never did—all they wanted was money. And since the transaction was transparent and short lived, some men asserted that they could be flirtatious, affectionate, and even emotionally intimate with passenger women—behaviors some were wary or uncomfortable enacting with wives. Thus, as one man was quoted as saying earlier in this chapter, "You can have fun, relaxed conversations with a girlfriend or a sex worker but not with your wife; if you do, she'll use that information to dominate you."

Because this study was part of a larger, multisited project, the interview protocol included questions that allowed for the possibility that men's extramarital sexuality might take the form of more enduring relationships, such as what are referred to as "outside wives" in some African countries, a pattern that was found by the researchers working in Nigeria and Uganda (see chapter 9; also Smith 2002, 2006; Parikh 2005). None of the Huli men interviewed had extramarital relationships of this more permanent kind, however, and the transient nature of their more commercial liaisons was associated with a wide range of freedoms—particularly, freedom from the ongoing social and economic responsibilities that come with being a husband, father, and in-law but also freedom from the burdens of having to constantly assess conjugal relations of power and whether a wife was being properly subordinate. Moreover, men routinely described passenger women as "women who don't belong to anyone," "women from broken marriages," or "women whose husbands have abandoned them." Seeing them as socially unconnected, men dismissed the possibility that sex with these women might lead to social conflict (with a woman's natal kin or former husband, for example) or to demands that a man support a passenger woman's children. As one man said, "I've always liked the times when I migrated to cities to find work. Passenger women there are free—there's no one to protect them or ask for bridewealth for them to take us to village court for having sex with them."

Perhaps counterintuitively, passenger women were also associated with freedom from the sexual pollution that a man incurred through marriage. In other words, many men suggested that passenger women's bodies posed less of a health risk to them than their own wives' bodies because passenger women's bodies were not connected to the men through bridewealth, commensalism, shared space, and regularly shared reproductive fluids. As discussed earlier, men expressed fewer concerns about the physical dangers of marital sexuality than the threats to male dominance posed by excessive emotional intimacy. So, for example, few men seemed terribly distressed about menstrual pollution per se, which, according to both Huli men and women, can occur when a woman's menstrual or other sexual fluids enter a man's body—either directly through food or more indirectly, such as when a man inhales smoke made from firewood that his menstruating wife has stepped over—and cause acute constipation, indigestion, or even death from his intestines' twisting into swollen knots and eventually bursting inside his body (see also Frankel 1980, 1986). Nevertheless, men did express both anxiety and resignation about the inevitable yet quotidian sexual pollution sustained through years and years of being married and producing children. Sharing food, breathing in a wife's exhaled breath, being in spaces and among things that a wife had walked through and over, and, of course, being perpetually exposed to her sexual fluids throughout one's reproductive life led slowly but ineluctably to the aging of a man's body (Wardlow 2006b; see also Biersack 1995). The more sex with one's wife and the more time spent in the domestic sphere with her, the more quickly this inevitable aging took place.

In contrast, none of the men in the study expressed fears about sexual pollution from passenger women, and a few men said explicitly that men could not be polluted by passenger women, both because a man usually had sex with each passenger woman only a few times and because passenger women were not connected to a man through the exchange of bridewealth. While anthropologists have conventionally treated bridewealth as a trans-action that establishes political and economic ties between families, Huli people speak about the consequences and effects of bridewealth in other, more phenomenological ways as well. As I discussed earlier, the giving of bridewealth creates a kind of physical bond between spouses that helps to ensure fertility, but it also means that they are affected more by each other's bodies and actions than by those of other people. Because a man has not given bridewealth for passenger women, her body is not bound to him, and he is therefore less vulnerable to the hot powers of her body. Indeed, some men said that they sought out extramarital sex with passenger women as a means of avoiding too much time in the domestic sphere in the presence of their wife's body and that they were encouraged to do so by older men who explicitly told them that they were endangering themselves and hastening the male aging process by spending too much time with their wife (see also chapter 6 in Wardlow 2006b). Christian missionaries' claims that spouses should live together in one home had, ironically, only exacerbated the issue, men said: now that they did not have their own residence to escape to, and now that they often found themselves feeling vaguely soiled from spending too much time in "the women's house" (as a number of men referred to the house they shared with their wife), the more appealing it was to assert their authority and autonomy and literally get a breath of fresh air, by going out with male peers, especially to *dawe anda* (traditional courtship parties that are now more like brothels; see Wardlow 2006b; see also Jolly 2001).

***

In sum, for many Huli men marriage, though gratifying and fulfilling in many ways, was also associated with at least a modicum of anxiety, not least because there seem to be so many different ways to do marriage now, and every choice a man makes—separate residence or one residence, sex anytime or only on days 11–14, "style-style" sex or "traditional" sex, emotional candor or emotional opacity—is consequential: each choice is a moral statement about the kind of man he is, and each choice has potential unforeseeable implications for the future health and stability of his marital and reproductive life. In contrast, many Huli men described commercial sex as a gendered transaction that was transparent, inconsequential, and less emotionally fraught than marriage. It was also appealing because of its association with modern, autonomous, urban masculinity (see also Nihill 1994). Thus one pattern that appears to be emerging in the Huli context is a kind of bifurcation or compartmentalization of men's sexual identities, in which they engage in more "modern" sexual and emotional practices with women who sell sex but to whom the men have no ongoing obligation, and the men engage in more "traditional" sexual and emotional practices with their wives, in part because of the long horizon of marriage and the sense that performing tradition may be the safest course of action. I want to emphasize that this pattern is certainly not universal among Huli men: some middle-aged men described relatively emotionally open, easy, and affectionate relationships with their wives, and the men of the younger generation appeared to feel less anxiety about the marital relationship, although it is unclear whether this difference represents real generational change or merely the "honeymoon" stage in the marital life course.

Men similarly compartmentalized the potential physical repercussions of these two different kinds of sexual relationship, suggesting roughly that a man gets sexual pollution from his wife and *gonolia* (the blanket term for all sexually transmitted infections, as the Huli construct them) from passenger women (Wardlow 2002). There is considerable conceptual overlap between these two illness conditions. For example, when asked what they would do if they suspected they had *gonolia,* a number of men said that they would attempt to cure it in the same manner they would treat sexual pollution—that is, by drinking mountain springwater, preferably ritually bespelled by a *gamuyi.* As one man said, "After sex with passenger women I drink lots of water. And I wash myself. I wash my penis immediately after, and I drink lots and lots of water—a whole containerful. [Interviewer: What does the water do?] The water will get rid of all the germs inside my penis because I will urinate out all the germs. It's the same as what the ancestors said. They used to drink water and give ritually bespelled water to young bachelors. If you drink lots of this kind of water, it will remove sickness."

On the other hand, *gonolia*—although socially humiliating if one's illness becomes public knowledge—was seen by many men as ultimately less grave than marital sexual pollution because the hospital had medicine that could cure it. The interviews with men who had been diagnosed with syphilis or gonorrhea showed that public humiliation was considered the worst consequence (and the potential shame of public exposure did delay or even prevent some men from seeking treatment). Physical symptoms, on the other hand, were viewed quite cavalierly by some men because they knew that effective drugs were available. As one man said, when asked what he knew about HIV/AIDS: "*Gonolia* I've had lots of times—I know what that feels like. Now I recognize when I have it, and I go to the hospital and get medicine. And then I'm fine. . . . So I know what happens to my body when I have *sik gonolia.* But AIDS I don't understand very well. I only know about it from what I've seen happen to other men—when the sickness gets inside their blood, and their bodies change, and then they die."

Very little AIDS awareness or prevention had been done when I was in Tari in 2004. However, people spoke frequently about what they perceived as a quite sudden surge in HIV-related deaths: Many people knew someone who had died of HIV-related illnesses, and almost everyone had seen the bodies of people who had died in the capital city being unloaded from planes on the Tari airstrip. These were people who had been flown home to be buried. A few men interviewed said mournfully that they had given up having extramarital sex because of their fear of contracting HIV. As one man said, "I got a blood test, and when they told me it was negative, I was so happy. It was at this time that I gave up having sex with other women. I had heard about AIDS from the hospital staff, and also some of my kin and one of my good friends died of AIDS. So now, when I sleep in the clan men's house, I try to talk to other men about AIDS and teach them to be careful."

Other men claimed to have become devout condom users, although the Christian missions' message that condoms were "fifty-fifty" (that is, very unreliable) appeared to be having more success in eroding men's confidence in condoms than in deterring extramarital sex.

There are some indications that knowledge about HIV/AIDS has spurred wives to attempt to be more assertive with their husbands—although the emphasis on male dominance and wifely obedience makes this quite difficult. As one man said in response to the question of whether knowledge about AIDS had changed his behavior, "There have been some women I've wanted to have sex with, but I knew that lots of other men had had sex with them, and so I decided not to. . . . Also my wife has heard these stories about AIDS, and now my wife follows me around and has told me not to sleep with other women. She didn't used to follow me or ask about my activities when I wasn't at home, but now she does. Now if I come home late at night, my wife will still be awake, and she'll interrogate me about what I have been up to." It remains to be seen, however, how men's increasing knowledge of, and experiences with, HIV/AIDS will shape their marital and extramarital sexual practices.

Notes

1. I recognize that women also engage in extramarital sexual liaisons. However, because survey research suggests that married men "stray" more than married women, and because men's unprotected extramarital sex is married women's greatest risk for HIV infection, in Papua New Guinea and elsewhere, in this chapter I focus on men's marital and extramarital relationships (Foreman 1999; UNAIDS/UNFPA/UNIFEM 2004).

The interview subjects were selected with the objective of achieving diversity in the sample along three axes: generation, socioeconomic status, and postmarital migration experience. The forty male participants were thus categorized in the following way: (1) as low or high socioeconomic status (whether a man had a waged or salaried job or made enough money selling coffee to live in a fiberboard house with a metal roof; participants who did not have jobs and lived in bush material housing were categorized as low SES); (2) as young (newlywed up to five years of marriage), middle aged, or old (defined as being a grandparent or having adult children); and (3) as having or not having postmarital migration experience (defined as having lived outside Tari for at least six months after marriage or making overnight trips away from Tari at least a few times a month).

2. The four other investigators and their respective research sites are Jennifer Hirsch, Mexico; Shanti Parikh, Uganda; Harriet Phinney, Vietnam; and Daniel Smith, Nigeria. The project as a whole is entitled "Love, Marriage, and HIV: A

Multi-Sited Study of Gender and HIV Risk," and it was funded by the U.S. National Institutes of Health. See Hirsch et al., Parikh, Phinney, Smith, and Wardlow, all in press for a special issue about this project in the *American Journal of Public Health.*

3. More recently, questions about how often a person has sex, with how many different partners, and whether condoms are used are intended to assess the risk of exposure to HIV.

4. From 1970 to 1995 a demographic database was maintained by the Tari Research Unit, a branch of the Papua New Guinea Institute of Medical Research, through a system in which Huli men were hired to keep track of five hundred to one thousand people in their own clan territories and report all demographic events monthly. This demography project was shut down in 1995 because of lack of funds and increasing crime and tribal fighting in the Tari area.

5. The concept of "sexual debut" is important for public health practitioners who do research on young people's contraceptive use or risk for sexually transmitted infections (STIs) and HIV. Typically, public health workers attempt to delay young people's sexual debut in order to (1) shorten the lifetime period of potential exposure to STIs and HIV, if only by a year or two, and (2) give young people the opportunity to mature and to gain the education, life skills, and relative security that might enable them to make less risky sexual choices. Implicit in some of this work is the notion that the interpersonal nature and social context of a person's first sexual experience can influence the sexual choices she or he subsequently makes. Thus, for example, if a young woman's first sexual experience is of a commercial nature and made in a context of desperation among female peers who are making similar choices, this pattern may endure. I am similarly suggesting here that the nature and context of men's first extramarital sexual experiences (for example, commercial sex, far from home, surrounded by one's drunk male peers) may likewise influence their subsequent sexual choices.

REFERENCES

Adams, Vincanne and Stacy L. Pigg, eds. 2005. *Sex in Development: Science, Sexuality, and Morality in Global Perspective.* Durham, N.C.: Duke University Press.

Biersack, Aletta. 1995a. "Heterosexual Meanings: Society, Economy, and Gender among Ipilis." In Biersack, *Papuan Borderlands,* pp. 1–54.

——, ed. 1995b. *Papuan Borderlands: Huli, Duna, and Ipili Perspectives on the Papua New Guinea Highlands.* Ann Arbor: University of Michigan Press.

Borrey, Anou. 2000. "Sexual Violence in Perspective: The Case of Papua New Guinea." In S. Dinnen and A. Ley, eds., *Reflections on Violence in Melanesia,* pp. 105–18. Annandale, Australia: Federation Press.

Clark, Jeffrey. 1997. "State of Desire: Transformations in Huli Sexuality." In Manderson and Jolly, *Sites of Desire, Economies of Pleasure,* pp. 191–211.

Clark, Jeffrey and Jenny Hughes. 1995. "A History of Sexuality and Gender in Tari." In Biersack, *Papuan Borderlands,* pp. 315–40.

Elliston, Deborah. 1995. "Erotic Anthropology: 'Ritualized Homosexuality' in Melanesia and Beyond." *American Ethnologist* 22 (4): 848–67.

Foreman, M., ed. 1999. *AIDS and Men: Taking Risks or Taking Responsibility.* London: Panos Institute, 1999.

Frankel, Stephen. 1980. "'I am Dying of Man.'" *Culture, Medicine, and Psychiatry* 4:95–117.

———. 1986. *The Huli Response to Illness.* Cambridge: Cambridge University Press.

Glasse, Robert M. 1968. *Huli of Papua: A Cognatic Descent System.* Paris: Mouton.

———. 1974. Le masque de la volupte: symbolisme et antagonisme sexuels sur les hauts plateaux de Nouvelle-Guinee. *L'Homme* 14 (2): 79–86.

Goldman, Laurence. 1983. *Talk Never Dies: The Language of Huli Disputes.* London: Tavistock.

Hammar, Lawrence. 1999. "Caught between Structure and Agency: The Gender of Violence and Prostitution in Papua New Guinea." *Transforming Anthropology* 8 (1–2): 77–96.

Harris, G. T. 1972. "Labor Supply and Economic Development in the Southern Highlands." *Oceania* 43 (1972): 123–39.

Herdt, Gilbert, ed. 1993. *Ritualized Homosexuality in Melanesia.* Berkeley: University of California Press.

Herdt, Gilbert and F. J. P. Poole. 1982. "Sexual Antagonism: The Intellectual History of a Concept in the Anthropology of New Guinea." *Social Analysis* 12:3–28.

Hirsch, Jennifer. 2003. *A Courtship after Marriage: Sexuality and Love in Mexican Transnational Families.* Berkeley: University of California Press.

Hirsch, Jennifer and Holly Wardlow, eds. 2006. *Modern Loves: The Anthropology of Romantic Courtship and Companionate Marriage.* Ann Arbor: University of Michigan Press.

Hirsch, Jennifer, Jennifer Higgins, Margaret Bentley, and Constance Nathanson. 2002. "The Social Constructions of Sexuality: Marital Infidelity and Sexually Transmitted Disease–HIV Risk in a Mexican Migrant Community." *American Journal of Public Health* 92:1227–37.

Hirsch, Jennifer S., Sergio Meneses, Brenda Thompson, Mirka Negroni, Blanca Pelcastre, and Carlos del Rio. In press. "The Inevitability of Infidelity: Sexual Reputation, Social Geographies, and Marital HIV Risk in Rural Mexico." *American Journal of Public Health.*

Hughes, Jenny. 1995. "After the Gold Rush: A Medical Anthropological Study in Papua New Guinea." In J. Perry and J. Hughes, eds., *Anthropology: Voices from the Margins,* pp. 35–60. Geelong, Australia: Deakin University Press.

Jenkins, Carol. 1996. "The Homosexual Context of Heterosexual Practice in Papua New Guinea." In Peter Aggleton, ed., *Bisexualities and AIDS: International Perspectives,* pp. 191–206. London: Taylor and Francis.

Jolly, Margaret. 2001. "Damming the Rivers of Milk? Fertility, Sexuality, and Modernity in Melanesia and Amazonia." In T. Gregor and D. Tuzin, eds., *Gender in Amazonia and Melanesia: An Exploration of the Comparative Method,* pp. 175–206. Berkeley: University of California Press.

Jolly, Margaret and Lenore Manderson. 1997. Introduction to Manderson and Jolly, *Sites of Desire, Economies of Pleasure,* pp. 1–25.

Kelly, Raymond. 1976. "Witchcraft and Sexual Relations: An Exploration in the Social and Semantic Implications of the Structure of Belief." In P. Brown and G. Buchbinder, eds., *Man and Woman in the New Guinea Highlands,* pp. 36–53. Washington, D.C.: American Anthropological Association.

Knauft, Bruce. 1986. "Text and Social Practice: Narrative 'Longing' and Bisexuality among the Gebusi of New Guinea." *Ethos* 14:252–81.

——. 1993. *South Coast New Guinea Cultures: History, Comparison, Dialectic.* Cambridge: Cambridge University Press.

——. 1997. "Gender Identity, Political Economy, and Modernity in Melanesia and Amazonia." *Journal of the Royal Anthropological Institute* 3:233–59.

Langness, L. L. 1967. "Sexual Antagonism in the New Guinea Highlands: A Bena Bena Example." *Oceania* 37:161–77.

——. 1974. "Ritual Power and Male Dominance in the New Guinea Highlands." *Ethos* 2 (3): 189–212.

Leavitt, Stephen. 1991. "Sexual Ideology and Experience in a Papua New Guinea Society." *Social Science and Medicine* 33 (8): 897–907.

Lehman, Deborah. 2002. "Demography and Causes of Death among the Huli in the Tari Basin." *Papua New Guinea Medical Journal* 45:51–62.

Lehman, Deborah, John Vail, Peter Vail, Joe Crocker, Helen Pickering, Michael Alpers, and the Tari Demographic Surveillance Team. 1997. *Demographic Surveillance in Tari, Southern Highlands Province, Papua New Guinea: Methodology and Trends in Fertility and Mortality between 1979 and 1993.* Goroka, Papua New Guinea: Papua New Guinea Institute of Medical Research.

Manderson, Lenore and Margaret Jolly, eds. 1997. *Sites of Desire, Economies of Pleasure: Sexualities in Asia and the Pacific.* Chicago: University of Chicago Press.

Meggitt, Mervin J. 1964. "Male–Female Relationships in the Highlands of Australian New Guinea." *American Anthropologist* 66 (2): 204–24.

Nihill, Michael. 1994. "New Women and Wild Men: 'Development': Changing Sexual Practice and Gender in Highland Papua New Guinea." *Canberra Anthropology* 17 (2): 48–72.

NSRRT (National Sex and Reproduction Research Team) and Carol Jenkins. 1994. *National Study of Sexual and Reproductive Knowledge and Behavior in Papua New Guinea.* Papua New Guinea Institute of Medical Research Monograph no. 10. Goroka, Papua New Guinea: Institute of Medical Research.

Parikh, Shanti. 2005. "From Auntie to Disco: The Bifurcation of Risk and Pleasure in Sex Education in Uganda." In Adams and Pigg, *Sex in Development,* pp. 125–58.

———. In press. "'My Husband Has Many Girlfriends': The Political Economy of Male Infidelity and Married Women's HIV Risk in Uganda." *American Journal of Public Health.*

Phinney, Harriet. In press. "'Rice Is Essential but Tiresome, You Should Get Some Noodles': The Political-Economy of Married Women's HIV Risk in Ha Noi, Viet Nam." *American Journal of Public Health.*

Pigg, Stacy and Vincanne Adams. 2005. Introduction to Adams and Pigg, *Sex in Development,* pp. 1–38.

Smith, Daniel J. 2002. "'Man No Be Wood': Gender and Extramarital Sex in Contemporary Southeastern Nigeria." *Ahfad Journal* 19 (2): 4–23.

———. 2006. "Love and the Risk of HIV: Courtship, Marriage, and Infidelity in Southeastern Nigeria." In Hirsch and Wardlow, *Modern Loves,* pp. 135–53.

———. In press. "Modern Marriage, Extramarital Sex, and HIV Risk in Southeastern Nigeria." *American Journal of Public Health.*

Tuzin, Donald. 1997. *The Cassowary's Revenge: The Life and Death of Masculinity in a New Guinea Society.* Chicago: University of Chicago Press.

UNAIDS (United Nations Programme on HIV/AIDS), UNFPA (United National Population Fund), and UNIFEM (United National Development Fund for Women). 2004. *Women and HIV/AIDS: Confronting the Crisis.* New York: UNAIDS/UNFPA/UNIFEM.

Vail, John. 2002. "Social and Economic Conditions at Tari." *Papua New Guinea Medical Journal* 45:113–27.

Wardlow, Holly. 1996. "*Bobby Teardrops:* A Turkish Video in Papua New Guinea." *Visual Anthropology Review* 12 (1): 30–46.

———. 2002. "Giving Birth to *Gonolia*: 'Culture' and Sexually Transmitted Disease among the Huli of Papua New Guinea." *Medical Anthropology Quarterly* 16 (2): 151–75.

———. 2004. "Anger, Economy, and Female Agency: Problematizing 'Prostitution' and 'Sex Work' in Papua New Guinea." *Signs: Journal of Women in Culture and Society* 29 (4): 1017–40.

———. 2006a. "All's Fair When Love Is War: Romantic Passion and Companionate Marriage among the Huli of Papua New Guinea." In Hirsch and Wardlow, *Modern Loves,* pp. 51–77.

———. 2006b. *Wayward Women: Sexuality and Agency in a New Guinea Society.* Berkeley: University of California Press.

———. In press. "Usually I Just Try to Find Passenger Women. You Know—Women Who Don't Belong to Anyone": Men's Extramarital Sexuality and Married Women's HIV Risk in Rural Papua New Guinea." *American Journal of Public Health.*

Zimmer-Tamakoshi, Laura. 1997. "'Wild Pigs and Dog Men': Rape and Domestic Violence as 'Women's Issues' in Papua New Guinea." In Caroline Brettell and Carolyn Sargent, eds., *Gender in Cross-Cultural Perspective,* pp. 538–53. Dallas: Southern Methodist University.

9. Intimacy, Infidelity, and Masculinity in Southeastern Nigeria

Daniel Jordan Smith

Marital infidelity is as ancient as marriage itself. Cultures vary in the degree to which they tolerate extramarital sex. Further, infidelity is highly gendered in both its moral and behavioral dimensions. In most societies it is more acceptable for married men than married women to engage in extramarital sex, and it is generally perceived that married men are also actually more likely to do so. Despite the prevalence of extramarital sex and the popular and moral preoccupation with infidelity in so many cultural contexts, remarkably little ethnographic research has examined the social organization of extramarital sexual relationships and elucidated the motives and meanings that can situate and explain infidelity from a social and cultural perspective.

Studying infidelity is difficult precisely because sex is so morally charged and extramarital sexual behavior takes place largely in private, out of sight from interested observers—whether they are jealous spouses, judgmental neighbors, or curious anthropologists. The moral valences and social risks associated with sexual behavior in general and infidelity in particular mean that extramarital sex is often shrouded in secrecy. Yet despite—or perhaps partly because of—the secrecy that surrounds infidelity, people talk a lot about illicit sexual behavior. Discourse about sexual morality is a powerful form of collective commentary, revealing shifting social fault lines with regard to gender, generation, and class.

This chapter examines men's extramarital sexual behavior in southeast-ern Nigeria, untangling the complex connections between masculinity and infidelity, particularly as they are shaped and revealed in the different arenas and relationships in which married men seek and experience various forms of social, sexual, and emotional intimacy. In presenting an ethnographic account of infidelity, I situate extramarital sexual behavior at the center of a confluence of significant patterns in the social organization of gender that are shaped by broader political, economic, and cultural transformations that are shifting the ground on which intimate relationships occur.

I focus on three intertwining dimensions of the social organization of gender in southeastern Nigeria: marriage, extramarital relationships, and sex-segregated social institutions. In various ways marriage and particular forms of sex-segregated social organization are central to a sociological explanation and cultural understanding of men's extramarital sexual be-havior. Marriage is changing in southeastern Nigeria, with young people increasingly insisting on choosing their own spouse, privileging conjugal re-lationships relative to broader kinship ties, and emphasizing an ideal of ro-mantic love as an important criterion for selecting a spouse. These changes appear to have heightened the importance of spousal intimacy, part of an increasingly common perspective regarding what constitutes a good mar-riage. But various forms of sex-segregated social organization remain pow-erful, despite such social transformations as near-universal participation in coeducational schooling, integration associated with migration to cities, and gender-mixed organization of urban commercial and employment opportunities in southeastern Nigeria—all of which have contributed to changes in the gender dynamics of courtship and marriage. Indeed, many Nigerians of both sexes feel that ongoing changes have produced too great a blurring of highly valued gender differences. People expect, enact, and experience intimacy in different valences across the complex constructions of gender that characterize relationships within and between the sexes. I argue that understanding men's infidelity in southeastern Nigeria requires tracing the interweaving of the different dimensions of intimacy that mat-ter in men's lives, and that male extramarital sexual behavior is partly a product of men's efforts to navigate the multiplicity of social expectations and individual needs created in different arenas of intimacy.

Specifically, I contend that men in southeastern Nigeria who cheat on their wives are seeking, experiencing, and performing distinctive forms or aspects of intimacy in different social arenas and relationships. Evidence from my ethnographic research suggests that men's extramarital sexual behavior must be understood in the context of the unique dimensions of intimacy that are associated with and fulfilled in men's relationships with their wife, their extramarital partners, and their male peers. I present examples from each type of relationship to illustrate the nature of intimacy in these distinct domains. I argue that the aspects of masculinity that help explain marital infidelity must be understood in the context of how men "do" intimacy rather than by an overly simplistic assumption that men are either incapable of intimacy or have failed to maintain intimate relationships.

BACKGROUND AND CONTEXT

I first began working in Nigeria in 1989 as an adviser to an internationally funded public health project. During the three years that I lived in the Igbo-speaking southeastern Nigerian city of Owerri, the prevalence and social importance of extramarital sexual relationships was striking. During those three years I became good friends with many married men. The majority of my male friends had extramarital sexual relationships. I heard their stories about those relationships and observed men with their lovers and girlfriends in various public and semipublic spaces where men can safely interact with and entertain women who are not their wives. Owerri was a particularly auspicious place to observe men's extramarital sexual behavior because it had several colleges and universities, producing an exceptionally large population of unmarried young adult women.

The gendered and class dimensions of extramarital sexuality in Owerri were readily apparent—symbolized by a common scene and a memorable conversation. The common scene occurred every Friday night, when one could observe dozens of cars parked outside the gates of Alvin Ikoku Teachers College—cars owned by married men who were awaiting their young unmarried female lovers. Although Alvin Ikoku Teachers College had almost as many male students as female students, I never noticed any older women waiting for young male lovers. Further, poorer men—the kind of men who might own only a bicycle—could not expect to attract the attention of these university women. These men did not show up on foot or with their bicycles, and the young women who sought or submitted to married male lovers would have found such a prospect absurd.

The socioeconomic features and class-driven aspects of extramarital sexual relations are encapsulated in the term *sugar daddy,* which is the moniker typically used by Nigerians to describe married men who have sexual relationships with younger unmarried women. For both men and women in these relationships, age and gender inequality intersect with socioeconomic disparities but in ways that are not always self-evident. For example, economic need is commonly portrayed in both scholarly literature and popular Nigerian discourse as motivating and explaining young women's participation in these relationships (Machel 2001; Smith 2000). But for both older married men and their younger female lovers, the interconnections of economics and sexual behavior are complex, involving material aspirations and social presentations of the self that extend far beyond simple sexual desire on the part of men or abject economic needs on the part of women (Cornwall 2002; Hunter 2002; Luke 2003, 2005). For the relatively elite married men who make up the population of sugar daddies, it is no coincidence that their girlfriends are predominantly urban, educated young women. These women fulfill male aspirations to live up to and perform a modern masculinity in which having young, attractive, fashionable, and educated extramarital sexual partners is as much about social status as sexual gratification. Similarly, for many of the young women who participate in these relationships—particularly those whose youth, education, beauty, and fashion sense mean that they have a choice of potential lovers—the motives for having a sugar daddy exceed the need for money for basic necessities. Thus, while Nigerian schoolgirls and university students commonly assert that there is "no romance without finance," what they mean by this phrase has more to do with the high expectations a young woman should enforce on a married lover in terms of material support than with a sense of abject economic desperation.

A memorable conversation from my first years in Nigeria reinforced the clearly gendered nature of extramarital sexuality and suggested connections to gender inequality in marital relationships. One night an older married man, whom I knew from a sports club where I used to play tennis, described his understanding of the implicit rules for extramarital sex in southeastern Nigeria. He was a man who regularly brought his girlfriend to the club and seemed to take obvious pride in his sexual appetite, even as he approached sixty years of age. After a few beers I questioned him about how he managed to keep his girlfriend secret from his wife and about the seeming double standard with regard to marital infidelity, in which men were free but women were forbidden to cheat. He laughed and exclaimed: "If I catch my wife cheating, she is gone; if she catches me cheating, she is gone, too." While his assertion was partly the product of male bravado in an alcohol-influenced all-male social setting, even in exaggerated form it represented many Nigerian men's expectations about the gendered dimensions of extramarital sexual relations. Women were supposed to be faithful in marriage *and* tolerate men's extramarital affairs. Of course, not all married women are faithful to their husbands, and many women both object to and take actions to try to minimize or punish their husband's extramarital indiscretions. Further, although my friend's declaration would make it appear that men have no boundaries in their ability to take lovers, over time I learned that men observed many implicit and collectively shared rules about discretion in extramarital liaisons, rules that highlight the continuing social importance of marriage and suggest the ways in which a wife has and can exercise a degree of power vis-à-vis her husband and her husband's lovers (Smith 2001, 2002).

While I was working in Nigeria on the public health project, I met and courted my wife, an Igbo woman. We married in 1992, and she returned with me to the United States when I began a doctoral program in anthropology. It is perhaps not surprising that in the intervening years, family, marriage, and reproduction have become a significant focus of my research in Nigeria. My position as an in-law in the Igbo-speaking Southeast has provided a quasi-insider status that has complemented the ways in which one always aims to immerse oneself as an anthropologist conducting ethnographic research. Being married to an Igbo woman reinforced my understanding of the profound social importance of marriage in the region. Not only is it expected that all adults marry, but divorce is extremely uncommon. As Meyer Fortes (1978) noted for West African societies more generally, in Igbo-speaking southeastern Nigeria marriage and parenthood are the sine qua non of full personhood. Both men and women respect the institution of marriage tremendously—indeed, when I married my wife, one of the greatest initial fears of my in-laws was that I might share what they perceived to be a casual American attitude toward marriage, in which any small problem can lead to divorce.

To an outside observer, in the context of the overwhelming importance of marriage, the high prevalence of extramarital sexual behavior would appear to be something of paradox. Indeed, as the institution of marriage has begun to change in southeastern Nigeria, with young couples expecting to exercise individual choice of marriage partner and romantic love's becoming idealized as a criterion for a good marriage, the contradictions and conflicts created by extramarital sex have become salient issues for Nigerians as well. The multiple dimensions of intimacy and the ways they intertwine with men's projects of masculinity provide part of the context for understanding the enduring prevalence of extramarital sex.

The material I present in this chapter draws on almost seventeen years of experience in southeastern Nigeria but derives especially from research conducted in 2004 as part of a five-country comparative ethnographic study entitled "Love, Marriage and HIV: A Multi-site Study of Gender and HIV Risk."[1] I led the Nigeria component of the research, which focused on collecting marital case histories from twenty-two couples and undertaking an intensive study of the social organization of men's extramarital sexual behavior. The marital case studies were implemented through a series of extended conversations in which husbands and wives were interviewed separately about a wide range of topics regarding their marriages and, eventually, their experiences in extramarital sexual relationships. Couples were purposefully selected to represent a range of ages and marital durations, a diversity of socioeconomic positions, and a variety of migration and mobility histories. Given the gendered dimensions of extramarital sexuality in the region, it is not surprising that men were both more likely to admit to having had extramarital sex and more forthcoming in discussing their experiences. Women commonly talked about other people's extramarital sexual behavior and expressed their views mostly through narratives that focused attention away from their own marriage.

In addition to the marital case study interviews with men, the research was conducted through participant observation and informal interviews at public and semipublic venues such as bars, discos, hotels, restaurants, brothels, social clubs, sports clubs, barber shops, and male-dominated sectors of the market, as well as other places where men either meet and entertain their female lovers or talk to each other about women and extramarital sex. In some settings and on some occasions I simply observed behavior; in others I listened and sometimes participated in natural conversations (unprompted by me) about extramarital sex and related topics; in still others I purposely initiated discussions with men individually or in small groups about various issues related to extramarital sex. I also talked extensively to many young women who were involved with married men, sometimes at venues where men were present and sometimes in private contexts where women might talk more candidly. In this chapter I focus mainly on the interviews with men, using women's perspectives only to elucidate the understanding of how men "do" intimacy in the primary social relationships relevant to understanding extramarital sexual behavior.

Finally, before proceeding to the ethnography and analysis, I should note that while studying men's extramarital sex in southeastern Nigeria was challenging in the sense that some of the most intimate aspects of these relationships were unobservable, it was not at all difficult to insert myself in contexts in which the more public dimensions of men's extramarital sexual behavior occur, nor was it hard to find men talking or get men talking more about extramarital sex. Indeed, it was the ease with which I, as a man, was included in these contexts and conversations that began to highlight for me the crucial importance of intramale intimacy for understanding and explaining men's extramarital sexual behavior.

Changing Marriage and Marital Intimacy

Scholars of West African society have long recognized the pronounced social importance of marriage and fertility in the region (Fortes 1978; Bledsoe and Pison 1994; Feldman-Savelsberg 1999; Smith 2001). While there is no doubt that marriage serves fundamental social purposes in every society, polygyny and high fertility have been considered hallmarks of West African social organization—logical demographic strategies in a horticultural economy where labor rather than land was traditionally a scarce resource (Caldwell and Caldwell 1987). Historically, in Igbo society men married women with the idea that they would provide labor and produce children (Uchendu 1965). Among the older cohort in my study this attitude could still be found. I interviewed a seventy-one-year-old man who has been married to one wife for forty years and who lived almost all his adult life in his semirural community. He explained: "A man marries a woman for two main reasons: the work she can do and the children she will bear."

Since Nigeria's independence in 1960, and especially since the 1970s, Igbo society has changed dramatically, and with these changes the institution of marriage has also been transformed. The extent of social change is too spectacular to summarize here, but the intertwining factors that have contributed to the transformation of marriage include economic diversification and labor migration, urbanization, education, religious conversion, and globalization. Contemporary economic strategies hinge on rural-urban migration and a strong emphasis on the importance of education for children. As larger numbers of families move to the city in search of better education, employment, and other economic opportunities, family structure is changing. Modifications in family organization induced by economic and demographic transformation have been complemented by moral, ideological, and religious trends that also affect the institution of marriage.

On its face marriage in southeastern Nigeria seems to be changing in ways that make it increasingly similar to marriage in Western societies. Describing the differences between her marriage and her parents' marriage, a thirty-year-old woman married for three years said: "My father had three wives and fourteen children. Often it was every woman for herself. My husband and I have a partnership. We decide things. There is love between us." The modern marriages of young couples in southeastern Nigeria are clearly different from their parents'. Perhaps the most concise way to contrast modern Igbo marriages with the past is to note that young couples see their marriages as a life project in which they as a couple are the primary actors, whereas their parents' marriages were more obviously embedded in the structures of the extended family. The differences are most pronounced in narratives about courtship, descriptions of how husbands and wives resolve marital quarrels, and decision making about contributions to their children's education. In each of these arenas people in more modern marriages tend to emphasize the primacy of the individual couple, often in conscious opposition to the constraints imposed by ties to kin and community. For example, a forty-three-year-old teacher reported: "For me and my wife our marriage is our business, whereas in my parents' time everything was scrutinized by the extended family. If they had any little problem, everyone might become involved. We try to keep things within the married house. If we have any problem, we handle it ourselves and maybe pray over it, but we don't go running to the elders, broadcasting our problems here and there."

But it is important not to exaggerate these trends. Even in the most modern marriages ties to kin and community remain strong, and the project of marriage and child rearing continues to be a social project, strongly embedded in the relationships and values of the extended family system. Indeed, the continued importance of ties to family and community and ongoing concerns about the collective expectations of wider social networks permeate people's stories of modern courtship, the resolution of marital disputes, and decisions about child rearing. The choice of a future spouse based on love is, in almost all cases, still subjected to the advice and consent of families. That modern marriage in southeastern Nigeria remains a resolutely social endeavor creates contradictions for younger couples, who must navigate not only their individual relationship but also the outward representation of their marriage to kin and community. Most couples seek to portray their marriage to themselves and to others as being modern but also (often in opposition to modern) morally upright. The tension between being modern and being moral is crucial to explaining the dynamics of intimacy in marriage, the motives for men's extramarital sexual relationships, and married women's responses to their husband's infidelity.

The nature of sexual intimacy in marriage is directly related to men's extramarital sexual behavior, though not in the same ways, of course, for all men. Many young couples talked about the quality of their sexual relationship and the ability to communicate about sexual matters as important aspects of their marriage and as characteristics that distinguish their marriage from their parents' marriages. At the same time that young men and women have aspirations for modern sexualities, they also face enduring social pressures created by discourses that depict modern sexual behavior as immoral and constrict sexual freedom in marriage. Women in particular face a double bind: they need to satisfy their husband's modern sexual appetites to help keep him faithful, yet they risk being branded as sexually licentious—and even unfaithful—if they demonstrate too much sexual expertise or pleasure.

One man told me a story of a friend whose civil-servant wife had a job that required her to live apart from her spouse for an extended period of time. When she returned home permanently, the husband interpreted her sexual aggressiveness (apparently, she initiated a position they had not previously tried together) as evidence that she had been unfaithful. Men also are cautious about introducing new sexual styles during marital sex, for fear that their wife might suspect they had learned and practiced these positions with other women. One highly educated man who worked for the local government told me a funny story about a married couple who were both having extramarital affairs in which they were experimenting with many different sexual positions and styles but had only missionary sex in their matrimonial bed. Each wanted to hide from the other what she or he really knew and enjoyed. He added that there are probably many married people who know much more about sex than they ever show their spouse.

These stories illustrate the degree to which intimacy in modern Igbo marriages often requires a certain sexual decorum, in which men and women must appear to subscribe to social values about sexual morality. Ironically, in contemporary Nigeria sexual morality may be more powerful than ever because sexual immorality has come to stand for people's discontents about various aspects of social change—a phenomenon most evident in popular responses to the HIV/AIDS epidemic, in which people commonly associate risk with sexual decadence (Smith 2003, 2004). The nature of marital intimacy is also shaped—as it is in all societies—by the pragmatic economic and social projects of provisioning a household and raising children. It should not be surprising that marital relationships cannot always fulfill the full range of a person's needs for intimacy, a reality that has been well documented in Western societies as well (Swidler 2001; Coontz 2005). In Nigeria, as in many places, persistent gender inequality shapes how men and women respond to these realities. Extramarital sex is socially available to married men but not to married women. Understanding the nature of intimacy in men's extramarital sexual relationships is the next aspect of the relationship between intimacy, infidelity, and masculinity that I examine.

INFIDELITY AND EXTRAMARITAL INTIMACY

The prevalence of married men's participation in extramarital sex in Nigeria is well documented (Karanja 1987; Orubuloye, Caldwell, and Caldwell 1991; Lawoyin and Larson 2002; Mitsunaga, Powell, Heard, and Larsen 2005). As in many societies, people in southeastern Nigeria commonly attribute men's more frequent participation in extramarital sexual relationships to some sort of innate male predisposition, and this perspective is well represented in the literature (Isiugo-Abanihe 1994; Orubuloye, Caldwell, and Caldwell 1997). Some men and women interviewed in the marital case studies articulated this view. In response to a question about why married men seek extramarital lovers, a fifty-four-year-old civil engineer in Owerri repeated a pidgin English phrase heard frequently among Nigerian men: "Man no be wood. It's something men need, especially African men." Only a piece of wood, he implies, lacks an outward-looking sexual appetite.

While it is important to acknowledge that many Igbo men and women share a conceptualization of men's innate sexual needs and desires for multiple sexual partners, this popular view obscures much of the complexity of male motivation. Explaining men's extramarital sexual behavior in these terms inaccurately reduces men's motives to sexual pleasure. Interviews and observations from my research suggest that, in addition to sexual pleasure, men seek a range of kinds of intimacy that may be unavailable or insufficient in their marriage for reasons that can be understood structurally and culturally, as well as in terms of the specific dynamics and life course of individual marriages. I present three cases of men's extramarital sexual relationships to illustrate the different dimensions of intimacy that men seek and fulfill through infidelity. I try to situate men's motivations in the context of social structural and cultural forces that shape the nature of intimacy in marriage and channel men's actions and desires for intimacy toward extramarital sex. These aspects of intimacy are not necessarily mutually exclusive, but in each case I highlight one aspect for the sake of analytical clarity.

Many men described their extramarital sexual relationships as taking place in the context of prolonged absences from their wife because of work-related migration. In these cases men described their extramarital lover as temporarily replacing their wife, fulfilling dimensions of intimacy the men associated with their marital relationship, including sexual relations, intimate communication, and mutual provisioning of needs according to a gender-specific division of labor. For example, a thirty-eight-year-old civil servant named Chima described a two-year relationship he had with another woman when he was posted far away from his family:

My job makes it difficult. In 1999 I was posted to Afikpo [a distant and somewhat remote town]. Because of my wife's job and the children's schooling we decided she would stay at home. The distance and the high cost of transport meant that I could come home only every other weekend, sometimes only once a month. After a few months in Afikpo I met a young widow who came to my office for assistance on an official matter. I helped her with her problem, and she brought me food to say thank you. From there our relationship developed, and eventually we became lovers. She would cook and wash for me, and I would help her with her economic problems. She was a very good person. I used to tell her my struggles, and she was very sympathetic. It ended when I was transferred.

In the longer conversation Chima made it clear that he was extremely fond of the young widow but also emphasized—as nearly all Igbo men do when they speak of their extramarital lovers—that the woman and the relationship ultimately posed no threat to his marriage. Chima's primary loyalty was to his wife, and he would never have contemplated divorcing her for this—or any other—woman. Like many other married men, Chima did not feel that his extramarital relationship diminished his love for his wife. He was extremely careful to hide the affair from her, and I sensed he did so not only to protect his reputation but out of genuine affection. Patterns of work-related mobility produced by Nigeria's economic diversification, combined with a powerful and assumed gendered division of labor, created circumstances in which migrant men commonly sought intimate relationships to temporarily replace their wife.

Nevertheless many men had extramarital affairs even while they resided with their wife. In these cases one of the most common motivations appeared to be a desire for forms of sexual intimacy that were absent or impossible within marriage. I have already described the way in which notions of sexual morality and decorum affect marital relationships. This dynamic is fueled partly by men's contradictory perceptions and desires with regard to women. Gender double standards mean that it is hard for women to be both a good wife and an exciting lover, because many men perceive a wife who is an exciting lover as also dangerously liberated and even likely to be promiscuous. Igbo men commonly want their wife to be relatively sexually conservative in order to symbolize her faithfulness, yet they also desire forms of sexual intimacy that are perceived to be modern and exciting. To fulfill these desires while preserving the image they want to retain regarding their wife, some men seek an extramarital lover. Obi, a forty-two-year-old merchant, described his experiences with sexual intimacy in extramarital relationships in contrast to his expectations for his wife:

These young girls today *na war-o* [pidgin English, literally, "are a war," figuratively, "are incredible" or "are beyond the pale"]. I mean, there are things they will do in the bed that even I, as the man, would not have thought to initiate. You would think that with these small [young] girls, you would be teaching them, but at times they are teaching you! They do things that my wife dares not. If my wife ever did some of those things, I would probably throw her out, because I would know she had become some kind of professional [a common local synonym for a prostitute].

In the full interview it became evident that the kinds of sexual acts Obi was referring to included oral sex and various positions during intercourse but also the overt ways in which some of his young lovers directed him to satisfy their sexual desires. These were forms of intimacy that many married men found attractive but also problematic. Indeed, men like Obi often spoke openly of their misgivings about and even their condemnation of the sexual morality of their young lovers. Although a strong double standard is at work, most men viewed their wife as morally superior to their young girlfriends, even as the girlfriends fulfilled needs for these forms of sexual intimacy.

The third dimension of intimacy that emerged as a common element in many men's extramarital affairs must also be understood in relation to expectations about intimacy in marriage. While most men whom I interviewed viewed their wife as their primary and permanent partner in the lifelong social and economic project of creating a family and provisioning a household, this family-building partnership seemed to block some forms of intimacy even as it created others. For Igbo men the capacity to provide for one's family is the ultimate measure of manhood. In the precarious economic circumstances of contemporary Nigeria, some of the most important features of Igbo masculinity are constantly under threat. Because providing for one's family is such a difficult task for so many men in the current economic context, a man's relationship with his wife is often fraught with tensions around the family-building and household-provisioning projects. Many men experience their wife's demands and complaints as emblematic of their failure to provide as they should, and a lot of men seek extramarital lovers as a refuge from these problems. By taking care of a young girlfriend these men establish an intimate relationship in which they feel rewarded for their masculine capacity to provide. Ironically, spending limited resources on an outside lover only exacerbates the economic challenges of being a good husband and a good father. Njoku, a forty-three-year-old man who owned a small shop that sold drinks, spoke of these issues:

Everything is struggle in Nigeria. But at times my wife does not seem to understand my predicament. She will always pester me for more chop [food] money or school fees, even when the money is not there. Can I produce naira [Nigeria's currency] by magic? What I have, I always provide. No man wants to see his children suffer. But my wife does not always see with me. . . . [later in the interview:] With Ngozi [his twenty-year-old unmarried lover of several months] I am free of those problems. She is always happy with what I provide for her. And she is sympathetic with my situation. At times, when I am having problems with my business, I will tell her things I do not tell my wife.

The intimacy between Njoku and his young lover reinforced his sense of manhood. That manhood often felt threatened in his marriage, with his wife's complaints symbolizing the difficulties of achieving competent masculinity in Nigeria's struggling economy. Njoku's case represents a common phenomenon in southeastern Nigeria: men seek forms of intimacy with extramarital lovers that will bolster their masculine identity. The dimensions of masculinity at stake for men in these relationships are shaped by structural forces and cultural processes that require a complex and multidimensional understanding of extramarital sex, where men seek different kinds of intimacy in different social fields and relationships. A final central part of the story is men's relationships with other men.

MEN'S INSTITUTIONS, MASCULINITY, AND MALE INTIMACY

Masculinity is created and expressed both in men's relationships to women and in their relationships with other men (Connell 1995). In male-dominated settings such as social and sports clubs, specific sections of the marketplace, and particular bars and eateries, married Igbo men commonly talk about their girlfriends and sometimes show them off. Male peer groups are a significant factor in many men's motivations for and behaviors in extramarital relationships. Yet men also play a central role in regulating each other's extramarital conduct. It is important to identify and delineate the boundaries and social mores that men enforce on each other in their extramarital sexual relationships—rules that emphasize the social value of marriage even as they also permit infidelity.

Because I have always been an avid tennis player, during fieldwork in Nigeria I frequently spend evenings at local sports clubs where a relatively elite, educated, and mostly urban male population plays tennis, drinks beer, and socializes. These sports clubs are heavily male dominated. Indeed, with the exception of bartenders, kitchen staff, receptionists, and members' girlfriends, they are almost exclusively male social settings. The all-male context builds on a much longer history of sex-segregated social organization in Igbo society, where kinship groups and village associations meet in gender-separate forums, church activities and seating are distinctly divided between men's and women's sections, and forms of labor and social space are highly sex segregated at key rituals such as weddings and funerals (Uchendu 1965). The way in which Igbo men seek, construct, and experience intimacy in all-male social settings is itself worthy of extensive exposition. Here I focus only on how men's extramarital sexual behavior intersects with and is partly explained by male-male intimacy.

I describe two cases in which aspects of male intimacy facilitate men's participation in extramarital sex, followed by an example in which men reinforce the boundaries of acceptable conduct. I draw on my experience at one particular tennis club because these examples stand for a much larger corpus of similar situations that I have observed at this and other clubs but also in many other male-dominated social settings in southeastern Nigeria. In these predominantly male contexts, men encourage and reward extramarital relationships. Further, the ways in which men discuss, share, encourage, *and* regulate each other's extramarital behavior are part of how men create and navigate intimacy with each other. While it is perhaps common sense to connect male infidelity to performances of masculinity, the centrality of intramale intimacy in men's motives and conduct adds an ironic but crucial twist to the analysis of such behavior.

Seeing men encourage and reward each other for extramarital sex is an everyday experience in masculine spaces like the tennis club. Men will compliment each other about the beauty of their lover and listen admiringly to stories about recent sexual exploits. While sexual virility is one aspect of masculinity that is performed and reinforced when married men show off a younger unmarried lover, demonstrating socioeconomic status is equally central to men's public self-presentation. Although my friends commonly complained among themselves about the consumptive demands and desires of their girlfriend—symbolized most recently by the growing expectations for cellular phones—it was also true that the capacity to provide these things was precisely part of what men were demonstrating to themselves and their peers in keeping an expensive girlfriend. One man's nickname provides an emblematic example of the interconnections between masculine performances of sexual prowess, socioeconomic status, and the qualities of intramale intimacy that facilitate men's extramarital sex. A young businessman, who was both one of the richest members of the tennis club and one of the most blatant philanderers, earned the nickname "One-Man Show." Whenever he entered the club, his mates would shout this moniker in unison with great endearment and admiration. The nickname was in recognition of the parade of beautiful women he brought to the club but also an acknowledgment of the economic resources necessary to keep so many beautiful young girlfriends. It was obvious that One-Man Show enjoyed the accolades of his male peers at least as much as the attention from his female partners.

The degree to which intramale intimacy figures into men's extramarital sexual behavior was illustrated in a personal way in 2004 when I accompanied my teammates from the tennis club to play a match in the city of Nnewi. In typical fashion the host club provided us drinks and dinner after the match. Many of my teammates had brought a girlfriend along for the trip—these away matches are excellent opportunities for infidelity. In addition, our hosts made sure that plenty of local young women attended the party after the match. I left the party early—around 10 P.M.—because I had begun to feel feverish. By midnight I was shivering under my covers with chills despite the hot ambient temperature. I was coming down with a case of malaria. As I huddled under my covers I heard a knock. When I opened the door, a pretty young woman told me that her friend—the girlfriend of my teammate who had driven me to Nnewi—had told her I was alone and might want some company. I told her I was not feeling well and said no thank you, returning to my covers. A few minutes later came another knock. This time it was my teammate. He came to reiterate the offer of the young woman, expressing genuine concern about my lonely state. It was obvious that he had facilitated the initial visit of the young woman through his girlfriend, and it was clearly a gesture of friendship and male solidarity. I told him I thought I had malaria and couldn't manage a woman. He said that if I felt better, they would all be in the disco, and he would make sure the woman stayed available for me.

My malaria helped me out of a difficult spot, as I was so feverish that I could avoid confronting the temptation posed by the pretty young woman and save face with my teammates, who would, no doubt, hear about the evening's events. Although I was protected by my malaria, at stake in the interaction with my teammate were both the perception of my masculinity—after all, "man no be wood"—and an aspect of intimacy in my male friendship. In addition to whatever temptation I might have felt had I not been sick, the pressure to receive the young woman would have come not only from a socially prevalent expectation regarding how to maintain a culturally acceptable masculinity but also from my membership in an intimate male social group. While these two aspects are intertwined, I think it is important to emphasize the latter to highlight the ways in which men's intimacy with each other is part of what men are navigating in their extramarital sexual behavior.

My tennis teammates, and indeed all my friends and colleagues in Nigeria, know that I am married to a Nigerian woman. It is commonly this aspect of my identity that is most celebrated. My tennis mates typically call me *ogo*, which is the Igbo word for *in-law*. I always feel that I am the recipient of extra affection and respect because of my in-law status. That my male friends, who privilege my marriage to an Igbo woman so highly, would also go out of their way to help me have an extramarital relationship speaks volumes about the complexity of how Igbo men see infidelity in relationship to marriage. The irony is that in Igbo society marriage is so sacred that extramarital sex poses little threat, at least in terms of how men conceptualize their behavior.

The primacy of marriage and the ways in which Igbo men collectively enforce this primacy on each other is illustrated by the case of a man at the tennis club who was heavily sanctioned by his male peers for his behavior in an extramarital relationship. At the time the man, Chibuike, was a thirty-six-year-old married father of four. He was involved in an intense relationship with a student at a local university, and he brought her to the club almost daily. Chibuike conducted himself, however, in ways that other men found highly inappropriate. While it is acceptable to "show off" girlfriends in male-dominated social spaces like the club, Chibuike paraded around with his girlfriend in fully public and sex-integrated settings, such that his wife and in-laws became aware of his affair. He openly touched and kissed his girlfriend in these public environments (whereas most men restrict physical contact with girlfriends to private venues), and he would sometimes spend several nights away from his home, sleeping with his lover. Worst of all, from his peers' point of view, he squandered his money on his girlfriend to the extent that he was no longer adequately supporting his family. To make a long story short, the club members organized themselves and intervened. A group counseled Chibuike to stop the affair, threatened him with suspension from the club, and even visited the wife in solidarity with her predicament, urging her to endure while they acted to rein in her husband. From an Igbo male point of view, competent masculinity allows and even encourages extramarital sex but not at the expense of taking responsibility for one's family.

All these examples, whether they are enabling men's infidelity or checking it, demonstrate the key role played by men's relationships with each other in the motives and dynamics of male extramarital sexual behavior. Of course, not all men cheat on their wife, and understanding what distinguishes men who cheat from men who remain faithful is an important challenge, particularly in the era of HIV. I have focused on understanding male infidelity, including how infidelity is shaped by a social construction of masculinity that includes multiple dimensions of intimacy rather than being antithetical to it. When men cheat on their wife in southeastern Nigeria, it is often as much about their relationships with other men as it is about their relationship with their wife and their lovers.

***

Studies from many different societies suggest that one characteristic of modern marriage, despite its cross-cultural diversity, is a transformation of intimacy (Collier 1997; Rebhun 1999; Hirsch 2003; Coontz 2005). These accounts suggest that as the institution of marriage changes along with other processes of social transformation, men and women increasingly privilege forms of interpersonal intimacy that distinguish contemporary couples from previous generations. Much of the evidence I collected in Nigeria suggests that marriage is changing in similar ways in the Igbo-speaking Southeast. Yet the growing importance of the conjugal relationship vis-à-vis other kinship ties, the emergence of romantic love as an important criterion for choosing a spouse, and the increasingly acknowledged value of many forms of marital intimacy have not resulted in an obvious reduction in male infidelity.

Although it is common to think of male infidelity as a violation of intimacy between husband and wife (indeed, many Igbo women also think of it this way), attributing men's extramarital sexual behavior simply to men's failure or incapacity to maintain an intimate relationship obscures the degree to which male infidelity involves multiple and sometimes contradictory intimacies. In this chapter I have argued that both the way men "do" intimacy in marriage and the centrality of intimacy in all-male peer groups contribute to producing infidelity. Further, I have shown that men's extramarital relationships are partly the product of men's desires for forms of sexual intimacy that many men feel are inappropriate in marriage. Infidelity, I have argued, is a product of men's strong desire for intimacy rather than its negation.

The dimensions of intimacy that shape men's infidelity are inextricably intertwined with the social construction of masculinity. To the extent that it might be important to encourage men to behave differently with regard to infidelity—for example, because of the risks posed by HIV; because the families they value so much might be put in jeopardy by their behavior, even absent HIV; because constructions of masculinity that enable infidelity are fundamentally gender unequal; or because their wife would be happier—the evidence from southeastern Nigeria suggests that change will be difficult. Male infidelity is paradoxically tied to the exalted position of marriage in Igbo society and the superior status of wives vis-à-vis unmarried women. If married Igbo women challenge men's infidelity too openly, the women risk undermining their own position. Given how important men's intimate relations with their male peers are—perhaps especially in this society with such a long, wide-ranging, and powerful system of sex-segregated social organization—and given how instrumental men are in encouraging, rewarding, *and* restraining each other's extramarital sexual behavior, perhaps these male peer groups would be an appropriate place to think about initiating change. Such efforts could take advantage of masculinity rather than combat it.

Notes

1. The "Love, Marriage and HIV" study is funded by the National Institutes of Health (1 R01 41724–01A1). I am grateful to Jennifer Hirsch, Shanti Parikh, Harriet Phinney, and Holly Wardlow, my collaborators on the project, whose intellectual contributions to my thinking about these issues have been invaluable.

REFERENCES

Bledsoe, Caroline and Giles Pison, eds. 1994. *Nuptuality in Sub-Saharan Africa: Contemporary Anthropological and Demographic Perspectives*. Oxford: Clarendon.

Caldwell, John and Pat Caldwell. 1987. "The Cultural Context of High Fertility in Sub-Saharan Africa." *Population and Development Review* 13 (3): 409–37.

Collier, Jane. 1997. *From Duty to Desire: Remaking Families in a Spanish Village*. Princeton, N.J.: Princeton University Press.

Connell, R. W. 1995. *Masculinities*. Cambridge: Polity.

Coontz, Stephanie. 2005. *Marriage, a History: From Obedience to Intimacy, or How Love Conquered Marriage*. New York: Viking.

Cornwall, Andrea. 2002. "Spending Power: Love, Money, and the Reconfiguration of Gender Relations in Ada-Odo, Southwestern Nigeria." *American Ethnologist* 29 (4): 963–80.

Feldman-Savelsberg, Pamela. 1999. *Plundered Kitchens, Empty Wombs: Threatened Reproduction and Identity in Cameroonian Grassfields*. Ann Arbor: University of Michigan Press.

Fortes, Meyer. 1978. "Parenthood, Marriage and Fertility in West Africa." *Journal of Development Studies* 14 (4): 121–48.

Hirsch, Jennifer. 2003. *A Courtship after Marriage: Sexuality and Love in Mexican Transnational Families*. Berkeley: University of California Press.

Hunter, Mark. 2002. "The Materiality of Everyday Sex: Thinking beyond 'Prostitution.'" *African Studies* 61 (1): 99–120.

Isiugo-Abanihe, Uche. 1994. "Extramarital Sexual Relations and Perceptions of HIV/AIDS in Nigeria." *Health Transition Review* 4:111–25.

Karanja, Wambui. 1987. "'Outside Wives' and 'Inside Wives' in Nigeria: A Study of Changing Perceptions of Marriage." In D. Parkin and D. Nyamwaya, eds., *Transformations in African Marriage*, pp. 247–61. Manchester, U.K.: Manchester University Press.

Lawoyin, T. O. and U. M. Larsen. 2002. "Male Sexual Behavior during Wife's Pregnancy and Postpartum Abstinence Period in Oyo State, Nigeria." *Journal of Biosocial Science* 34 (1): 51–63.

Luke, Nancy. 2003. "Age and Economic Asymmetries in the Sexual Relationships of Adolescent Girls in sub-Saharan Africa." *Studies in Family Planning* 34 (2): 67–86.

——. 2005. "Confronting the 'Sugar Daddy' Stereotype: Age and Economic Asymmetries and Risky Sexual Behavior in Urban Kenya." *International Family Planning Perspectives* 31 (1): 6–14.

Machel, J. Z. 2001. "Unsafe Sexual Behavior among Schoolgirls in Mozambique: A Matter of Class and Gender." *Reproductive Health Matters* 9 (17): 82–90.

Mitsunaga, T. M., A. M. Powell, N. J. Heard, and U. M. Larsen. 2005. "Extramarital Sex among Nigerian Men: Polygyny and Other Risk Factors." *Journal of Acquired Immune Deficiency Syndrome* 39 (4): 478–88.

Orubuloye, I. O., John Caldwell, and Pat Caldwell. 1991. "Sexual Networking in Ekiti District of Nigeria." *Studies in Family Planning* 22 (2): 61–73.

——. 1997. "Perceived Male Sexual Needs and Male Sexual Behavior in Southwest Nigeria." *Social Science and Medicine* 44 (8): 1195–1207.

Rebhun, Linda-Anne. 1999. *The Heart Is Unknown Country: Love in the Changing Economy of Northeast Brazil.* Stanford, Calif.: Stanford University Press.

Smith, Daniel Jordan. 2000. "'These Girls Today *Na War-O*': Premarital Sexuality and Modern Identity in Southeastern Nigeria." *Africa Today* 47 (3–4): 98–120.

——. 2001. "Romance, Parenthood and Gender in a Modern African Society." *Ethnology* 40 (2): 129–51.

——. 2002. "'Man No Be Wood': Gender and Extramarital Sex in Contemporary Southeastern Nigeria." *Ahfad Journal* 19 (2): 4–23.

——. 2003. "Imagining HIV/AIDS: Morality and Perceptions of Personal Risk in Nigeria." *Medical Anthropology* 22 (4): 343–72.

——. 2004. "Youth, Sin and Sex in Nigeria: Christianity and HIV-related Beliefs and Behaviour among Rural-Urban Migrants." *Culture, Health and Sexuality* 6 (5): 425–37.

Swidler, Ann. 2001. *Talk of Love: How Culture Matters.* Chicago: University of Chicago Press.

Uchendu, Victor. 1965. *The Igbo of Southeast Nigeria.* Fort Worth, Texas: Holt, Reinhart and Winston.

10. "I Have His Heart, Swinging Is Just Sex"
The Ritualization of Sex and the Rejuvenation of the Love Bond in an American Spouse Exchange Community

William Jankowiak and Laura Mixson

*R*esearch into the foundations of enduring love has found that the intensity of a couple's emotional intimacy is often diluted whenever sexual infidelity is tolerated, if not encouraged (Collins and Gregor 1995; also see Person 1988). These observations find support in Benjamin Zablocki's comprehensive 1980 study of 120 communes that found a close relationship between the number of sex partners and an individual's inability to sustain a love bond. He also found a solid correlation between the feeling of being in love and the number of sex partners: the higher the number of sex partners, the lower an individual's feeling of love (Collins and Gregor 1995:76–79). In effect, love is dyadic or it is nothing. Zablocki's finding is consistent with other studies of every known group-marriage community (e.g., Oneida, Kerista, New Buffalo, and so forth). This finding illustrates the insurmountable difficulties that group-love arrangements hold for individuals and their society (Berger, Cohen, and Zelditch 1972:244). Because symbolic boundaries are vital for the maintenance and enhancement of a long-term intimate relationship (Person 1988), sex-inclusive communes *never* last beyond the life span of its founding generation. In fact, in a relatively short time they are often abandoned in favor of some type of pair-bond relationship (Hatfield, Traupmann, and Walster 1978; Zablocki 1980).

An alternative, albeit more philosophical, position (Berlant 2000; Reich 1973; Smith 1974) contends that the pursuit of sexual variety can readily be uncoupled from the love bond. Berlant, Reich, Smith, and other advocates of this position (Anapol 1997; Kipnis 2000; see overview in Wolfe 2003) maintain that because individuals are reflective beings who make choices about their lives, they can, at least in matters of sex and love, overcome societal conventions. From this perspective the pursuit of sexual variety within a loving relationship can easily be separated without negatively affecting the emotional strength of a couple's marriage. Advocates point out that American spouse exchange, or "swinging," involves having a large number of sex partners without the dilution of an enduring love bond. This is offered as proof of the feasibility of separating sex from love without diminishing marital love's intensity.

This raises several questions: (1) If passionate or romantic love is a dyadic bond that requires emotional exclusivity to survive and thrive (Jankowiak 1995, 2000; Jankowiak, Sudakov, and Wilreker 2005), what impact does spouse exchange have on the maintenance of symbolic borders and thus the overall quality of their love experience? (2) Are spouse exchange participants truly capable of developing close relationships? (3) If so, how do they manage emotional issues that tear apart sex-inclusive communes and most "open marriages"?[1] (4) If swinger marriages are relatively successful, does that suggest there are alternative means other than sexual exclusivity to signal emotional union? To this end American spouse exchange constitutes an excellent arena in which to study the relative success of efforts to uncouple sex from love within a satisfying marital union.[2]

A word on methodology: Many studies (notable exceptions are Bartell 1971; Gilmartin 1978) on American spouse exchange have been written from a partisan or advocacy perspective. Consequently, the researchers tend to become trapped by their own "utopian" conviction and highlight selective cases supportive of this conviction. We sought to avoid not becoming caught up in the utopian spirit by striving to retain a level of objectivity that meant exploring contradictions in participants' statements and behavior. Throughout the study we sought to understand the institution of spouse exchange as another way to interpret the often intertwined relationship between sex and love. Our study is not intended to serve as an advocacy position paper or a morality fable. It is written from an ethnographic perspective that seeks to understand how participants thought about their lives and behaved in a variety of contexts.

The data were collected between 1998 and 2000 in Las Vegas, Nevada. Sixty individuals who practiced spouse exchange were interviewed together and/or separately concerning their involvement with the swinging lifestyle. A few interviews ($n = 6$) were conducted with both researchers present. Other interviews ($n = 21$) were conducted with just one researcher present. The remaining thirty-three interviews were conducted by e-mail or the use of a survey questionnaire that was distributed by student aides. Twenty-seven interviews were conducted with both spouses/partners present. This method enables us to look for indirect indexes of attachment (i.e., eye contact, touching, facial expression, completion of sentences, and positive humor). Most interviews took place in public settings (e.g., coffee shops, local restaurants). A few took place in private homes. The age cohorts of our sample range from 21 to 29 years old (14 individuals); 30 to 39 years old (6); 40 to 49 years old (22); 50 to 59 years old (17); and older than 60 (1).

We wanted to determine the extent to which the participants were emotionally involved or withdrawn from one another. To this end we observed the frequency with which they interacted with, smiled at, or focused their attention on one another or completed each other's sentences. Married couples, many of whom had known one coauthor for a number of years, were also asked to discuss how they met one another, their favorite memories of being together, and crisis points that resulted in the transformation of their love during their marriage. From these and other questions we were able to compare swingers' attitudes and feelings of involvement with Collins and Gregor's Midwest couple survey, which is discussed in their insightful unpublished manuscript "Narratives of Love." In addition, we explored "problematic events" when couples had a serious disagreement about how to arrange and behave in a spouse exchange situation. By focusing on these problematic events we were able to identify some of the tacit norms that structure these swingers' marital relationship. Using these indicators also enabled us to form an overall impression of the quality of a couple's marital intimacy.

By asking each participant about her or his ground rules for selecting a sex partner within and outside a party environment, we sought to understand how swingers structure their spouse exchange transactions. How do they communicate with their partner about selecting or rejecting a sexual invitation? Who approaches whom about the idea? What style of spouse exchange do they prefer (e.g., full swing versus soft swing, couples or singles, bisexual or heterosexual)?[3] What do they find the most erotic about swinging? What do they like most and least about being involved in the life-style? Why do they prefer a swinging lifestyle to an open marriage lifestyle? We delved into participants' attitudes toward adultery or cheating. We also wanted to determine whether jealousy is a recurrent problem. If so, how do they deal with it? We make no claim for statistical representativeness. We asked the standard survey questions: age, gender, length time married, how long in the lifestyle, and types and frequency of sexual behavior. The validity of the interviews was cross-checked by Laura Mixson, a former participant and observer of interactions at swinger clubs (e.g., Red Roster, Green Door, and the like) and at private "invitation only" house parties.[4]

ARE SWINGERS CAPABLE OF LOVE?

Popular conceptions of swingers often hold that they are people who are either extremely eccentric or psychologically troubled. Researchers (Bartell 1971; Butler 1979; Constantine and Constantine 1973; Dixon 1985; Gilmartin 1978; Leavitt 1988; Rubin 2001) have repeatedly noted that participants did not demonstrate deep-seated emotional problems or show any visible social pathology. Today the consensus is that swingers are ordinary people en-gaged in a different, albeit for nonpractitioners, non-normative sex behav-ior (Bergstrand and Blevins Williams 2000; Jenks 1985a, 1985b; Jenks 1998).

Among the swingers interviewed, we found evidence of long-term com-mitment and material and social support, strong symbolic boundaries that define couples unity. For example, they often dreamed of one another, com-pleted each other's sentences (suggesting that they are familiar enough to know one another's thoughts), demonstrated attachment through touching and looking at one another, especially whenever a partner left or returned to the interview area. In every way participants demonstrated in subtle and not-so-subtle fashions their mutual involvement or love for one another.

We found that interviewees vividly recalled the beginnings of their rela-tionship. These memories were emblematic of the density of their bounded relationship (Collins and Gregor n.d.). Significantly, no one mentioned spouse exchange as a defining aspect of what made the pair a couple. Every-one could provide examples of a turning point, or an event or moment, in which a spouse became acutely aware of the other partner's commitment. These turning points usually occurred during some crisis point in the mar-riage: a serious personal illness or that of an in-law, a son or daughter's dilemma, or financial trouble. In many ways these events of sacrifice form the based for the stories that signal their transformation into a more united loving union and thus served as evidence of the strength of their marriage.

These acts of kindness, consideration, and commitment also served as the basis for the formulation of a couple's anchoring memories and as a statement of their mutual commitment. Because anchoring memories are symbolic of a strong bounded relationship (Collins and Gregor n.d.), they are an important index of the presence or absence of intimacy. A case in point is the memory of a forty-two-year-old woman, who had been married for more than seventeen years, of her first encounter with her future husband: "We met at a mutual friend's wedding," she giggled, "we were staring at each other across the room. She [the friend] said that it was obvious that we would be together." Her husband then pointed out (as his wife continued to giggle) that he thought she was already married and was immensely disappointed that such a strikingly beautiful woman was already taken. It was obvious to us that this was a tale the couple had repeated often. It was equally obvious that there remained a strong emotional connection between them. For most swingers their couple-origin story served, as it had for Collins and Gregor's sample of nonswinger couples, as their most vivid and emotionally salient anchoring memory.

THE MEANING OF LOVE

Swingers' model of love is a combination of a romantic love and companionship love organized around the pursuit of pleasure more than it is a confluent or self-actualized love (Giddens 1992). Swingers' notions of love, intimacy, and sexual pleasure are remarkably similar to those of mainstream Americans. Victor De Munck's (n.d.) research among East Coast Americans found their model of love had the following attributes: spending time together, trust, honesty, caring, sacrifice, and sharing that may or may not include sexual intimacy (also see Swidler 2001; Canican 1987).

Swingers also thought that love includes focusing attention on the person you care deeply about. A twenty-seven-year-old woman acknowledged that she was obsessed with her husband. She said, "We are best friends. Not a minute goes by that we do not reassure each other that our relationship is the most important emotion in our lives. We never run out of things to talk about, and we support each other's thoughts and ideas." A thirty-four-year-old man also thought love involved sharing personal concerns and life goals. For him love is present in a "long-term relationship . . . [in which] you find true love that you can share yourself and your dreams with. Really, isn't that most people's goal?" A twenty-four-year-old woman thought love was being together: "I like lying in our apartment just cuddling and gazing into his big brown eyes. He looks like this little puppy dog that is in the window of the pet store just waiting for you to take him with you. I wouldn't give up those moments for anything in the world."

Another woman thought feelings of trust were an important aspect of a loving commitment. She told us that "crazy as it may sound, the lifestyle taught me to trust Charles and be honest with him, regardless of the outcome. He brain fucks me; he makes love to my mind, along with my body. I give him that, because the love that I feel for Charles in my heart doesn't compare to the grains of sand in the ocean." A forty-four-year-old woman thought love was best recognized through the sacrifice spouses made for one another. She offered the following event that altered the way she perceived her husband: "I love him, but it was a kind of ordinary love—a comfort love. When my mother got brain cancer, she came to live with us (really at my husband's insistence) as opposed to being placed in a nursing home. He was so kind to her. He really took charge after my mother died and handled the details of her estate. It was during this long time that I came to see him for who he really was: a caring, kind, and immensely generous man. I knew I would always and forever love him, and I have." What stands out from these interviews is the immense appreciation partners have for one another. In effect, they have deep, sustained attachment.

If the quality of love can be identified through its nonverbal expressions of intimacy, commonality of memories, stories of love's beginnings, and acts of personal sacrifice as reported by Collins and Gregor (n.d.), then Las Vegas swingers in our sample have created and sustained enduring love bonds (see Cook 2005 for a similar finding among polyamours and polyfriendly groups in Northern California).

EROTIC VALIDATION AND MUTUAL PLEASURE

The swingers we interviewed enjoy the opportunity to explore their sexual fantasies as well as participate in real sexual adventures (see Gould 2000 for a national overview of swingers' erotic preferences and behaviors). Women overwhelmingly stressed an exhibitionistic delight in wearing sexy clothes, whereas men noted the importance of having a sexual experience with different women. Swinging has a voyeuristic quality: the women are excited by watching their mates receive pleasure, and the men are excited by watching their wife having sex with another man. The majority of women interviewed admitted becoming more sexually excited by verbal stimulation. Middle-aged (older than forty-five) men and women mentioned the youthfulness of their sex partner as a source of pride and pleasure. We also found within the twentysomething cohort ($n = 14$) a greater reluctance to share a spouse than in the thirtysomething cohort ($n = 46$). The disparity may arise out of a stronger interest in mate guarding among individuals in their reproductive prime, or it may arise from having a strong erotic desire for the spouse that diminishes interest in seeking an alternative erotic outlet, or it could arise from " a paucity of attractive exchange opportunities, as people in their 20's are a distinct minority in the swinging community" (Christopher Ryan, personal communication, 2006). Whatever an individual's sexual preference or experience, all interviewees noted their satisfaction in seeing their partner find sexual fulfillment with someone else. For both spouses this constituted what some refer to as a "special gift" that one gave the other. For example, a twenty-nine-year-old woman noted that she "loves to share my man with another woman and still know I am number one in his life. To be able to trust him and give him everything he wants . . . this is a tacit gift, and I enjoy him enjoying my gift."

To this end we wanted to understand how swingers were able to negotiate the difference between love and sex. Our sex survey found striking sex differences in the frequency of orgasm as well as the criteria used to select a sex partner. Men reported more frequent orgasm than women. Forty of 60 men acknowledged reaching an orgasm (through oral sex, sexual intercourse, or masturbation) all the time, whereas 20 of 59 women reported always having an orgasm. Four men reported having an orgasm less than 10 percent of the time compared with 8 women who acknowledged seldom reaching an orgasm. Performance anxiety affected half the men interviewed but only 10 percent of the women. The men's reasons for experience anxiety ranged from physical incompatibility to not feeling comfortable enough, in the words of a fortysomething man, "to relax and let themselves go."

AGE AND GENDER DIFFERENCES IN PARTICIPATION

A common expression that swingers readily invoke for "who talked who" into participating is "It is men who introduce their wife to swinging, but it is the wife who makes them stay." The point is clear: Once women discover the joys of sexual variety, they have a hunger for it that rivals and, in some incidences, surpasses men's. However, we found generational and sex differences. For couples forty and older, husbands overwhelmingly (33 of 41, or 80 percent) introduced their wife to the idea; among the 21–29-year-old cohort, nearly 50 percent of the couples (9 of 19) noted they had mutually agreed to the idea. This generational difference may arise from erotic satisfaction's being held as more of an end point in some marriages as well as women's increased economic autonomy in society. Whatever the reason(s), it is clear that young women found sexual enjoyment through participating in a spouse exchange arrangement.

There are also sex differences in that more women than men acknowledged a lack of interest in participating in spouse exchange transactions. Seven women ($n = 7$, or 23 percent) admitted not being satisfied with the arrangement. These women participate as a favor to their husbands, whom they clearly want to please. As one thirty-four-year-old woman noted: " I get very little out of it. I do not like sex with other women, and I never have an orgasm. . . . Maybe it is because I care too much for my husband." Significantly, more women ($n = 13$) than men ($n = 8$) stressed that their home sex is more emotionally fulfilling than the casual sex with strangers. Still, 77 percent of the women we interviewed ($n = 21$ of 30) enjoyed their participation in a spouse exchange arrangement and wanted to continue.

Men and women gave various reasons for participating in a swinger lifestyle. For a thirty-three-year-old man it is the opportunity "to try new things—if you get bored you find someone else. I like new bodies." For a twenty-eight-year-old couple who are open to everything, it is "threesomes with another woman." For a twenty-eight-year-old male it is "discovering that different people do different things in bed." He elaborates: "It's a turn-on to sleep with someone new every now and then. This way I get to have a steady relationship and big tits—my wife doesn't have a whole lot behind the bra strap and isn't into all that kinky stuff. She refuses to have anal sex." A fifty-year-old man said, "I get a lot out of it—it totally turned my libido on. After so many years you get tired of eating cheesecake—every now and then you need ice cream." A fifty-two-year-old woman's desire for oral sex motivated her to participate in spouse exchange. She added, "My husband just won't do it. Variety spices up everything between us and allows us to be closer to one another. It has renewed our interest in one another."

A twenty-eight-year-old woman noted that her enjoyment of having sex with other women was one of the reasons for participating in a group sex encounter. In fact, she added that "being able to fulfill my passion for women revitalized my sex life with my husband." A twenty-six-year-old woman who preferred hard-core swinging noted, "We work to ensure each other's gratification and satisfaction. We both enjoy it rough." A twenty-eight-year-old man stressed his enjoyment in "playing with my fantasies in the way most guys don't. I get to have rough sex with two women and still have a loving and great marriage." A forty-eight-year-old woman found that swinging rejuvenated her feelings for her husband, even though she initially thought she would be "too ashamed to be able to ever look at my husband's eyes again."

Swingers' erotic narratives also contained an overt concern for and a loyalty to upholding their marriage. A forty-eight-year-old swinger acknowledged the difference between sex and love could be thought of as a difference between emotional sacrifice and physical fun. He pointed out that "love is knowing that you would sacrifice anything for your wife and she will for you. Swinging is sex without a heart. It is fun and exciting, but that's it." Another man, who was thirty-nine, acknowledged that "I'm not in love with any of these other women, nor do I want to be with them everyday. I love my wife and my kids, and if there was ever a question of anything relating to swinging coming in between us, it would stop instantly." A twenty-nine-year-old woman emphasized the difference between sex with a stranger and sex with her husband: "We keep our emotions at home and save intimacy for our bedroom. Swinging is not to find a new relationship. Swinging is strictly sexual gratification." Perhaps the most poignant illustration of the difficulty in separating sexual from emotional exclusivity is voiced by a twenty-four-year-old man who acknowledged being erotically turned on by attending swinger parties. However, he and his spouse have never shared an orgasm under any circumstance. They preferred to wait until they got home to focus their sexual appetite on each other. Clearly, some swinger relationships are tightly bounded, intense, and authentic. We found clues to how this group of Las Vegas swingers has successfully decoupled love and sex where other sex-inclusive communities have failed.

RITUALS AND CULTURE MEANING

Rituals have many functions—"they can channel and express emotions, guide and reinforce forms of behavior, support or subvert the status quo, bring about change, or restore harmony and balance" (Bowie 2006:138). Because rituals are often used to overcome or manage anxiety (Frescska and Kulcsar 1988), they are "symbolic means for channeling unacceptable emotions" (Lindholm 2001:170; see also Shore 1996). In effect, rituals are inventions designed to resolve "potential threats to [humans'] fitness" (Boyer and Liénard 2006:2). The swingers' dilemma arises from trying to serve often-competing desires: erotic satisfaction through pursuing sexual variety, and emotional fulfillment through pair-bond exclusivity. We will argue that the participants' ability to insulate themselves from overt expressions of sexual jealousy arises from conforming to specific action sequences that ensure that the couple remains within a ritualized setting that serves to promote emotional fidelity and with it the continuing importance of the marital union.

Charles Stafford (2000:20) was the first anthropologist to point out that rituals contain elements that encourage individuals to become separated from their surroundings and then reintegrated or reunited in those surroundings or social order. Rituals are often organized to promote distance so that people can reunite and thus reexperience a sentiment of belonging to a community or to one another. Stafford thought that much of the emotional force that individuals experience while participating in a ritual performance derives from this process.

Spouse exchange is not unique to contemporary Euro-American societies. Ford and Beach (1951:115) found spouse exchange practiced in 55 of 139 cultures, or 39 percent. Spouse exchange around the globe shares several common features: It is seldom based on spontaneous choice but rather is organized around a *ritualized* code of conduct that highlights each spouse's authority to approve or reject the transaction. The reasons given for engaging in spouse exchange range from the need to form closer male alliances to establishing a social insurance in terms of extra male support for offspring (Hrdy 1999) to possible female romantic attraction (Stern and Condon 1995) to erotic satisfaction (Wolfe 2003).[5] From a comparative perspective American spouse exchange should be perceived not as an oddity but as another variation of a rather ubiquitous cultural institution.

It is our thesis that American swingers usually communicate the primacy of *the pair bond* over unrestricted sex choice when they participate in a spouse exchange arrangement. Because the process of separation also involves the process of reintegration, the process of separation contributes to the production of a special sentiment of belonging or mutuality. Contrary to a self-actualization model, which emphasizes agency or will power as the primary means to separate sex from love within a pair-bond relationship, swingers relied more upon a ritualization of the sex encounter that makes the couple and not the individual the more central and thus more valued unit. In this way swingers implicitly understand the importance of ritual practices for muting sexual jealousy while upholding the central place of their marital bond. We hope to make this statement clearer as we continue the discussion.

The Performance Phases of Swinging

We found three distinct phases or action sequences to American swinging. These involve preparation, participation, and rejuvenation of the pair-bond phase. In each phase the spouses remain acutely conscious of one another's needs, interests, and desires.

The Preparation Phase

In the preparation phase many spouses verbally and nonverbally seek to reassure one another through overt acts of consideration. In every way participants remain conscious that they are a couple.

In preparing to attend a swinger party most couples engage in acts of reassurance that are manifested in a spouse's demonstrating greater consideration, such as offering more frequent compliments, acts of consideration (e.g., opening the car door, selecting attractive clothes to wear, and agreeing to a spouse's request to enter into a sexual exchange with a specific person). This phase can also be a time of rising insecurities. One thirty-four-year-old woman reported how she and her husband "try to discuss our anxieties and concerns with each other. . . . For example, I used to be against him being attracted to blondes with overdeveloped breasts. I had a hard time with him being attracted to a girl who looked different than me. I felt that he was looking for something that I didn't have or couldn't offer. . . . I am now less worried about that, but there can be other small things that may arise, and it is good to discuss them." Not everyone discussed things with her or his spouse. Six people ($n = 3$ couples) acknowledged that they often were too self-absorbed in anticipation of the pending event to focus on their spouse. For them, spouse exchange appears to be more of an opportunity to momentarily escape their marriage than a time to rejuvenate their feelings for each other.

THE PARTICIPATION PHASE

It is common in large American urbanite social parties for couples to separate upon arrival, only to link up later in the evening. In contrast, the majority of participants at a swinger party/club seldom separate from one another. For swingers this is the time of heightened anticipation and anxiety: Will they be able to attract someone they find appealing? It is also the time when the spouses continue to focus their attention on one another. For example, many wives are pleased when their spouse wants to escort them to the bar or to the restroom. Women considered this presentational ritual to be further evidence of their husband's concern for their well-being and commitment to the marriage. Moreover, many women commented that they did not like unattached single men "hitting" on them. Being accompanied by their husband signaled the unavailability of these women. At these events couples often sat next to one another and frequently touched each other's arm, hand, or hair while quietly discussing or nonverbally signaling their sex-partner preference.

"All sexual practices function within some kind of moral system" (Davenport 1965:211). Swingers are no different. There are standard rules (e.g., be courteous, arrive together and leave together, dress appropriately) that couples can and often modify. Ideally, unless otherwise discussed and agreed upon, each spouse has the right to veto another's sex-partner selection. In a way, arranging a spouse exchange can be more complicated than single dating. First, four people have to agree. If one partner does not want to participate but prefers someone else, the entire arrangement may be canceled. This is not always the case, however. If one spouse, for example, is not attracted to another swinger but knows that his or her partner is attracted to that person, the reluctant spouse will agree with a reminder that at the next swinger outing she or he will have first choice and that it cannot be vetoed.

Not every swinger believes it is important to seek a spouse's approval before having sex. Leanna Wolfe's research among Californians found that 35 percent of her sample population (which included more polyamory participants than swingers) did not seek partner approval before having sex (2003:161). In contrast, we found that 80 percent of our sample population thought it was essential to receive a spouse's approval before having sex. Whatever the variation, for the majority of these swingers the importance of the marital bond remains a stabilizing force throughout the spouse exchange negotiation.

Selecting a potential sex exchange partner is never a free-for-all. There are patterns in swingers' selection criteria. First, it is based on relative age, looks, intelligence (as demonstrated in conversational ability), dress, and cleanliness (i.e., social class). Swingers tend to pick someone from a similar social class. Because of an uneasiness about the possibility of being rejected as a desirable sex partner, participants, especially middle-aged men, prefer to select someone who is in a similar age cohort. There are exceptions. This is especially true of mixed-age couples. Mixed-age spouses tend to swing only with couples who are also of mixed age. But even this arrangement is not without potential drawbacks. For example, a twenty-five-year-old woman married to a middle-aged man often wonders: "Will a young man's twenty-five-year-old wife want my fifty-plus husband?" The answer is often no.

Another exception to the selection of a partner from a similar age cohort occurs when older women (that is, older than fifty) choose younger unmarried men. Since single men have no partner to exchange, it is harder for them to participate in marriage exchange negotiations. The primary way that single men participate is as extra(s). Because some husbands are erotically stimulated by watching their wife having sex with other men, they (with their wife's approval) organize single or multiple sex-partner encounters. This type of arrangement is frequent enough that single men hang out at the bars in anticipation of being asked to participate.

When a couple agrees to a spouse exchange, they have to decide whether to have sex in the same room or different rooms. Our survey found that more men than women wanted separate rooms. However, we found that the majority of "swinging" took place in each other's presence. This may be because of the wife's concern with emotional mate guarding, as she thereby ensures that encounter remains strictly a physical experience.

THE REAFFIRMATION OF THE PAIR-BOND PHASE

After the sexual encounter, couples demonstrate concern for one another by getting back together as quickly as possible to discuss what transpired. One way a couple can achieve this is to provide specific details of the sex encounter (e.g., flirting acts, request offered or made, sexual positions taken) to their spouse. By conveying this information in an emotionally detached matter, each spouse seeks to reassure the other of his or her continued involvement. Laura Mixson observed that spouses keenly study one another for evidence of detachment or growing detachment. Individuals are often quick to assume the worst. Because of this tacit assessment, swingers are acutely conscious of the importance of being attentive to their partner in the postsex-encounter phase. A point made by a twenty-seven-year-old woman was that she needed to be reassured that "it was not better with someone else." So powerful is this concern that men strive to reassure their wife that she is loved. A thirty-year-old man admitted that after completion of the sex act, "I try to make sure my wife knows I love her and that I think she really is a good person." This point is echoed by a thirty-three-year-old man's account of how he and his wife interact after a spouse exchange encounter: "We repeatedly embrace one another after having sex with strangers and sometimes before having sex, too." A thirty-eight-year-old woman noted the importance of emotional reassurance: "He makes me feel like I am the most beautiful woman in the world when we are in bed alone. So when other people are involved, I know I am the one he really wants." Another thirtysomething man thought demonstrating consideration for a spouse was vital to any marriage, especially if the couple engaged in a swinger lifestyle. He added, "If my wife is upset [after a spouse exchange], I will do something special for her." This can range from going to dinner to taking a vacation together to enhance their sense of exclusiveness.

DANGERS OF UNCOUPLING LOVE AND SEX

Swingers assume that out of sex can come an emotional entanglement. They therefore are hypersensitive to signs of emotional betrayal. Our survey found that 25 percent (or 20 of 80) participants acknowledged that, at one time or another, swinging had threatened their relationship.[6] We found an unvoiced fear that a partner may become more interested in someone else, as evidenced in the spouse's wanting to see that person again, spending too much time with that person after reaching an orgasm, or becoming aloof upon returning home. Swingers use these indirect indicators to assess what actually transpired, and these indicators suggest that sexual jealousy, albeit muted, remains a concern. Not informing another about a sexual encounter often results in heightened suspicion. This was a point made by a forty-three-year-old woman who acknowledged: "I felt that he kind of cheated on me because he hid it from me. It would have been fine if I knew about it. I guess I felt that he was more attracted to her than just in a sexual way." For this woman the centrality of the pair bond—emotional exclusiveness—may have been violated.

Clearly, following the prescribed rituals does not guarantee success, at least not for everyone. For example, after reaching an orgasm, a man continued to kiss, fondle, and hug his sex partner. Laura Mixson recalls that it was clear to everyone present that they liked one another. The man's spouse observed the interaction and burst into tears. Another example of emotional betrayal occurred when a twentysomething couple new to the lifestyle had sex with different people in the same room. Afterward an intense argument ensued, with the woman demanding an explanation for her husband's continued physical involvement with someone with whom he had climaxed, whereas he wanted to know why she continued to "suck his dick after he [her partner] came."

POTENTIAL BENEFITS OF UNCOUPLING SEX FROM LOVE

If enduring love "requires engagement in something outside the relationship, whether in a shared project, or even periods of separation" (Collins and Gregor 1995:75; see also Person 1988:331), extramarital sex could provide couples with a diversion useful for overcoming a sense of habituation. For some swingers spouse exchanges can have a positive impact by reeroticizing their marriage. For example, a forty-one-year-old man pointed out that he "still thinks my wife is the sexiest person in the world, and [swinging] has enhanced our sexual relationship as a couple." Another couple had an agreement that they would only hug and kiss but never have sexual intercourse with other partners. They had decided to wait, the man explained, "until they returned home to have great passionate sex." In this way mild jealous feelings and related insecurities can serve as an important stimulus for the rejuvenation of the marital bond. Upon seeing that a mate is sexually desirable to a stranger(s), a couple often tries to sexually repossess each other. As one woman noted, "You see others wanting your man and you want him, too." For many couples spouse exchange offers a way out of sexual habituation (King 1996) toward the rejuvenation of their erotic selves.

David Buss's (2000a) research among nonswingers found jealousy could be a positive force for igniting sexual passion toward one's spouse. He argues that jealousy should be seen as "a kind of old-fashioned mate insurance, an evolutionary glue that holds modern couples together" (Buss 2000b:54). In concurrence, Laura Kipnis noticed a similar reaction among individuals who had an extramarital affair: there was "a reawakening of passion" (2000:13). For swingers the pursuit of erotic satisfaction with strangers often results in an adrenaline rush toward renewed sexual excitement for their spouse (for similar findings with different sample populations see Bartell 1971; Varni 1974; Gilmartin 1979; Wolfe 2003). Our questionnaire on sexual frequency among married couples found that 26 of 30 middle-aged couples had sexual intercourse at least twice a week, which Christopher Ryan (personal communication) points out is "about double the national average" for that age cohort. This further supports the view that sexual jealousy can, at times, have a positive influence on the quality of a marriage or relationship.

The clandestine nature of the experience may also contribute to the enhancement of the marital union. Collins and Gregor (1995) point out that sharing a secret can produce a more intense bond of fellowship. Swingers are aware that spouse exchange is viewed as deviant activity that can negatively affect their profession or reputation in the wider community. To protect themselves they are highly circumspect in acknowledging to nonswingers their extramarital activities. By maintaining a code of secrecy, couples bracket their lifestyle while heightening a sense of commitment and feelings of closeness toward one another.

***

American spouse exchange is organized around the pursuit of erotic satisfaction outside the marital bond.[7] In redefining sexual infidelity as a sex encounter without a spouse's permission, swingers have removed sexual exclusivity as a defining feature of marital borders. For most swingers uncoupling sex from love is relatively easy and does not diminish their marital love bond. In effect, love and sex are separate experiences independent of each other.

American swingers appear to constitute an ideal example of Giddens's thesis that modernity has resulted in the production of utilitarian individualists engaged in exclusive pragmatic encounters. Closer examination reveals, however, that American swingers are anything but utilitarian pragmatists. For swingers the monopolization of a spouse's sexual behavior is not as critical as the monopolization of a spouse's emotional commitment. This may account for the relative success of swingers' marriages compared with those "open marriages" that are organized around unrestricted free choice in pursuit of erotic satisfaction. In this arrangement couples, lacking few means to rejuvenate their sense of belonging, simply drift apart. In contrast, swingers deemphasize individual choice in favor of a couple's consensus.

Communities and individual relationships that uncouple sexual exclusivity from a love bond have not fared well. In the end something is lost, and it usually is the intensity of a spouse's love. In most situations the separation of sex from love would result in the dilution of the love bond (Collins and Gregor 1995). American swingers, like many bisexual couples (Weinberg, Williams, and Pryor 1994:115), are able to avoid emotional dilution, largely because of their continued dedication to upholding the marital bond as the more important symbolic, ethical, and emotional value. In this way they are the exception that proves the rule.

Institutionalization of the spouse exchange transaction, and not free will or personal conviction, accounts for the muting of sexual jealousy. Sex and love can be separated without the dilution of the love bond when the spouse exchange transaction is conducted within a ritualistic setting that emphasizes the authority and value of the marital union.[8] In a regulated or ritualistic context the pursuit of sexual adventure with multiple sex partners appears not to diminish the quality or density of a couple's love. For most American swingers sexual pragmatism is confined only to the arena of spouse exchange, which enables them to remain at heart romantic/companionate sentimentalists dedicated to preserving their marriage.

***

I want to thank the following people for their insights, comments, and suggestions for improving the paper: Helen Gerth, Stacy Garreston, Tom

Gregor, David Hall, Elaine Hatfield, Libby Hinson, Tom Paladino, Jennifer Thompson, Christopher Ryan, Alice Schlegel, Dave Suggs, Benjamin Wilreker, and Leanna Wolfe.

NOTES

1. A "full swing" includes sexual intercourse; a "soft swing" consists of only kissing and touching.

2. "Open marriage" is a vague term that implies many things—it can range from being a statement of complete sexual independence to more restricted sexual openness. It appears that few empirical studies have sought to investigate how these types of marriages actually function. We suspect that the more successful (i.e., relationships that sustain enduring love sentiments) adopt ritual practices discussed in the chapter.

3. Carol Cassell, a specialist on family and sexual relationships and program director for the Society for the Scientific Study of Human Sexuality, informed me (in a telephone conversation) that sex therapists and health practitioners agree that "open marriages" do not work as they are organized around individual freedom to the exclusion of the importance of the couple. Over time this results in undermining the couple bond. Advocates point out, however, that health practitioners work with the dysfunctional, and thus their sample set is not representative.

4. The Lifestyles Organization's annual convention for swingers regularly attracts four thousand attendees (Wolfe 2003:57). The mean age is forty-six (Gilmartin 1978). It is overwhelmingly white (94 percent; Wolfe 2003). We also found this consistent with our own sample. Swingers tend to move around the country and tend to be professionals, with a high number of college graduates (40 percent; Wolfe 2003). In our sample 79 percent had gone to or graduated from college or a technical school. Their jobs were ordinary. Twenty-one percent of men were in the police force or the military, and 31 percent were employed in a professional career. In contrast, 30 percent of the women worked in an administrative occupation, with 37 of 62 (or 60 percent) earning an income of $35,000 or more. Wolfe's participants ranged in age from twenty-three to sixty-six. In our sample population the length of marriage ranged from three to thirty years, with the median length about twelve years.

5. We found that 18 percent of the men had had at least one bisexual encounter. In contrast, 77 percent of the women had had a bisexual experience.

6. It is not uncommon for participants, especially men, to form or enter into a business relationship as a result of sharing a sexual exchange. In this way American swingers are no different from spouse exchangers in non-Western societies. Wives can also form social relationships such as going to lunch together or participating in a common activity.

7. Humans do not have to form a dyadic love relationship to survive. A group-love ethos (e.g., contemporary Mormon polygamous talk of plural love as being superior to dyadic love) is easy to invoke. However, a close examination finds that the ethos may endure while the quality of love that people actually feel is muted. This was the case for the Oneida community, a utopian commune founded in 1848, and we suspect the Kerista commune, too. Our interpretation of the swinger lifestyle is that it is an attempt to account for why love does not diminish when a couple is involved with a large number of sex partners. The ethnographic data—what little we have—on spouse exchange are supportive of this analysis. This does not mean that people cannot have a good life with lots of sexual variety—but it does strongly suggest that swinging will diminish the quality of their love bond—unless the swinging is organized around an ethos of dyadic love.

8. Cross-cultural research has documented that even in double-standard societies, most women do not appreciate, encourage, or are indifferent to extramarital sexual liaisons (Jankowiak, Nell, and Buckmaster 2001). Daniel Smith (see chapter 9) observed that Igbo men who actively participated in extramarital affairs still sought to follow tacit ethical rules that kept these encounters "secret" from their spouse. Clearly, sexual fidelity is central to Igbos' idealized model of the proper marriage.

References

Anapol, D. 1997. *Polyamory: The New Love without Limits: Secrets of Sustainable Intimate Relationships.* San Rafael, Calif.: IntiNet Resource Center.

Bartell, G. 1971. *Group Sex: A Scientist's Eyewitness Report on the American Way of Swinging.* New York: Peter Wyden.

Berger, J., B. P. Cohen, and M. Zelditch Jr. 1972. "Status Characteristics and Social Interaction." *American Sociological Review* 37:241–55.

Bergstrand, C. and J. Blevins Williams. 2000. "Today's Alternative Marriage Styles: The Case of Swingers." *Electronic Journal of Human Sexuality* 3:1–11.

Berlant, Lauren. 2000. *Intimacy.* Chicago: University of Chicago Press.

Bowie, F. 2006. *The Anthropology of Religion: An Introduction.* Malden, Mass.: Blackwell.

Boyer, P. and P. Liénard. 2006. "Why Ritualized Behavior? Precaution Systems and Action Parsing in Developmental, Pathological and Cultural Rituals." *Behavioral and Brain Sciences* 29 (6): 595–613.

Buss, D. 2000a. *The Dangerous Passion: Why Jealousy Is as Necessary as Love and Sex.* New York: Free Press.

———. 2000b. "Prescription for Passion." *Psychology Today* (June): 55–61.

Butler, E. 1979. *Traditional Marriage and Emerging Alternatives.* New York: Harper and Row.

Canican, F. 1987. *Love in America.* Cambridge: Cambridge University Press.

Collins, J. and T. Gregor. 1995. "Boundaries of Love. " In William Jankowiak, ed., *Romantic Passion: A Universal Experience?* pp. 72–92. New York: Columbia University Press.

——. n.d. "Narratives of Love." Unpublished paper.

Constantine, L . and J. Constantine. 1973. *Group Marriage: A Study of Contemporary Multilateral Marriage.* New York: Collier.

Cook, E. 2005. "Commitment in Polyamory." Master's thesis, Regis University, Denver, Colorado.

Davenport, W. 1965. "Sexual Patterns and Their Regulation in a Society of the Southwest Pacific." In Frank Beach, ed.. *Sex and Behavior,* pp. 209–34. New York: John Wiley and Sons.

De Munck, V. n.d. "Cultural Models Approach to Romantic Love." Unpublished paper.

Dixon, D. 1985. "Perceived Sexual Satisfaction and Marital Happiness of bisexual and Heterosexual Swinging Husbands." *Journal of Homosexuality* 11 (1–2): 209–22.

Ford, C. and F. Beach. 1951. *Patterns of Sexual Behavior.* New York: Harper and Brothers.

Frescska, E. and Zsuzsanna Kulcsar. 1988. "Social Bonding in the Modulation of the Physiology of Ritual Trance." *Ethos* 17 (1): 70–87.

Giddens, A. 1992. *The Transformation of Intimacy: Sexuality, Love, and Eroticism in Modern Societies.* Stanford, Calif.: Stanford University Press.

Gilmartin, B. 1978. *The Gilmartin Report.* Secaucus, N.J.: Citadel.

Gould, T. 2000. *The Lifestyle: A Look at the Erotic Rites of Swingers.* San Francisco: Firefly Books.

Hatfield, E., J. Traupmann, and G. W. Walster. 1978. "Equity and Extramarital Sexuality." *Archives of Sexual Behavior* 7:127–41.

Hrdy, S. 1999. *A History of Mothers, Infants, and Natural Selection.* New York: Pantheon.

Jankowiak, W. 1995. Introduction to William Jankowiak, ed., *Romantic Passion: A Universal Experience?* pp. 1–20. New York: Columbia University Press.

——. 2000. "Femme Fatale and Status Fatale: A Cross-Cultural Perspective." With Angela Ramsey. *Cross Cultural Research* 34, no. 1 (February): 57–69.

Jankowiak, W., D. Nell, and A. Buckmaster. 2001. "Managing Infidelity: A Cross-Cultural Perspective." *Ethnology* 41 (1): 85–101.

Jankowiak, W., M. Sudakov, and B. Wilreker. 2005. "Co-wife Conflict and Cooperation." *Ethnology* 44 (1): 81–98.

Jenks, R. 1985a. "A Comparative Study of Swingers and Nonswingers: Attitudes and Beliefs." *Lifestyles* 8 (1): 5–20.

——. 1985b. "Swinging: A Test of Two Theories and a Proposed New Model." *Archives of Sexual Behavior* 14 (6): 517–27.

———. 1998. "Swinging: A Review of the Literature." *Archives of Sexual Behavior* 27 (5): 507–21.

King, B. 1996. *Human Sexuality Today*. Englewood, N.J.: Prentice-Hall.

Kipnis, L. 2000. "Adultery." In Lauren Berlant, ed., *Intimacy*, pp. 9–47. Chicago: University of Chicago Press.

Leavitt, E. 1988. "Alternative Lifestyle and Marital Satisfaction: A Brief Report." *Annals of Sex Research* 1 (3): 455–61.

Lindholm, C. 2001. *Culture and Identity: The History, Theory, and Practice of Psychological Anthropology*. Boston: McGraw-Hill.

Person, E. 1988. *Dreams of Love and Fateful Encounters: The Power of Romantic Passion*. New York: W. W. Norton.

Reich, W. 1973. *The Discovery of the Orgone*. Translated by Vincent R. Carfagno. New York: Farrar, Straus and Giroux.

Rubin, R. H. 2001. "Alternative Lifestyles Revisited, Or Whatever Happened to Swingers, Group Marriages, and Communes?" *Journal of Family Issues* 22 (6): 711–26.

Shore, B. 1996. *Culture in Mind*. New York: Oxford University Press.

Smith, J. 1974. *Beyond Monogamy: Recent Studies of Sexual Alternatives in Marriage*. Baltimore: Johns Hopkins University Press.

Stafford, C. 2000. *Separation and Reunion in Modern China*. Cambridge: Cambridge University Press.

Stern, P. and R. Condon. 1995. "A Good Spouse Is Hard To Find: Marriage, Spouse Exchange, and Infatuation among the Copper Inuit." In William Jankowiak, ed., *Romantic Passion: A Universal Experience?* pp. 196–219. New York: Columbia University Press.

Swidler, A. 2001. *Talk of Love: How Culture Matters*. Chicago: University of Chicago Press.

Varni, J. 1974. "An Exploratory Study of Spouse Swapping." In J. Smith and L. Smith, eds., *Beyond Monogamy: Recent Studies on Sexual Alternative in Marriage*, pp. 230–45. Baltimore: John Hopkins University Press.

Weinberg, M., C. Williams, and D. Pryor. 1994. *Dual Attraction: Understanding Bisexuality*. Oxford: Oxford University Press.

Wolfe, L. 2003. "Jealousy and Transformation in Polyamorous Relationships." Ph.D. diss., Institute of Advanced Study of Human Sexuality, San Francisco.

Zablocki, B. 1980. *Alienation and Charisma: A Study of Contemporary American Communes*. New York: Free Press.

APPENDIX: THE ETHNOGRAPHIC EVIDENCE FOR THE UNIVERSALITY OF ROMANTIC LOVE

A number of scholars retain reservations about the "universality" of or the accuracy of the coding procedure used to document its presence within a given culture. Because of continued professional skepticism I have included a list of the cultures where the ethnographer or folklorist provides evidence of romantic love's presence, if not vitality. I am not claiming that everyone or even the majority of people in a given culture experience romantic love. There are no ethnographic data available to assess the degree to which the emotion was experienced in a particular culture. I am claiming, however, that the emotion was recognized and experienced by some, if not many, individuals within a particular culture. I invite the diligent student of the phenomenon to visit the sources used to argue for its universality.—William Jankowiak

Abkhaz
Benet, S. 1974. *Abkhasians.* New York: Holt, Rinehart and Winston, p. 64.
Ainu
Batchelor, J. 1927. *Ainu Life and Lore.* Tokyo: Kyobunkwan, pp. 437–48.
Aleut
Jochelson, W. 1933. *History, Ethnology, and Anthropology of the Aleut.* Washington, D.C.: Carnegie Institution, p. 73.
Alorese
DuBois, C. 1944. *The People of Alor.* New York: Harper and Row, pp. 92–111.
Amhara
Beier, U. 1966. *African Poetry.* Cambridge: Cambridge University Press, pp. 51–52.

Andamanese
Radcliffe-Brown, A. R. 1948. *The Andaman Islanders.* Glencoe, Ill.: Free Press, pp. 70–73.
Aranda
Bell, D. 1983. *Daughters of the Dreaming.* Melbourne: McPhee Gribbe, pp. 58, 166–71.
Spencer, B., and I. J. Gillen. 1927. *The Arunta.* London: Macmillan, pp. 466–67.
Armenians
Von Haxthausen, B. 1854. *Transcaucasian.* London: Chapman and Hall, p. 226.
Ashanti
Rattray, R. S. 1929. *Akan-Ashanti Folk Tales.* Oxford: Clarendon, pp. 45–51.
Aweikoma
Henry, J. 1941. *Jungle People.* New York: Vintage, pp. 17–29.
Ayamara
Hickman, J. 1963. "The Ayamara of Chinchera, Peru." Ph.D. diss., Cornell University, p. 66.
Azande
Seligman, C. G., and B. Z. Seligman. 1933. *Pagan Tribes of the Nilotic Sudan,* pp. 514–17.
Aztec
Leon-Portilla, M. 1985. "Nahuatl Literature." In Munro Edmonson, ed., *The Supplement to the Handbook of Middle American Indians: Vol. 3, Literature,* pp. 31–33. Austin: University of Texas Press.
Babylonians
Morris, J. 1915. *The Civilization of Babylonia and Assyria.* Philadelphia: J. B. Lippincott, p. 453.
Badjau
Nimmo, H. A. 1972. *The Sea People of Sulu.* San Francisco: Chandler, p. 22.
Baiga (Tribes of India)
Elwin, V. 1939. *The Baiga.* London: J. Murray, p. 253.
Balinese
Bello, J. 1970. *Traditional Balinese Culture.* New York: Columbia University Press, p. 73.
Geertz, H., and C. Geertz. 1975. *Kinship in Bali.* Chicago: Chicago University Press, pp. 110–11, 137.
Jennaway, Megan. 2002. *Sisters and Lovers: Women and Desire in Bali* Lanham, Md.: Rowman and Littlefield, p. 143 (overview of studies of love in Bali).
Wikan, U. 1990. *Managing Turbulent Hearts.* Chicago: University of Chicago Press, p. 10.
Bambara
Courlander, H., with Ousmane Sako. 1982. *The Heart of the Ngoni.* New York: Crown, pp. 77, 127.

Basques

Gorostiaga, J. 1955. *Antologia de Poesia Popular Vasca*. San Sebastian: Vascongada de los Amigos del Pais, chaps. 11 and 15.

Bellacoola

McIlwraith, T. F. 1948. *The Bell Coola Indians*. Vol. 1. Toronto: University of Toronto Press, pp. 419–21, 714–15.

Bribri

Stone, D. 1990. Personal communication.

Burmese

Nash, M. 1965. *The Golden Road to Modernity*. New York: John Wiley.

Burusho

Lorimer, D. L. R. 1935. *The Burushaki Languages*. Oslo: H. Aschehoug, pp. 15–19.

Callinago

Taylor, D. 1938. "The Caribs of Dominica." *Bureau of American Ethnology Bulletin* 119:103–59.

Carib

Gillin, J. 1936. *The Barama River Caribs of British Guiana*. Cambridge, Mass.: Peabody Museum, pp. 74–75, 80.

Cayapa

Barrett, S. A. 1925. *The Cayapa Indians of Ecuador*. New York: Museum of the American Indian, pp. 321–23.

Chambri (New Guinea)

Errington, F., and D. Gewertz. 1993. "The Historical Course of True Love in the Sepik." In Victoria Lockwood, Thomas Harding, and Ben Wallace, eds., *Contemporary Pacific Societies: Studies in Development and Change*, pp. 233–48. Englewood Cliffs, N.J.: Prentice-Hall.

Chinese

Diamond, N. 1969. *K'un Shen*. New York: Holt, Rinehart, and Winston.

Jankowiak, W. 1993. *Sex, Death and Hierarchy in a Chinese City*. New York: Columbia University Press, pp. 192–97 (folklore literature on love from Han dynasty to present day).

Chiricahua Apache

Opler, M. E. 1969. *Apache Odyssey*. New York: Holt, Rinehart and Winston, pp. 74–75.

Chuckchee

Bogoras, W. 1970. *The Chuckchee*. New York: Johnson Reprint, pp. 556–79.

Comanche

Wallace, E., and E. A. Hoebel. 1952. *The Comanches*. Norman: University of Oklahoma Press, pp. 132–35.

Copper Inuit (Eskimo)

Stern, P., and R. Condon. 1995. "A Good Spouse Is Hard to Find: Marriage, Spouse Exchange, and Infatuation among the Copper Inuit." In William Jankowiak, ed.,

Romantic Passion: A Universal Experience? pp. 196–218. New York: Columbia University Press.

Cubeo

Goldman, I. 1979. *The Cubeo.* Urbana: University of Illinois Press, pp. 142–43, 183.

Cuna

Herrera, T. P. 1978. *Cuna Cosmology.* Washington, D.C.: Three Continents Press, pp. 9–11, 46–48.

Egyptian Bedouin

Abu-Lughod, L. 1990. "Shifting Politics in Bedouin Love Poetry." In Catherine Lutz and Lila Abu-Lughod, eds., *Language and the Politics of Emotion,* pp. 24–45. New York: Cambridge University Press.

Egyptians

Ammar, H. 1954. *Growing up in an Egyptian Village.* London: Routledge and Kegan Paul, pp. 186–87.

Eyak

Birket-Smith, K., and F. De Laguna. 1938. *The Eyak Indians of the Copper River Delta, Alaska.* Copenhagen: Levin and Munksgaard, pp. 202–3 (suggestive, but inconclusive).

Fulani

Regis, Helen. 1995. "The Madness of Excess: Love among the Fulbe of North Cameroun." In William Jankowiak, *Romantic Passion: A Universal Experience?* pp. 141–51. New York: Columbia University Press.

Stenning, D. J. 1959. *The Savannah Nomads.* London: Oxford University Press, pp. 141–44.

Garo

Burling, G. 1963. *Rengsanggri.* Philadelphia: University of Pennsylvania Press, p. 85.

Gilbertese

Grimble, A. 1957. *Return to the Islands.* New York: William Morrow, pp. 90–96.

Gilyak

Shternberg, L. 1964. *The Gilyak, Orochi, Goldi, Megida, Aiunu Articles and Materials.* Translated by L. Bromwich. New Haven, Conn.: Human Area Relations Files, pp. 367–69.

Goajiro

Bolinder, G. 1957. *Indians on Horseback.* London: Dennis Dobson, pp. 80, 95.

Gond

Fuchs, S. 1960. *The Gond and Bhumia of Eastern Mandla.* New York: Asia Publishing House, p. 294.

Gros Ventre

Flannery, R. 1953. *The Gros Ventres of Mountain: Part 1.* Washington, D.C.: Catholic University of America Press, pp. 174–77.

Hadza

Marlowe, F. W. 2004. "The Hadza." In Carol R. Ember and Melvin Ember, eds., *Encyclopedia of Sex and Gender*. New York: Kluwer/Plenum.

——. 2004. "Mate Preferences among Hadza Hunter-Gatherers." *Human Nature* 15:365–76.

Haida

Swanton, J. 1905. "Haida Texts and Myths." *Bureau of American Ethnology Bulletin* 29:354–55.

Haitians

Niles, B. 1926. *Black Haiti*. New York: Grosset and Dunlap, pp. 106–10.

Hausa

Cohen, A. 1971. *Customs and Politics in Urban Africa*. Berkeley: University of California Press, pp. 56–57.

Tremearne, A. J. N. 1970. *Hausa Superstitions and Customs*. London: Frank Cass, pp. 304–6.

Havasupai

Smithson, C. L. 1959. *The Havasupai Woman*. Salt Lake City: University of Utah Press, pp. 73–89.

Hebrews

Ecclesiastes, 11:19.

Hidatsa

Bowers, G. 1965. "Hidatsa Social and Ceremonial Organization." *Bureau of American Ethnology Bulletin* 194:138–39, 150–51.

Huichol

Zingg, R. M. 1977. *The Huichols: Primitive Artists*. Millwood, N.Y.: Kraus Reprint, pp. 127–28, 138.

Huli (Highlands of Papua New Guinea)

Wardlow, H. 2006. *Wayward Women: Sexuality and Agency in a New Guinea Society*. Berkeley: University of California Press.

Iban

Howell, W. 1963. *The Sea Dyaks and Other Races of Sarawak*. Hong Kong: Borneo Literature Bureau, pp. 240–43, 268–69.

Ibo

Ottenberg, P. 1981. Marriage Relations in the Double Descent System of the Afrikpo Ibo of Southeastern Nigeria. New Haven, Conn.: Human Relations Area File Press, pp. 49–50.

Ifuago

Barton, R. F. 1930. *The Half-Way Sun*. New York: Brewer and Warren, pp. 48–49, 56–57.

Igbo

Smith, Daniel J. 2001. "Romance, Parenthood and Gender in a Modern African Society." *Ethnology* 40 (2): 129–51.

Inca

Vega, G. de la. 1966. *Royal Commentaries of the Inca.* Austin: University of Texas Press, pp. 126–27.

Ingalik

Osgood, C. 1959. *Ingalik Mental Culture.* New Haven, Conn.: Yale University Press, pp. 143–49.

Irish

Glassie, H. 1985. *Irish Folk Tales.* New York: Pantheon, p. 257.

Japanese

Riyang, S. 2006. *Love in Modern Japan.* New York: Routledge, p. 27.

Wagatsuma, H., and G. DeVos. 1984. *Heritage of Endurance.* Berkeley: University of California Press, p. 193.

Javanese

Geertz, H. 1961. *The Javanese Family.* New York: Free Press of Glencoe, p. 58.

Jivaro

Stirling, M. W. 1938. "Historical and Ethnographical Material on the Jivaro Indians." *Bureau of American Ethnology Bulletin* 17:109.

Kapauku

Pospisil, L. 1963. *The Kapauku Popuans.* New York: Holt, Rinehart and Winston, pp. 66, 76, 87.

Kaska

Honigmann, J. J. 1949. *Culture and Ethos of Kaska Society.* New Haven, Conn.: Yale University Press, pp. 159, 290.

Kazak

Winner, T. 1958. *The Oral Art and Literature of the Kazakhs of Russian Central Asia.* Durham, N.C.: Duke University Press, pp. 186–88.

Kikuyu

Kenyatta, J. 1953. *Facing Mount Kenya.* London: Seeker and Warburg, chap. 8.

Konso

Hallpike, C. R. 1972. *The Konso of Ethiopia.* Oxford: Clarendon, pp. 112–13.

Khalka Mongols

Jagchild, S., and P. Ayer. 1979. *Mongolia's Culture and Society.* Boulder, Colo.: Westview, p. 95.

Khmer or Cambodians

Groslier, B., and J. Arthaud. 1957. *The Arts and Civilization of Angkor.* New York: Praeger.

Kimam

Serpenti, L. M. 1965. *Cultivators in the Swamps.* Assen, The Netherlands: Van Goreom, pp. 172–75.

Koreans

Osgood, C. 1951. *The Koreans and Their Culture.* New York: Ronald Press, p. 257.

!Kung

Marshall, L. 1976. *The !Kung of Nyae Nyae.* Cambridge, Mass.: Harvard University Press, p. 279.

Shostak, M. 1981. *Nisa.* New York: Vintage, pp. 266–69.

Kurds

Kinnane, D. 1964. *The Kurds and Kurdistan.* Oxford: Oxford University Press, p. 6.

Kwoma

Whiting, J. W. M. 1941. *Becoming a Kwona.* New Haven, Conn.: Yale University Press, pp. 83–85.

Lahu

Du, Shanshan. 2002. "Chopsticks Only Work in Pairs": Gender Unity and Gender Equality among the Lahu of Southwest China. New York: Columbia University Press.

———. 2004. "Choosing between Life and Love: Negotiating Dyadic Gender Ideals among the Lahu of Southwest China." *Critical Asian Studies* 36 (2): 239–63.

Lakher

Parry, N. E. 1932. *The Lakhers.* London: Macmillan, pp. 292–93, 318–19.

Lamet

Izikowitz, K. G. 1951. *Lamet.* Elanders, Sweden: Gottenburg, pp. 78–79. Republished in 1979 by AMS Press of New York.

Lapps

Turi, J. 1931. *Turi's Book of Lappland.* Oosterhout, The Netherlands: Anthropological Publications, pp. 202–7.

Lepcha

Gorer, G. 1967. *Himalayan Village.* New York: Basic Books, pp. 158, 169, 316–17.

Lolo (Yi)

Lin, Y. 1961. *The Lolo of Llang Shan.* New Haven, Conn.: Human Relations Area File Press, pp. 49–50.

Luguru

Beidelman, T. O. 1983. *The Kaguru.* Prospect Heights, Ill.: Waveland, p. 66.

Manchu

Shirokogoroff, K. 1924. *Social Organization of the Manchus.* Shanghai: Royal Asiatic Society, p. 152.

Mangaians (Polynesia)

Harris, H. 1995. "Rethinking Heterosexual Relationships in Polynesia: A Case Study of Mangaia, Cook Island." In William Jankowiak, ed., *Romantic Passion: A Universal Experience?* pp. 95–127. New York: Columbia University Press.

Manus

Romanucci-Ross, L. 1985. *Mead's Other Manus.* South Hadley, Mass.: Bergin, pp. vii–ix, 120–21.

Maori
Reed, A. W. 1948. *Wonder Tales of Maoriland.* Wellington, N.Z.: A. H. and A. W. Reed,
     pp. 28–37.
Mapuche
Faron, L. C. 1968. *The Mapuche Indians of Chile.* New York: Holt, Rinehart and Win-
     ston, p. 41.
Marquesans
Kardiner, A., and R. Linton. 1939. *The Individual and His Society.* New York: Colum-
     bia University Press, p. 174.
Marshallese
Kramer, A., and H. Nevermann. 1938. *The Marshall Islands.* Hamburg: Aldine de
     Gruyter, p. 185.
Masai
Spencer, P. 1988. *The Masai of Matapato.* London: Manchester University Press,
     p. 32.
Mbau Fijians
Brewster, A. B. 1922. *The Hill Tribes of Fiji.* Philadelphia: J. B. Lippincott, pp. 202–3
     (suggestive, backed up by Reed and Hames).
Reed, A. W., and I. Hames. 1967. *Myths and Legends of Fiji.* Wellington, N.Z.: A. H.
     and A. W. Reed, pp. 239–41.
Mbundu
Courlander, H. 1976. *A Treasury of Afro-American Folklore.* New York: Crown,
     p. 299.
Mbuti
Turnbull, C. 1955. *Wayward Servants.* New York: Natural History Press, p. 141.
Mende
Little, K. 1967. *The Mende of Sierra Leone.* London: Routledge and Kegan Paul, pp.
     153–57.
Micmac
Rand, S. T. 1971. *Legends of the Micmacs.* New York: Johnson Reprint, pp. 154–59,
     440–42.
Miskito
Conzemius, E. 1932. "Ethnographical Survey of the Miskito and Sumo Indians of
     Honduras and Nicaragua." *Bureau of American Ethnology Bulletin* 106:14–115,
     144–45.
Munduroccu
Murphy, R. F. n.d. "Deviance and Social Control II," pp. 22–33.
Murphy, Yolanda. 1990. Personal communication.
Muria (Hill Tribes India)
Elwin, V. 1947. *The Muria and Their Ghotul.* London: Oxford University Press.
Gell, S. 1992. *The Ghotul in Muria Society.* Philadelphia: Harwood Academic,
     p. 219.

Murik (New Guinea)

Lipset, David. 2004. "Modernity without Romance?" *American Ethnologist* 31 (2): 205–24.

Nama

Schapera, I. 1951. *The Khorsan Peoples of South Africa*. London: Routledge and Kegan Paul, pp. 244–45.

Nambicuara

Lévi-Strauss, C. 1961. *A World on the Wane*. New York: Criterion Books, p. 277.

Natchez

Swanton, J. 1911. "Indian Tribes of the Lower Mississippi Valley and Adjacent Coast of the Gulf of Mexico." *Bureau of American Ethnology Bulletin*, no. 43:96–99.

Negri Sembilan

Ahmand, R. 1922. *The Akuan or Spirit-Friends*. pp. 381–82.

Nepalese

Ahearn, L. 2001. Invitations to Love: Literacy, Love Letters, and Social Change in Nepal. Ann Arbor: University of Michigan Press.

New Irelanders

Powdermaker, H. 1933. *Life in Lesu*. New York: W. W. Norton, pp. 228, 232, 238–39.

Nkundo Mongo

Hulstaert, G. 1938. *Le Marriage des Nkunde*. Bruxelles: Givan Campenhout, p. 37.

Northern Brazilians

Rehbun, Linda-Anne. 1999. *The Heart Is Unknown Country: Love in the Changing Economy of Northeast Brazil*. Stanford, Calif.: Stanford University Press.

Nyakyusa

Wilson, M. 1951. *Good Company*. Boston: Beacon, pp. 76–77.

Omaha

Fletcher, A., and F. La Flesche. 1893. *A Study of Omaha Music*. Cambridge, Mass.: Peabody Museum, pp. 52–54.

Otoro

Nadel, S. F. 1947. *The Nuba*. London: Oxford University Press, p. 111.

Paiute

Whiting, B. 1950. *Paiute Sorcery*. New York: Viking Fund, p. 59.

Palauans

Barnett, H. G. 1960. *Being a Palauan*. New York: Holt, Rinehart, and Winston, pp. 46–49.

Papagoans

Underhill, R. 1939. *Social Organization of the Papago Indians*. New York: Columbia University Press, pp. 183–85.

Pawnee

Weltfish, G. 1965. *The Lost Universe*. New York: Basic Books, p. 52.

Pentecost

Harrison, R. 1937. *Savage Civilization*. London: Victor Gollance, pp. 361–63.

Pomo
Aginsk, B. W., and Ethel Aginsky. 1967. *Deep Valley.* New York: Stein and Day, pp. 42–45, 135.

Punjabi
Eglar, Z. 1960. *A Punjabi Village in Pakistan.* New York: Columbia University Press, pp. 93–94.

Quiche
Bunzel, R. 1981. *Chichicastenango.* Guatemala City: Seminario de Integracion Social Guatemalteca, pp. 152–54.

Riffians
Joseph, R., and T. B. Joseph. 1987. *The Rose and the Thorn.* Tucson: University of Arizona Press, pp. 86–112.

Romans
Cowell, I. R. 1975. *Life in Ancient Rome.* New York: Capricorn, p. 57.

Russians
Benet, S. 1970. *The Village of Viriatino.* New York: Anchor, pp. 106–7.

Rwala
Musil, A. 1928. *The Manner and Customs of the Rwala Bedouins.* New York: American Geographical Society, pp. 138–39.

Samoans
Holmes, L. 1974. *Samoan Village.* New York: Holt, Rinehart and Winston, p. 83.
Shore, B. 1996. *Culture in Mind.* Chicago: University of Chicago Press, pp. 291–301.
Turner, G. 1884. *Samoa.* London: Macmillan, pp. 95–107.

Santal
Bompas, C. H. 1972. *Folklore of the Santal Parganas.* New York: Arno, pp. 300–301.

Saramacca
Herskovits, M. J., and F. S. Herskovits. 1934. *Rebel Destiny.* New York: Whittlesey House, pp. 277, 233.
Price, S. 1984. *Co-Wives and Calabashes.* Ann Arbor: University of Michigan Press.
Wekker, G. 2006. *The Politics of Passion: Women's Sexual Culture in the Afro-Surinamese Diaspora.* New York: Columbia University Press, p. 205.

Saulteaux
Hallowell, I. 1988. *Culture and Experience.* Prospect Heights, Ill.: Waveland, pp. 298–99.

Semang
Schebesta, P. 1962. *The Negritos of Asia.* Vol. 2. Translated by Frieda Schutze. New Haven, Conn.: Human Relations Area File Press, pp. 216–45.

Shavanti
Mayberry Lewis, David. 2004. Personal communication.

Siamese or Central Thai
Gordon, Y. 1962. *The Hill Tribes of Northern Thailand.* Bangkok: Siam Society, pp. 32–36.

Siuai

Oliver, D. 1955. *A Solomon Island Society.* Boston: Beacon, pp. 130–44, 234.

Somali

Lewis, I. M. 1962. *Marriage and the Family in Northern Somaliland.* Kampala, Uganda: East African Institute of Social Research, pp. 12–13.

Songhai

Miner, H. 1953. *The Primitive City of Timbuctoo.* Princeton, N.J.: Princeton University Press, pp. 176–77.

Sri Lankans

De Munck, V. 1998. "Lust, Love and Arranged Marriages in Sri Lanka." In Victor De Munck, ed., *Romantic Love and Sexual Behavior: Perspectives from the Social Sciences,* pp. 285–300. Westport, Conn.: Praeger.

Sulawesi

Rossler, Birgitt Rottger. 2005. Personal communication.

Taita (of Kenya)

Bell, J. 1995. "Notions of Love and Romance among the Taita of Kenya." In William Jankowiak, ed., *Romantic Passion: A Universal Experience?* pp. 152–65. New York: Columbia University Press.

Tallensi

Fortes, M. 1949. *The Web of Kinship among the Tallensi.* London: International African Institute, p. 86.

Tanala

Linton, R. 1956. *Analysis of Tanala Culture.* New Haven, Conn.: Human Relations Area File Press, pp. 321–29.

Tehuelche

Wilbert, J., and K. Simoneau. 1984. *Folk Literature of the Tehuelche Indians.* Los Angeles: University of California Press, pp. 21, 201.

Thonga

Junod, H. 1962. *The Life of a South African Tribe.* New Hyde Park, N.Y.: University Books, pp. 100–101, 190–201.

Tikopia

Firth, R. 1936. *We the Tikopia.* London: Allen and Unwin, pp. 196–97, 524.

Tiv

Bergsma, H., and R. Bergsma. 1969. *Tales Tiv Tell.* London: Oxford University Press, pp. 9–14, 19–20.

Tiwi

Berndt, Roland. 1976. *The Love Songs of Arnhem Land.* Chicago: University Chicago Press, pp. 160–61.

Goodale, J. 1971. *Tiwi Wives.* Seattle: University of Washington Press, p. 131.

Toda

Emeneau, M. B. 1937. "The Songs of the Todas," *Proceedings of the American Philosophical Society* 77 (4): 543–60.

Torajda

Hickson, S. 1889. *A Naturalist in the North Celebes.* New York: McClure, Phillips, p. 272.

Hollan, Doug, and Janet Wellenkamp. 1994. *Contentment and Suffering: Culture and Experience in Toraja.* New York: Columbia University Press, p. 71.

Trobrianders

Malinowski, B. 1948. *The Sexual Life of Savages.* New York: Harcourt, Brace, Johanovich, pp. 63, 64, 264.

Trukese

Goodenough, W. 1951. *Property, Kin and Community on Truk.* New Haven, Conn.: Yale University Press, pp. 120–23.

Tuareg

Briggs, L. C. 1960. *Tribes of the Sahara.* Cambridge, Mass.: Harvard University Press, pp. 130–33.

Turks

Makal, M. 1954. *A Village in Anatolia.* London: Vallentine, Mitchell, p. 73.

Turu (Tanzania)

Schneider, Harold. 1971. "Romantic Love among the Turu." In Donald S. Marshall and Robert C. Suggs, eds., *Human Sexual Behavior: Variation in the Ethnographic Spectrum.* New York: Basic Books, pp. 59–70.

Twana

Eells, M. 1985. *The Indians of Puget Sound.* Seattle: University of Washington Press, p. 35.

Uttar Pradesh

Beck, B., P. Claus, P. Goswami, and J. Handoo, eds. 1987. *Folk Tales of India.* Chicago: University of Chicago Press, pp. v, 256.

Freeman, J. 1979. *Untouchable: An Indian Life History.* Stanford, Calif.: Stanford University Press, chap. 23.

Vedda

Parker, H. 1910. *Village Folk Tales of Ceylon.* London: Luzac, pp. 67–68.

Seligmann, C. G., and B. Z. Seligmann. 1969. *The Veddas.* Osterhout, The Netherlands: Anthropological Publications, p. 96.

Vietnamese

Dumoutier, G. 1907. *Les Cultes Annamites.* New Haven, Conn.: Human Relations Area File Press, pp. 23–24.

Warrau

Wilbert, J. 1970. *Folk Literature of the Warrau Indians.* Los Angeles: University of California Press, pp. 28, 35, 88.

Wolof

Gamble, D. 1967. *The Wolof of Senegambia.* London: International African Institute, pp. 65–68.

Yamana

Gusinde, M. 1961. *The Yamana*. New Haven, Conn.: Human Area Relations File, pp. 387–392 (suggestive; backed up by Wilbert).

Wilbert, J. 1977. *Folk Literature of the Yamana Indians*. Berkeley: University of California Press, p. 269.

Yanomamo

Lizot, J. 1985. *Tales of the Yanomamo*. Cambridge: Cambridge University Press, p. 35.

Chagnon, N. Personal communication.

Yapese

Hunt, E., D. Schneider, N. Kidder, and W. Stevens. 1949. *The Micronesians of Yap and Their Depopulation*. Washington, D.C.: Pacific Science Board, National Research Council, pp. 89, 91.

Yukaghir

Jochelson, W. 1928. *Peoples of Asiatic Russia*. New York: American Museum of Natural History, pp. 224–25.

Yurak Samoyed

Popov, A.A. 1964. "The Nganasans." In M.G. Levin and C.P. Potapov, eds., *The Peoples of Siberia*, p. 571. Chicago: University of Chicago Press.

Yurok

Powers, S. 1976. *Tribes of California*. Berkeley: University of California Press, pp. 58–60.

Zuni

Cushing, F.H. 1979. *Zuni*. Edited by J. Green. Lincoln: University of Nebraska Press, pp. 365–86.

LIST OF CONTRIBUTORS

Denise Brennan is an associate professor of anthropology in the Department of Sociology and Anthropology at Georgetown University in Washington, D.C. She is the author of *What's Love Got to Do with It? Transnational Desires and Sex Tourism in the Dominican Republic* (Duke University Press, 2004). She is writing a book on the resettlement of trafficked people to the United States; its working title is *Life after Trafficking: Forced Labor and Servitude in the United States Today.*

Shanshan Du is an associate professor of anthropology at Tulane University. She is the author of "*Chopsticks Only Work in Pairs*": *Gender Unity and Gender Equality among the Lahu of Southwest China* (Columbia University Press, 2002), and coeditor of "Negotiating Women's Roles and Power: The Practice of World Religions in Contemporary Asia" (a special issue of *Religion,* 2007). Her current research projects include a comparative study of gender-egalitarian societies and an ethnographic examination of the extraordinary outbreak of love suicide and its remarkable persistence among the Lahu in China since the 1950s.

Barry S. Hewlett is a professor of anthropology at Washington State University, Vancouver. He is the coeditor of *Hunter-Gatherer Childhoods* (with Michael Lamb; Aldine Transaction, 2005), and the author of *Intimate Fathers* (University of Michigan Press, 1991), and *Emerging Disease: Ebola, Culture and Politics* in Africa (with Bonnie Hewlett; Wadsworth, 2007). He has conducted research with African forest foragers and farmers for more than thirty years, and his research interests include biocultural evolution, parent-child relations, and the anthropology of infectious diseases.

Bonnie L. Hewlett is an adjunct professor of anthropology at Washington State University, Vancouver. Her research interests include medical anthropology, adolescent development, hunter-gatherers, evolutionary cultural anthropology, and sub-Saharan Africa. Recent publications include (with Barry Hewlett) "Providing Care and Facing Death: Nurses and Ebola in Central Africa," *Journal of Transcultural Nursing* 16, no. 10 (2005): 289–97; and "Vulnerable Lives: The Experience of Death and Loss among Aka and Ngandu Adolescents of the Central African Republic," in Barry Hewlett and Lamb, *Hunter-Gatherer Childhoods*.

William Jankowiak is a professor of anthropology at the University of Nevada, Las Vegas. He is the editor (with Dan Bradburd) of *Drugs, Labor, and Colonial Expansion* (University of Arizona Press, 2003), guest editor of "Well-Being, Family Affections, and Ethical Nationalism in Urban China," a special joint issue of the *Journal of Urban Anthropology* and *Studies of Cultural Systems and World Economic Development* 33, no. 2–4 (2004); and the author of *Romantic Passion* (Columbia University Press, 1995), and *Sex, Death and Hierarchy in a Chinese City* (Columbia University Press, 1993).

Laura Hicks Mixson graduated summa cum laude from the University of Nevada, Las Vegas, in 2000 with a bachelor of arts degree in anthropology. After working as a financial analyst and controller, she moved to upstate New York and now owns and operates a boutique day spa. In her spare time she is an active member of her business community and is researching trends in the spa industry with the goal of developing her own line of antiaging skin-care products.

Victor De Munck is an associate professor in the Anthropology Department of the State University of New York, New Paltz. For his dissertation he conducted thirty-four months of fieldwork in a Sri Lankan village, focusing on cultural change, particularly how villagers have responded to the many national and transnational forces that have affected their lives. He is the editor of *Romantic Love and Sexual Practices* (Praeger, 1998) and the author of *Culture, Self and Meaning* (Waveland Press, 2000). He was the recipient of a Fulbright lecture award to teach theory and method at Vilnius University in Lithuania. His recently completed ethnography on Vilnius has been submitted for publication.

Thomas Paladino is a senior instructor at the Boston Center for Adult Education where he teaches American and English literature. He the recipient of the center's Special Teacher Award in 1999. He is the coeditor of *Romantic Passion* (Columbia University Press, 1995). He is also a poet, the author of a sequential ling poem entitled *Presences*. He has also published poems in a wide variety of literary journals such as *Antioch Review, Kansas Quarterly, Paterson Review,* and *New England Review,* among others.

Birgitt Röttger-Rössler is a research professor at the Max Planck Institute of Social Anthropology in Halle, Germany. She studied anthropology as well as Ibero-Romanic and Malay languages and literature at the universities of Gottingen, Zurich, Cologne, and Bonn. During several years of fieldwork in Indonesia, mainly in Sulawesi and Sumatra, she investigated systems of social stratification; local forms of transgenderism; and the relation between culture, person, self, and (auto-)biographical narrating; as well as the role of emotions in social interaction. She is the author of two monographs and numerous articles, as well as editor and coeditor of several books.

Holly Wardlow is an assistant professor of anthropology at the University of Toronto. She is the author of *Wayward Women: Sexuality and Agency in a New Guinea Society* (University of California Press, 2006). Her research interests include gender, sexuality, international health, institutional medications of HIV/AIDS, and the lived experience of being on antiretrovirals.

Daniel Jordan Smith is an associate professor of anthropology at Brown University. He has published widely on Nigeria in journals such as *Africa, Africa Today, American Anthropologist, American Ethnologist, Canadian Journal of African Studies, Cultural Anthropology, Medical Anthropology, Population and Development Review,* and *World Development.* He is the author of *A Culture of Corruption: Everyday Deception and Popular Discontent in Nigeria* (Princeton University Press, 2006).

Geetanjali Tiwari has a Ph.D. in anthropology and a master's degree in wildlife ecology. She was born and raised mostly in India and has worked on various research projects in India, including ecotourism, wildlife filming, illegal trade in wildlife, herpetology, and large mammal conservation. Her current research focus is on social and economic explanations for polyandry in Kinnaur, a high-altitude Himalayan community in India. Although she is also a full-time mother of two, she remains in continuous contact with Kinnaur and returns regularly to conduct field research.

INDEX